MW01621006

Images of Modern America

SIOUX FALLS

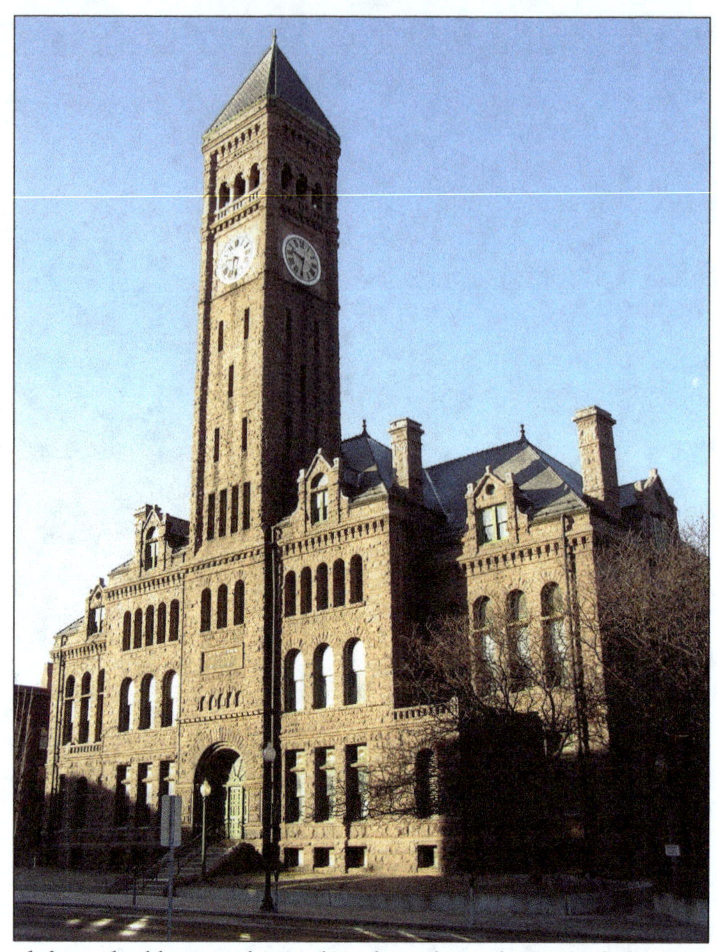

One of the most defining buildings in the city has always been the Minnehaha County Courthouse. Until 1962, this building was used as a courthouse; it also housed other Minnehaha County offices. There was a period when the building sat vacant, and at one point, there was a movement to have it demolished to make space for a parking lot. In 1974, the building was officially safe from the wrecking ball and became part of the Siouxland Heritage Museums. The outside is ornately designed and built with Sioux quartzite from a local quarry. Not only is the exterior amazing, but the interior is as well. There are several large painted murals, a restored circuit courtroom, and beautiful woodwork throughout. Pioneer architect Wallace Dow designed this beautiful building, and it was constructed in 1890 with an addition completed to the north in 1937. (Author's collection.)

Front Cover: The cover photograph, taken in 1958, is a view of Phillips Avenue and Ninth Street looking south. The downtown area was at its peak at this time. Note the three lanes of heavy one-way traffic. Most of the buildings to the right have since been torn down. (Courtesy Charles Cushman Collection: Indiana University Archives, P10228, see page 47.)

Upper Back Cover: Richard Nixon campaigning in Sioux Falls. (Author's collection, see page 88.)

Lower Back Cover (from left to right): The beautiful Falls of the Big Sioux River, the namesake of Sioux Falls (author's collection); Raven Industries showing an early hot-air balloon (courtesy Orvin Olivier, see page 17); parade on Main Avenue (courtesy R. Kolbe Dakota collection, see page 70).

Images of Modern America

SIOUX FALLS

Dr. Rick D. Odland

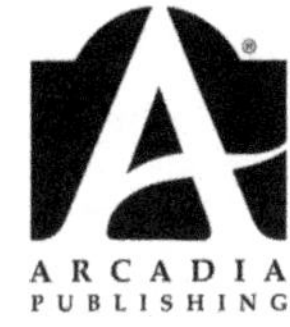

ISBN 978-1-5402-2584-9

Published by Arcadia Publishing
Charleston, South Carolina

Library of Congress Control Number: 2017933761

For all general information, please contact Arcadia Publishing:
Telephone 843-853-2070
Fax 843-853-0044
E-mail sales@arcadiapublishing.com
For customer service and orders:
Toll-Free 1-888-313-2665

Visit us on the Internet at www.arcadiapublishing.com

To Amy—we share so many Sioux Falls memories together: growing up two blocks apart and going to the same elementary, junior high, high school, and college together. Thank you for supporting me while I was collecting and writing some of the memories of our Sioux Falls childhood and adult life.

Contents

Acknowledgments		6
Introduction		7
1.	Historic Buildings with a New Life	9
2.	Businesses Then and Now	17
3.	Street Views	47
4.	Landmarks of Sioux Falls	71
5.	Aerial Views	77
6.	Local Legends, Events, and More	85

Acknowledgments

I am so honored to share other people's precious pictures and delightful memories. I was welcomed around dining room tables and felt privileged to be able to hear stories about their time while living in Sioux Falls. I drove a few of you crazy trying to get the pictures I knew you had—a special thanks to you. I am always amazed and greatly appreciative when building owners allow me to climb on their roofs to catch a bird's-eye view of changes in the city—I may ask again.

A large percentage of the pictures in this book were shared by other people. For those pictures, I want to thank William Pay, Orvin Olivier, Merlin Sundvold, Cory Hansen, Paul and Karen Van Bockern, Olin Odland, Gary Hanson, Hubert "Skip" Benz, Mark Griffin, Hayley Zeigler, Jim Coppock, Joe Alick, Bob Hanson, Judy Eisenbraun, Doris and Wally Johnson, Robert Kolbe, Tom Olsen, Gerald and Patricia Bruget, Ed Limke, Jerry Wallenstein, Joe Swenson, Jim and Joan Dresch, Christian Begeman, Angie Roth, Jessica Potter, Joe Henkin, Susan (Henkin) McGowan, the Opland family, Sean Cox, Bruce Millikan, Vonita Gardner, Carl Musselman, Shelly Sjovold, Paul Farmer, Ray Campbell, Heather Howe, Wayne Prostrollo, Jay Olson, Jon Brown, Pat Marso, Brittany Christensen, Lyn Hahn, and Denise Turner. Thanks also go to the following businesses: William Pay Photography, Ideal Yardware, Lewis Drug, Cliff Avenue Greenhouse, Arthur's Shoes, Alick Drug, Harold's Photo, Pizza Inn, B&G Milky Way, Happy Joe's, Vern Eide Motorcars, Buck's Muffler Shop, Handy Man, Indiana University, Clipper Jim's, Parker Transfer & Storage, Christian Begeman Photography, Avera, Sanford Health, Keloland Television, Sioux Falls Jaycees, Siouxland Heritage Museums, Centurylink, Great Western Bank, Davenport Evans, and Hurwitz & Smith. Unless otherwise noted, all images appear courtesy of the author.

Thank you to Arcadia Publishing for allowing me to write this book. A special thanks to Liz Gurley at Arcadia for helping me through the process and your patience with all my questions.

A special thank you to my wife, Amy, and our children, Alex, Bekah, Sam, and Laura, for encouraging me along the way.

Introduction

This book is meant to show changes within Sioux Falls as it became a modern city and, as some would say, a metropolitan area. The years included in this book are from the 1950s to the present. This began a postwar era, and during the modern years, life for many changed dramatically. Most of the changes have been for the good of the community, but changes bring challenges as well.

Many have said the 1950s were a wonderful time. This was soon after the end of World War II. It was a slower, simpler time when neighbors acted "neighborly" and you could count on the neighborhood to look out for one another. Life felt secure during these times. Many people would have left their homes and cars unlocked.

Sioux Falls had a postwar population boom that lasted well into the 1960s. During World War II, Sioux Falls was home to the Army Radio Technical Training School and trained 50,000 servicemen during its three and a half years here. The school was like its own city by the airport. It was a catalyst for a boom in the population and provided stability to the local economy.

Things like pizza, television, the jukebox, and certain styles of music were relatively new. Little did anyone know then that the future would bring computers, cell phones, and advances in medicine and technology. The movie *Back to the Future* tried to show us the difference in culture between the years 1955 and 1985. It is staggering to think we are already another 30 years past 1985, when the movie was released.

Sioux Falls has prospered in modern times. Before the 1950s, the city's economy was largely agricultural. Since the 1950s, Sioux Falls has added other boosts to the economy with construction, credit card companies, and health care. John Morrell's has continued to be a large employer, offering much to the economy since 1909. In 1981, Citibank came to Sioux Falls and added many jobs to the city. Raven Industries began in 1956 and has greatly expanded to have a worldwide impact on space exploration and environmental preservation; it is known for significantly more than just hot-air balloons. Health care has taken off in the last decade and has brought many new medical specialties and advanced medical research to Sioux Falls.

T. Denny Sanford has made history with his generosity to Sioux Falls organizations. He has given approximately $1 billion to create Sanford Health, which has greatly expanded the availability of medicine in Sioux Falls. Sanford also gave a large donation for the building of the Denny Sanford Premier Center. Since the new state-of-the art facility opened, locals and visitors alike have enjoyed concerts, sporting events, and many other forms of entertainment at the center. Prior to the Denny Sanford Premier Center, big name performers overlooked Sioux Falls due to the size of the old arena. Not only has this new venue brought entertainment, but it has helped the restaurant, hotel, and shopping industries.

Sioux Falls has a history of being a vibrant community with a stable economy. The modern era helped to create what we have today. As Sioux Falls has grown, it has been able to offer its people many new restaurants, shops, arts, and other forms of entertainment. People from "big cities" like Omaha, Minneapolis, and Chicago are often surprised that Sioux Falls offers many of the same things that they are accustomed to in their larger cities. Although it is a different time, Sioux Falls has continued to offer a wonderful life to those who call it their home.

There are so many other stories and pictures that make up the modern era of Sioux Falls, but due to space, only certain events and pictures were used. It was decided to not include certain events and pictures that have been documented in other books. The goal was to share pictures or stories of the past that are not well documented. It is my hope that this book will teach you, entertain you, and possibly surprise you about how great Sioux Falls is—Enjoy!

One

Historic Buildings with a New Life

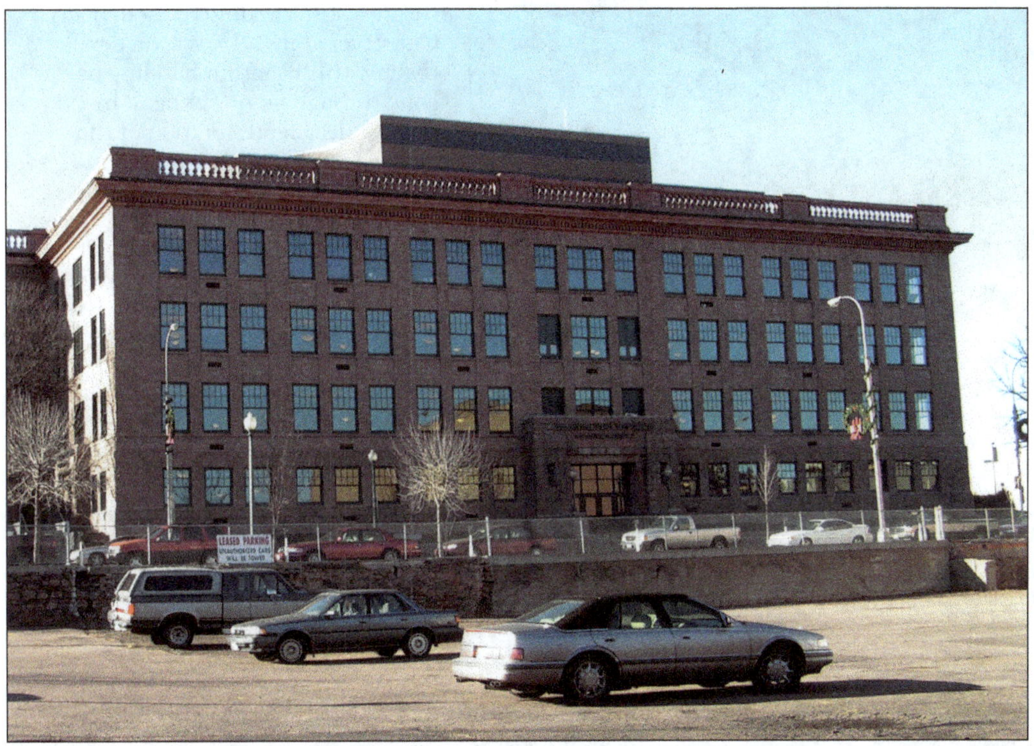

One of the most historic buildings, which has seen significant changes, is the original Washington High School, now the Washington Pavilion. The school building was constructed in sections around Central School, one of the first schools in Sioux Falls. In 1906, the north section was built. The west section was the final section to be completed, in 1936. Central School was razed in 1935, prior to the west section completing the square. In the fall of 1992, students began attending the new Washington High School at 501 North Sycamore Avenue. The old school was totally remodeled and became the Washington Pavilion. The pavilion offers arts, entertainment, and science to educate and entertain people of all ages. These cars are parked in a parking lot where the Washington Square building is now being constructed. This will be an eight-story structure with residential, office, and commercial space.

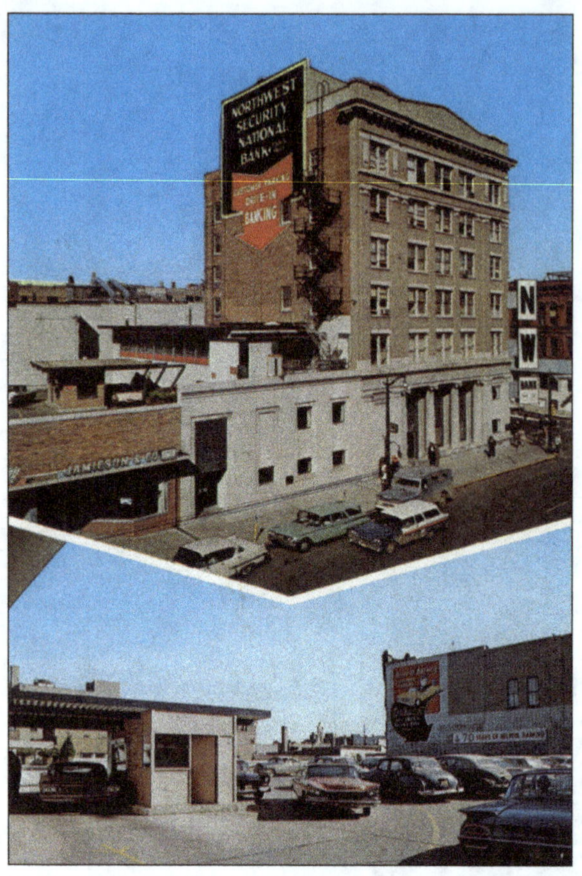

The Northwest Security Bank was a very modern bank for its time. It provided a new service, "drive-in banking," and customer parking on the roof of the adjacent building. Although never proved, this bank was rumored to be shot up and robbed by John Dillinger and his gang on March 6, 1934. The building is located on the southwest corner of Ninth Street and Main Avenue.

The Orpheum is the last of the oldest theaters still standing in Sioux Falls. Constructed in 1913 as a vaudeville theater, this beautiful building has gone through many changes. In the last decade, restoration of the original murals in the theater and remodeling of the theater and the two connecting south buildings have made this a beautiful reminder of what existed during the early years of Sioux Falls. (Courtesy Siouxland Heritage Museums, Sioux Falls, SD.)

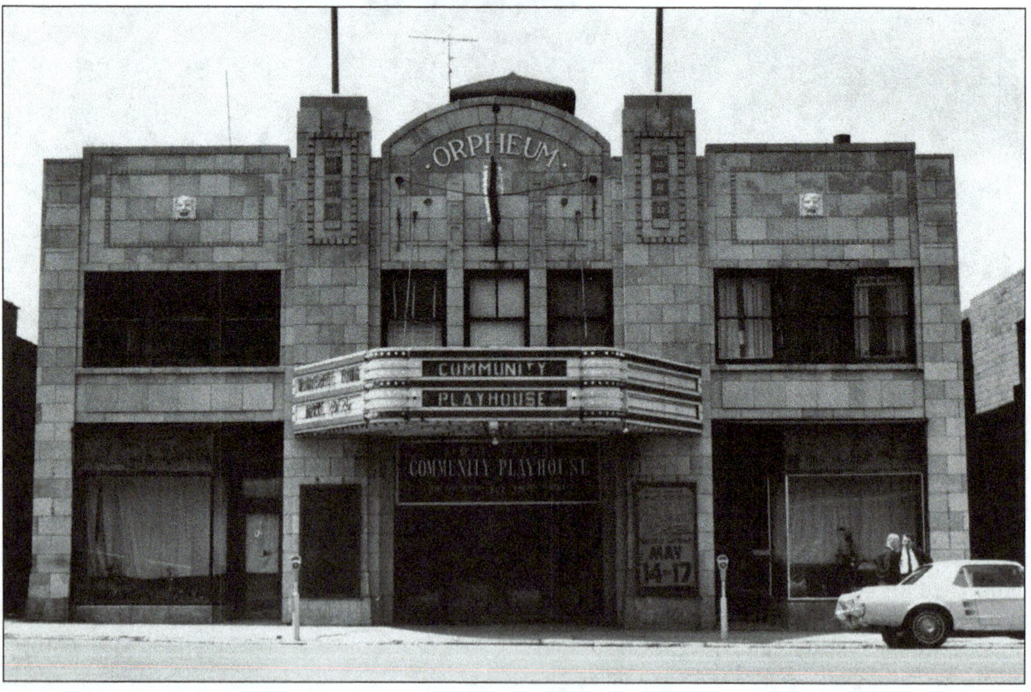

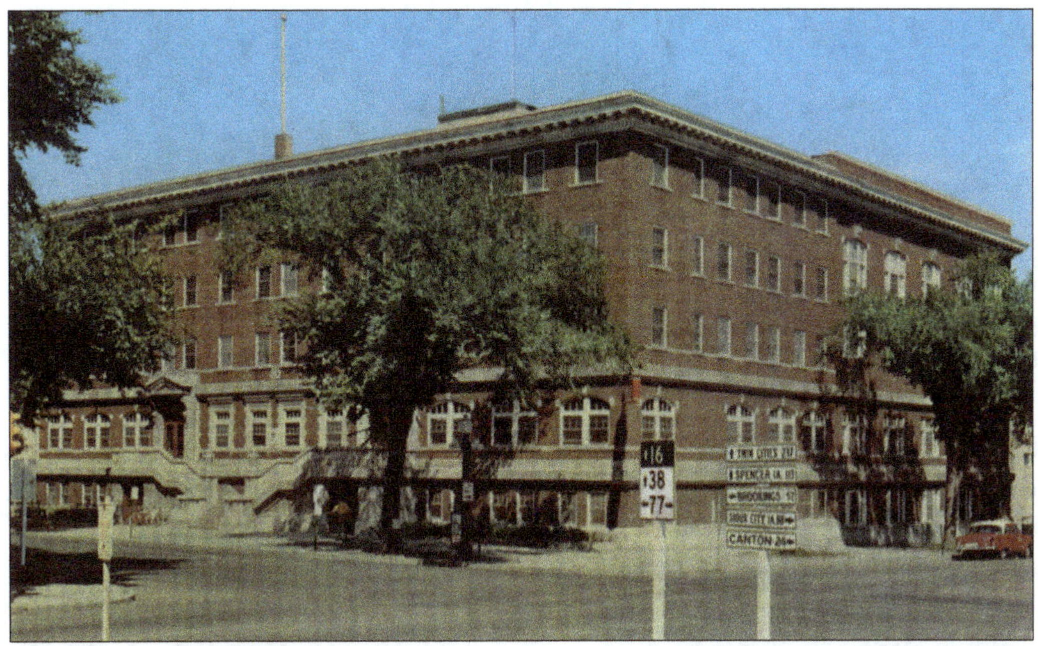

Located on the northeast corner of Eleventh Street and Minnesota Avenue, the YMCA was in front of a major intersection that led to the Black Hills, Minnesota, and Iowa. The intersection included Highway 16 (Twelfth Street), Highway 77 (Minnesota Avenue continuing north to Cliff Avenue), Highway 42 (heading west from Sioux Falls), and Highway 38 (Tenth Street as it leaves the city on the east side).

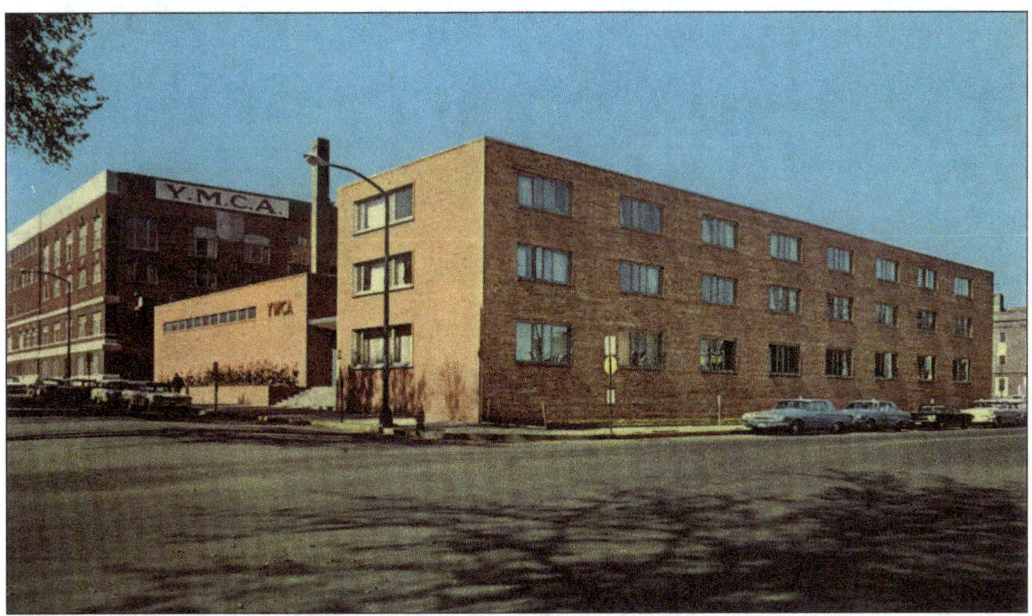

The YWCA building was completed to the east side of the YMCA in 1936. For nearly 80 years, the YWCA served the community. On April 2013, the local YWCA disbanded from the national organization to form EMBE, short for "EMpowering you to BE." This new organization would have better control on seeing and meeting the needs of the Sioux Falls community.

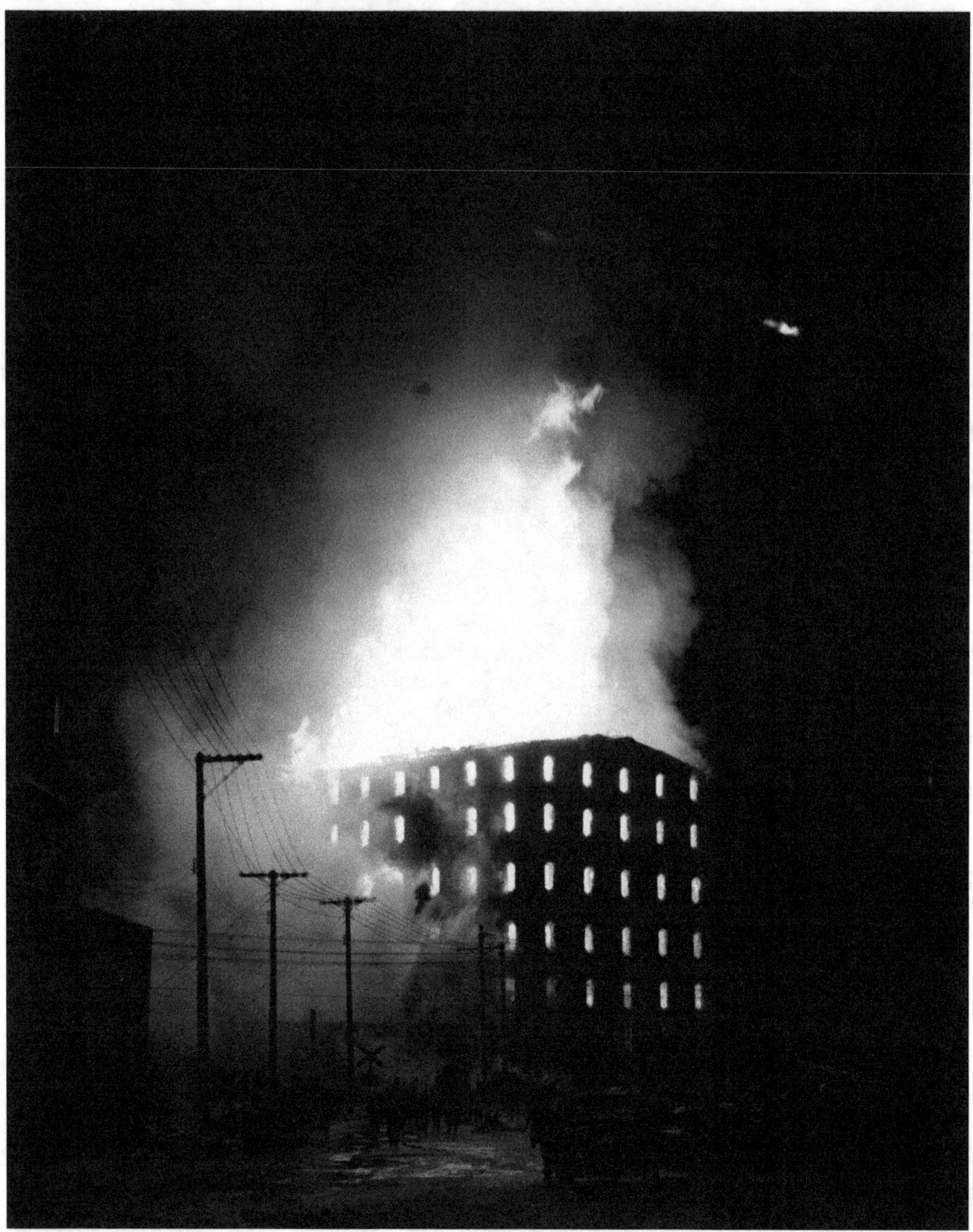

The Queen Bee Mill was completed in 1881 and destroyed by fire in 1956; this beautiful seven-story quartzite structure was doomed from the beginning. R.F. Pettigrew promoted it to have enough waterpower, from the Falls, to be able to grind flour. Soon, it was determined there was not enough wheat to keep the mill going, and it failed within two years. In 1911, it was purchased by United Flour Milling Company and converted to electric power, but that soon failed too. Larabee Flour Company ran it for about a year, closing it after World War I. Today, the remnants of the foundation are used during the summer for plays and other performances. (Courtesy Siouxland Heritage Museums, Sioux Falls, SD.)

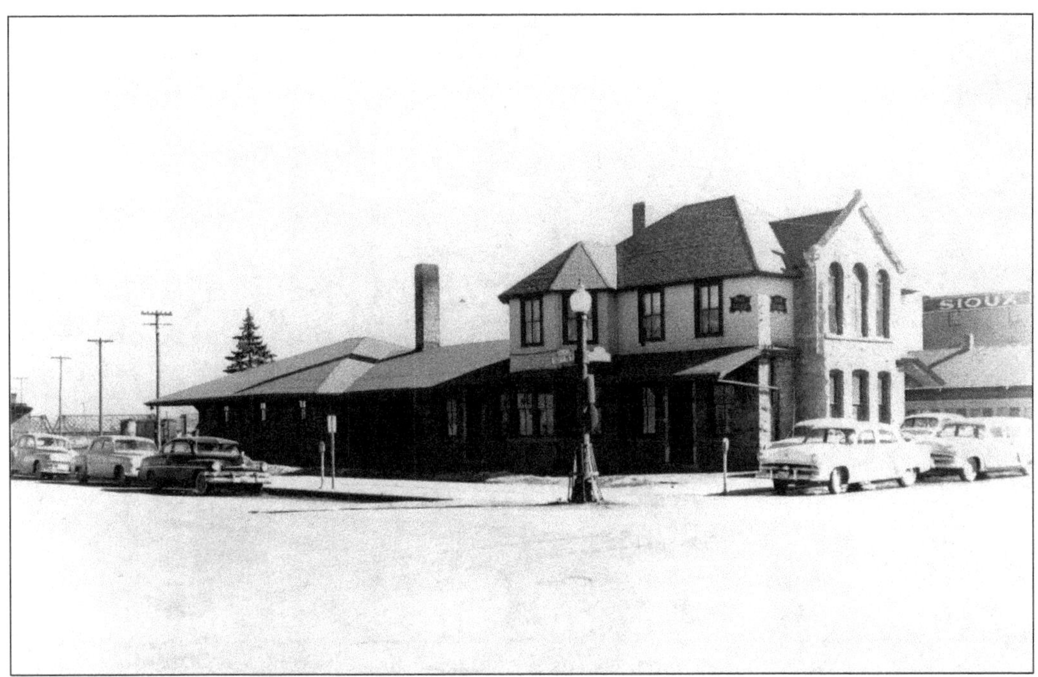

This is a wonderful view of the Rock Island train station in 1954 by famous Sioux Falls photographer William Pay. The building still sits on the southeast corner of First Avenue and Tenth Street. Note in the background, to the right, the Sioux Falls Paper Company building. This business began at a different location in 1906 and moved next to the train station in 1925. (Courtesy William Pay.)

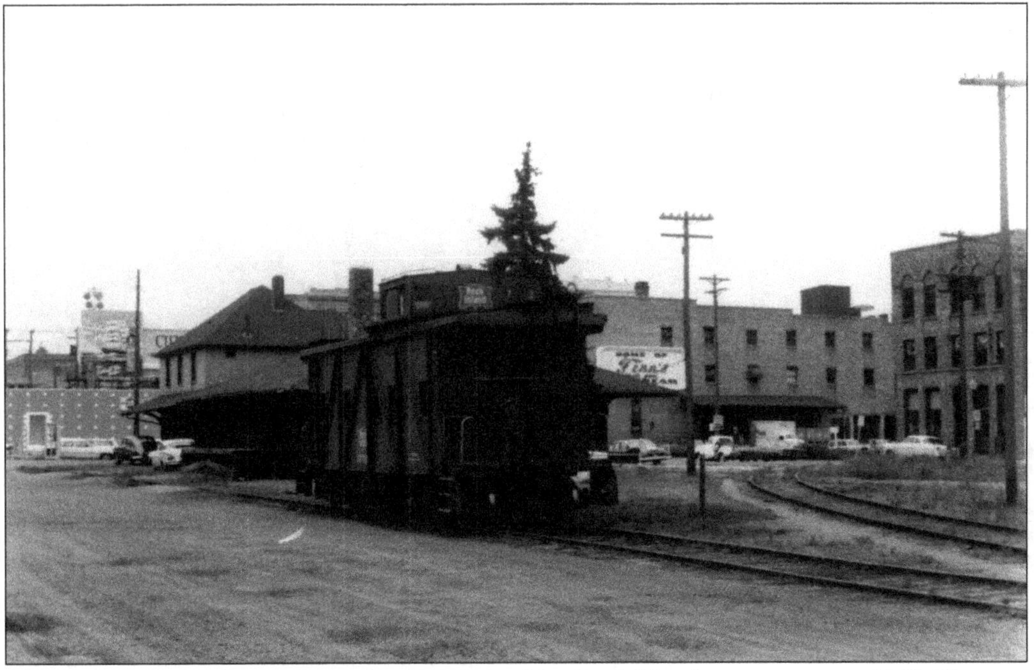

This picture shows the south-side loading area of the Rock Island train station in 1965. This was a depot for the Burlington, Cedar Rapids, and Northern Railroad from 1886 until 1970. Note Fenn's Ice Cream in the background.

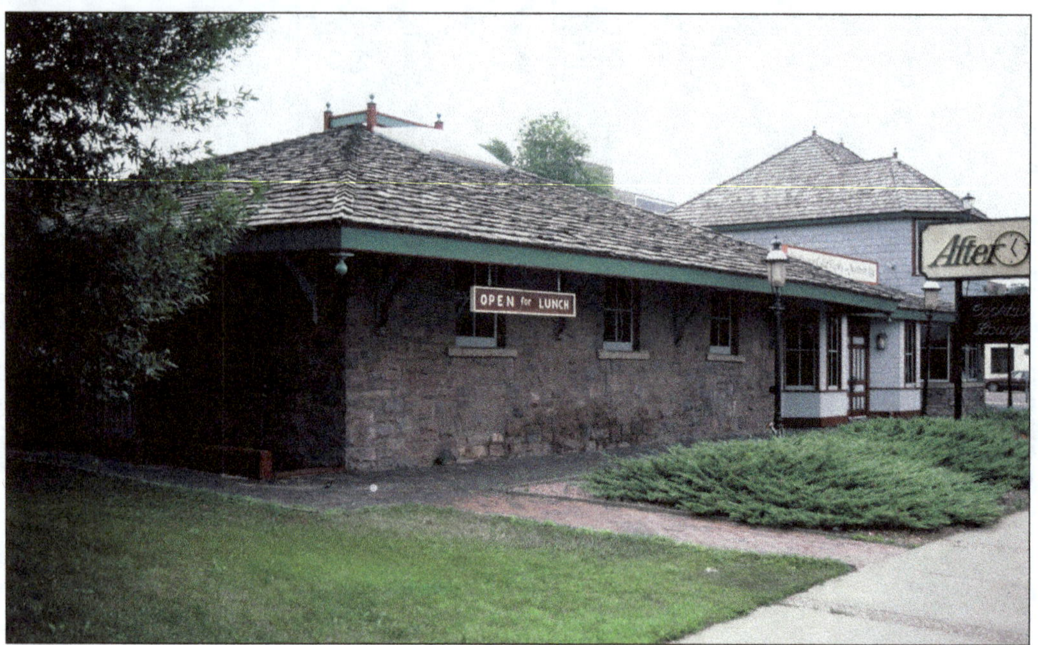

The Rock Island Depot, built in 1886, was used as a depot until 1970. Since then, the building has housed restaurants and stores. This picture shows the After Five Restaurant when it used the depot. Other restaurants here included Barco's, Maxwell's, and Sidetrack. Today, it is the Great Outdoor Store.

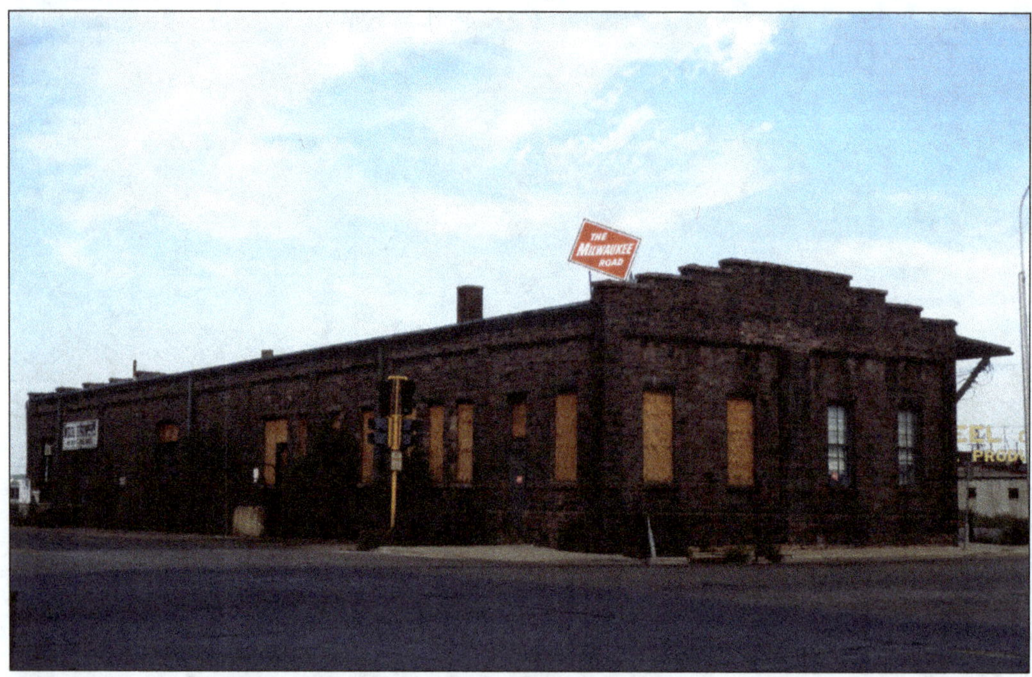

This picture of the Milwaukee freight depot was taken on September 6, 1980. It was constructed in 1894. This depot could have easily met the wrecking ball of urban renewal but was saved. Now 121 years old, this depot continues to sit proudly on the northeast corner of Sixth Street and Phillips Avenue. The Sioux Falls Parks and Recreation Department currently occupies the building.

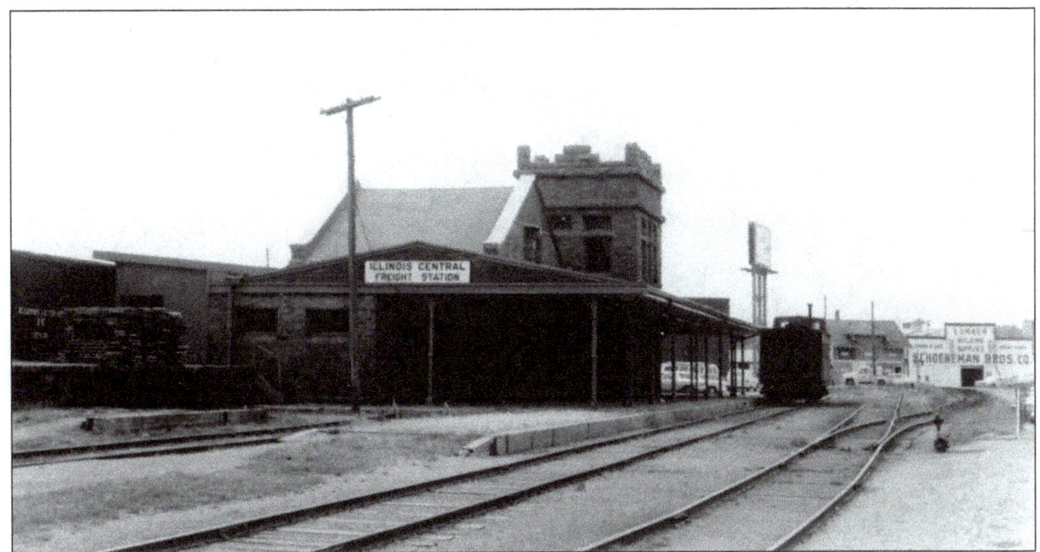

This view was photographed in 1965 looking south and shows the Illinois Central Depot. This depot, originally built in 1887, still stands today. At right is the Schoeneman Bros. Lumber Company, established in 1912. It was in business for nearly 100 years at the same location. In 2010, the downtown Schoeneman lumber yard buildings were torn down and the grounds excavated for new development.

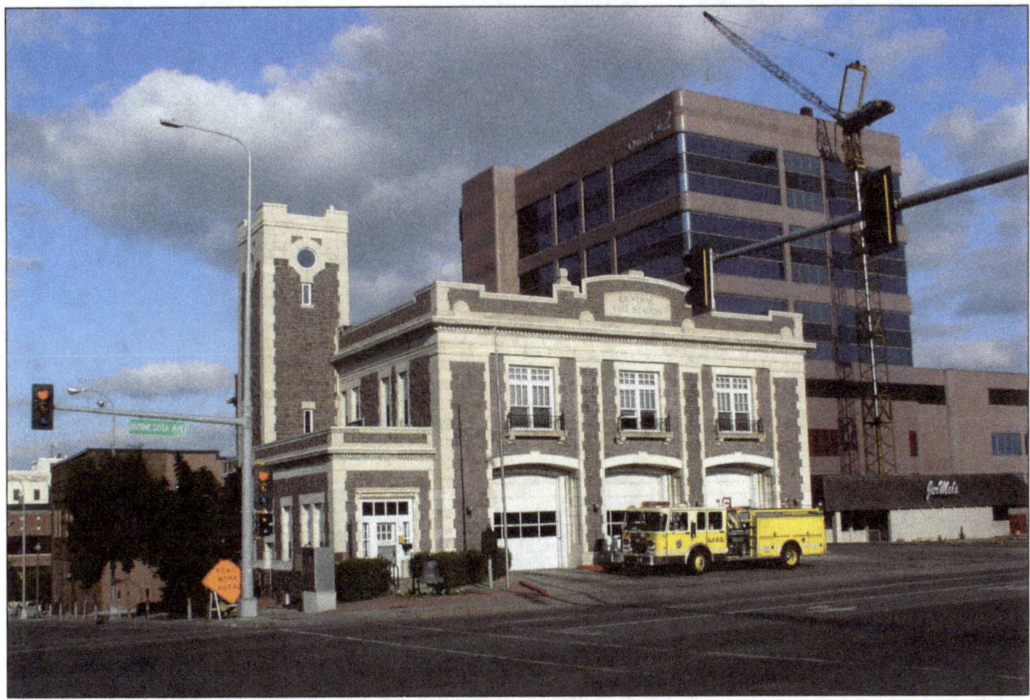

Central Fire Station, located on the southeast corner of Ninth Street and Minnesota Avenue, is the oldest fire station in Sioux Falls. It was built in 1912 and originally housed horses instead of fire trucks. Horses would pull the 1880 Silsby Steamer and hand pumper to fires until 1915, when a motorized Seagrave pumper truck replaced them. The original truck was restored and can be seen at the firehouse.

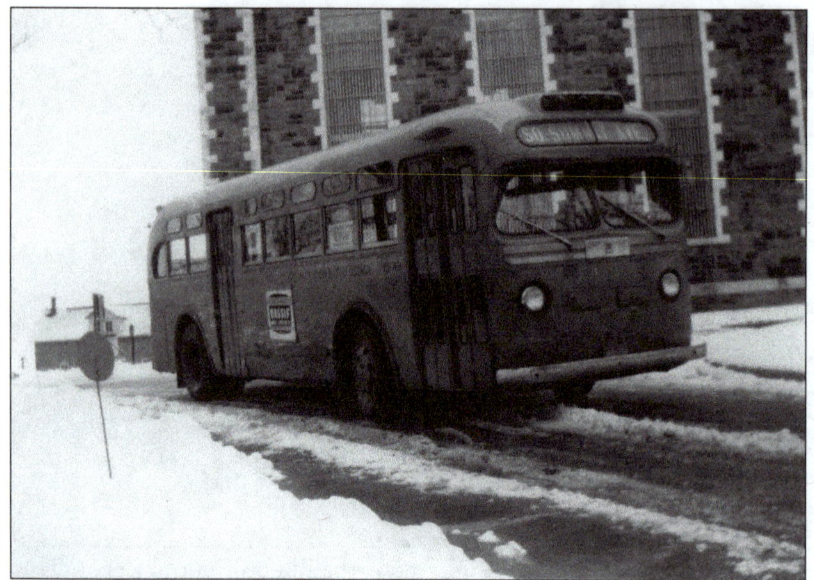

In 1907, the Sioux Falls Traction Company began offering trolley rides throughout the city on 16 miles of track. In 1929, bus service replaced the trolley. Here, a city bus is shown driving on the south side of the South Dakota State Penitentiary in 1969.

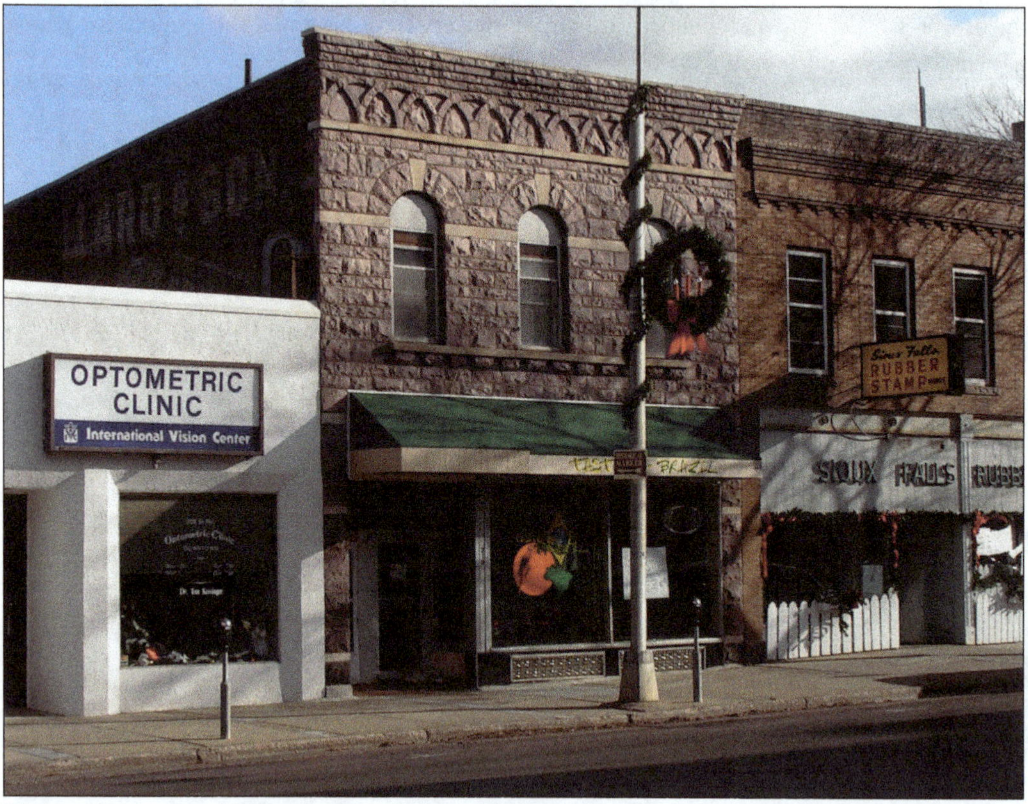

This pink quartzite building originally housed the Ballard and Son Monument Company. On the side of the building, their sign is still visible. This picture was taken in 2005; since then, it has been beautifully restored as Parker's Bistro. The home of the Ballard family can be seen on page 25.

Two

Businesses Then and Now

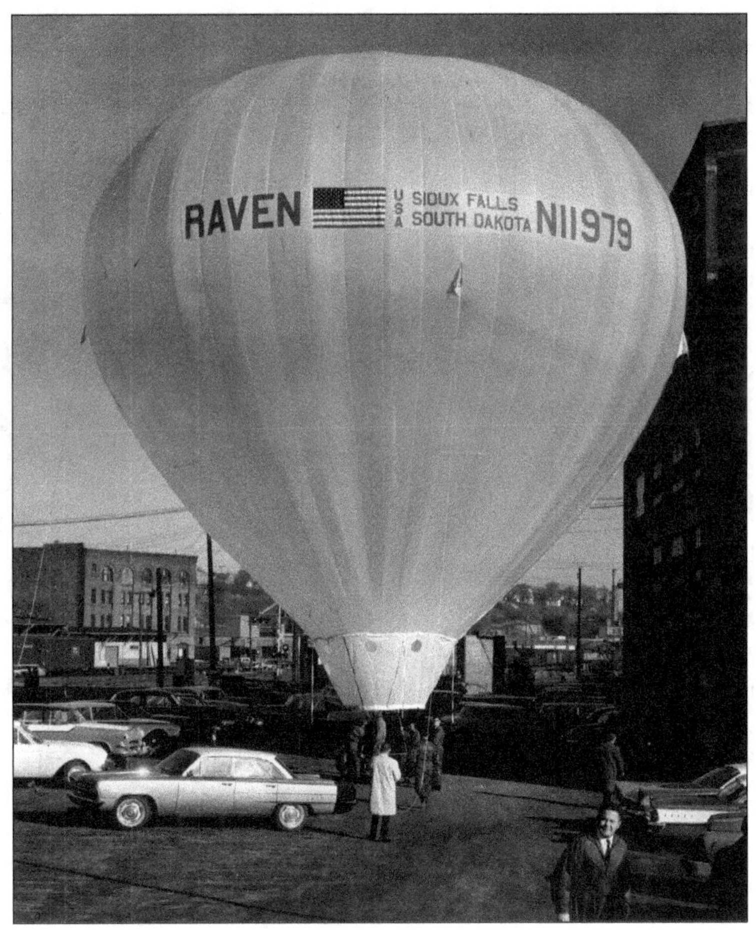

Hot-air balloons have floated across the skies of the world, but have roots in Sioux Falls, the birthplace of the modern hot-air balloon. Ed Yost started Raven Industries in 1956 to make high-altitude balloons. He is known as the inventor of the modern-day hot-air balloon. (Courtesy Orvin Olivier.)

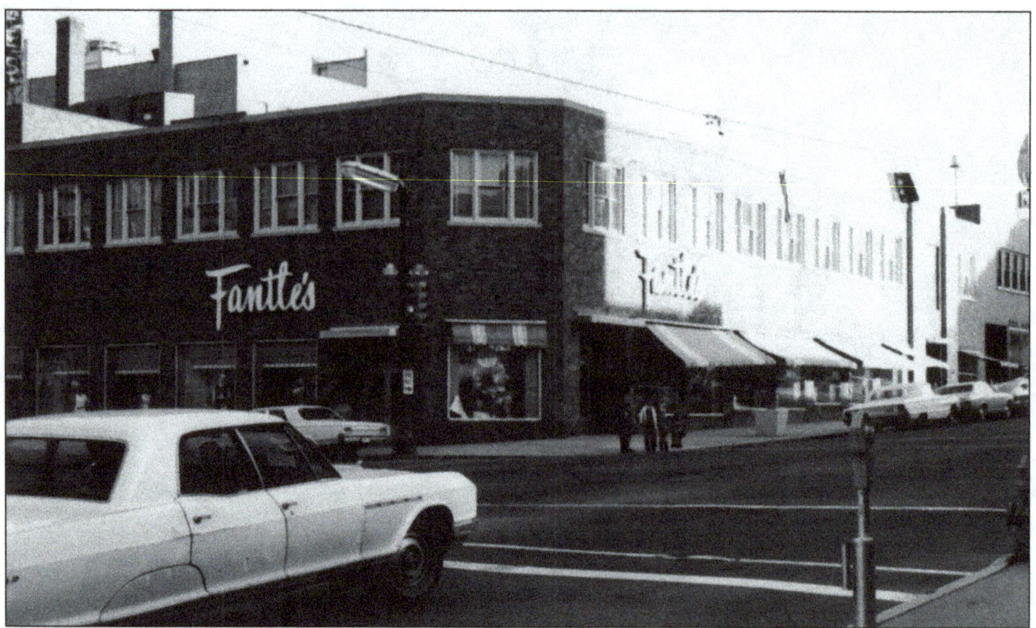

Fantle's department store was a longtime anchor for fashion in downtown Sioux Falls. Fantle's was originally located on the west side of Phillips Avenue between Ninth and Tenth Streets. It moved to a new building on the southeast corner of Ninth Street and Main Avenue in 1939. Soon after the Empire Mall opened in 1975, Fantle's moved to its final location at the mall. (Courtesy Siouxland Heritage Museums, Sioux Falls, SD.)

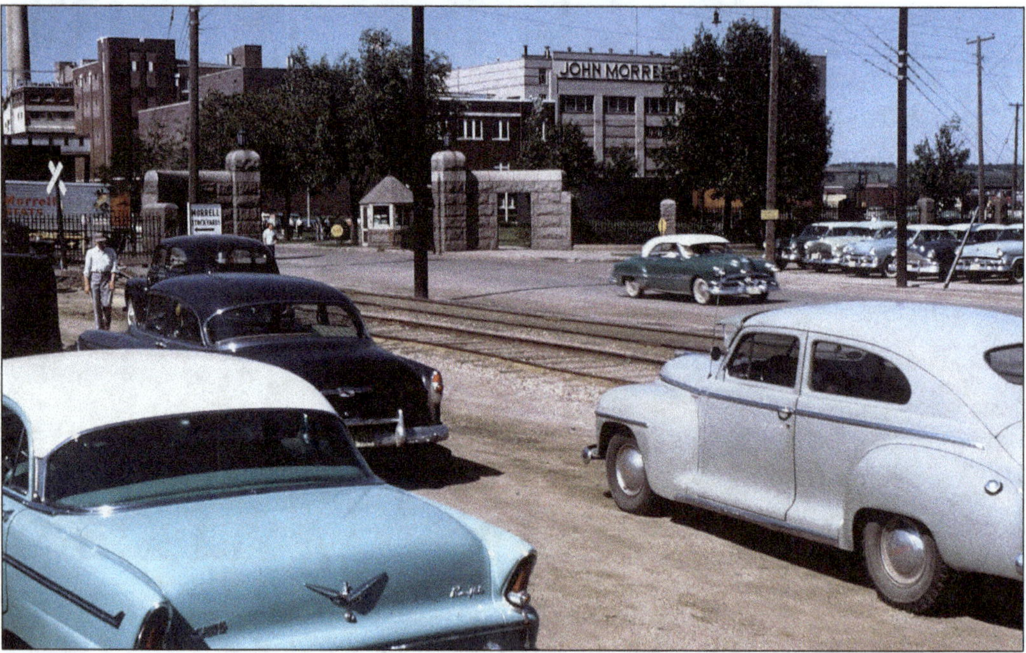

This picture shows John Morrell & Company in 1956. It was originally started in England by George Morrell, John's father. George started by selling oranges, and later, cured meats. In 1909, the company was established in Sioux Falls, and soon purchased the Green Meat Packing Plant, which was located between the river and the present-day Morrell & Company buildings.

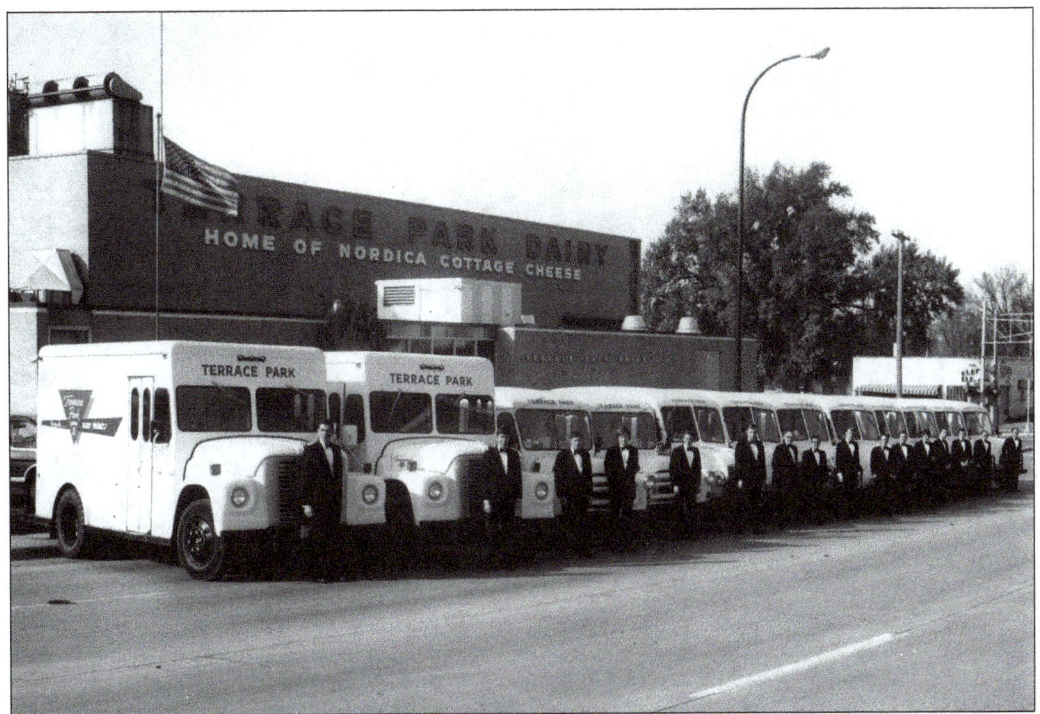

This is a rare view of the Terrace Park Dairy, located on the southwest corner of Tenth Street and West Avenue. Brothers Al and Ozzie Schock started Terrace Park Dairy in 1948. Up until this time, milk was delivered by horse. It is hard to believe that milk was once delivered to the house, and in style, too; these men were wearing tuxedoes. (Courtesy of Merlin Sundvold.)

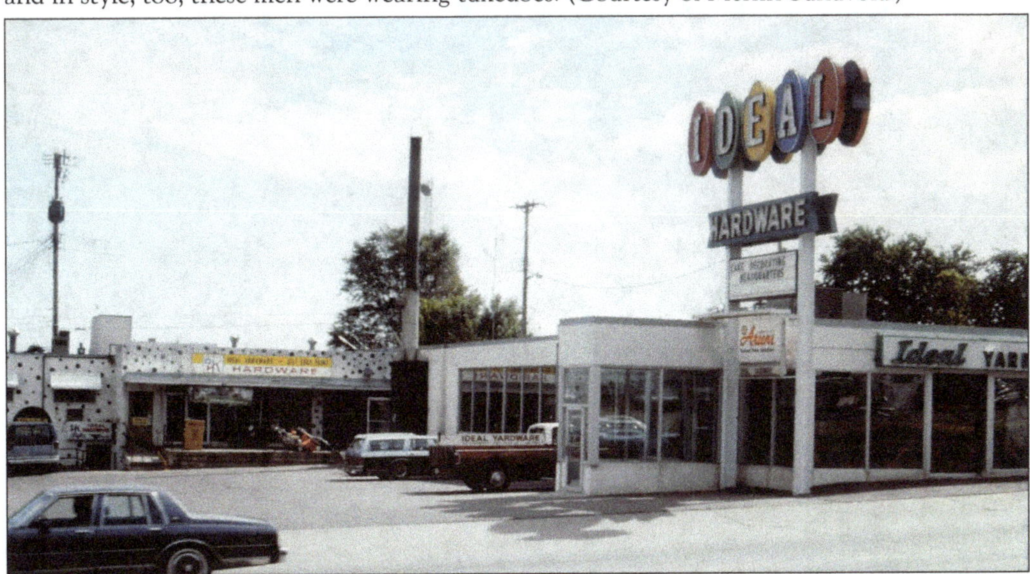

Ideal Hardware began in Sioux Falls in 1946. Adolph Hansen started the business, and his son Wayne and now his grandson Cory continue the business as Ideal Yardware. Most people remember the polka-dot building on the southeast corner of Twelfth Street and Minnesota Avenue. That was the location of the store for many years, until the business moved to the northwest corner of Louise Avenue and Interstate 229. (Courtesy Cory Hansen.)

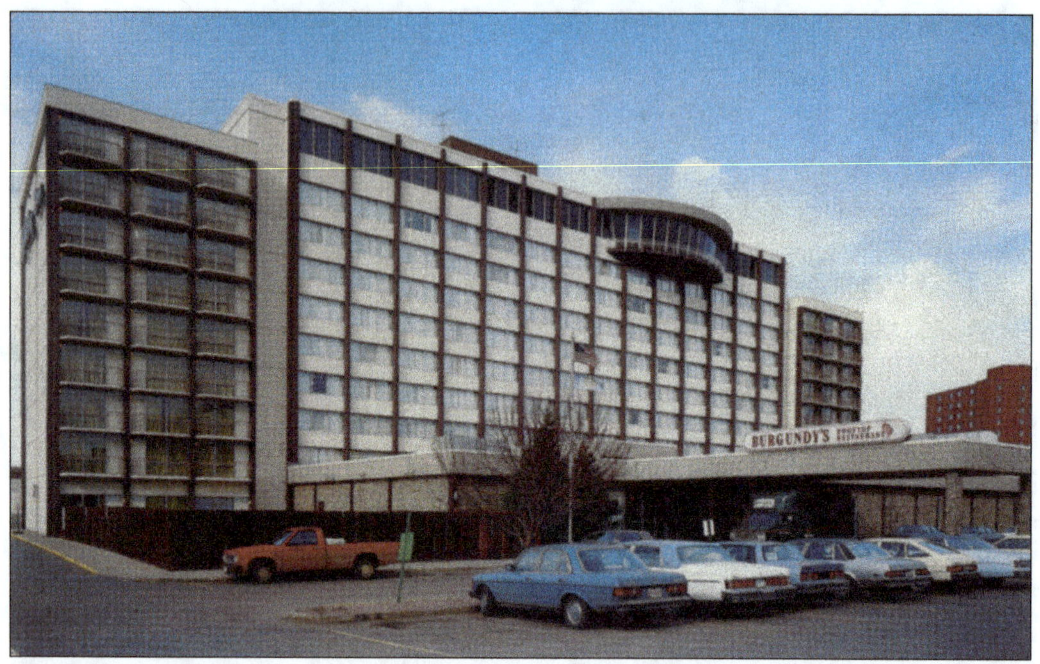

Since 1972, the Holiday Inn City Centre has been a fixture of downtown Sioux Falls. This fine hotel has housed many impressive guests, including rock and sports stars, presidents, and other important people, while they were guests in the city. The restaurant at top rotated and was known to be a fancy place for special occasions. This picture was taken in the late 1980s.

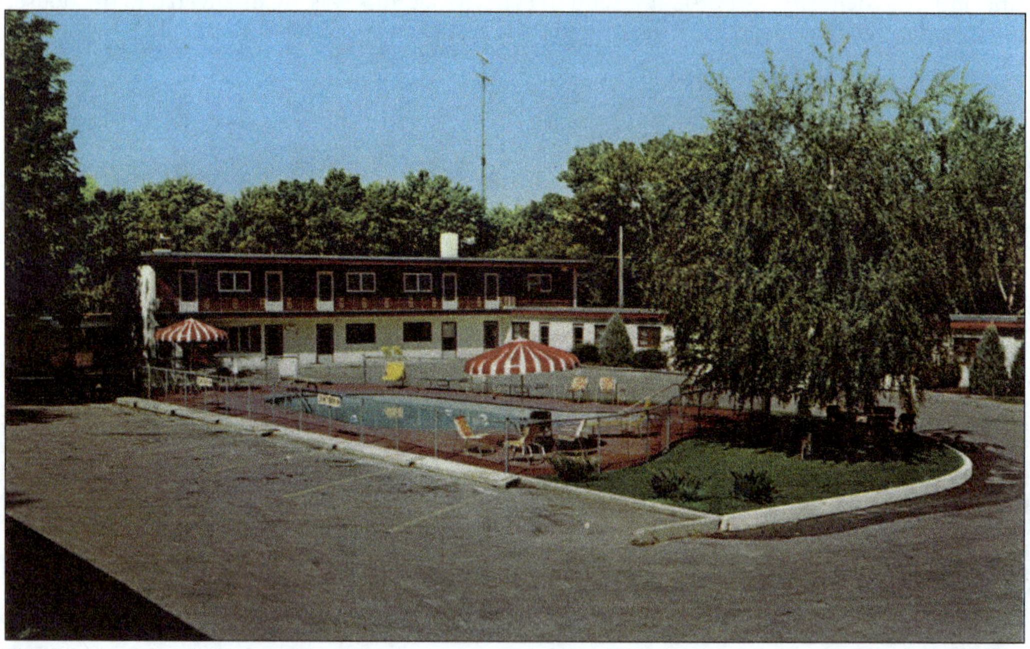

The Lindendale Motel was one of the properties in the Best Western Motel chain. It was tucked away in a beautiful wooded area south of Interstate 229, on Highway 77 (Minnesota Avenue section), at 4201 South Minnesota Avenue. It was in business from the late 1950s to the late 1980s. Currently, a medical and law office building is located on the same parcel of land.

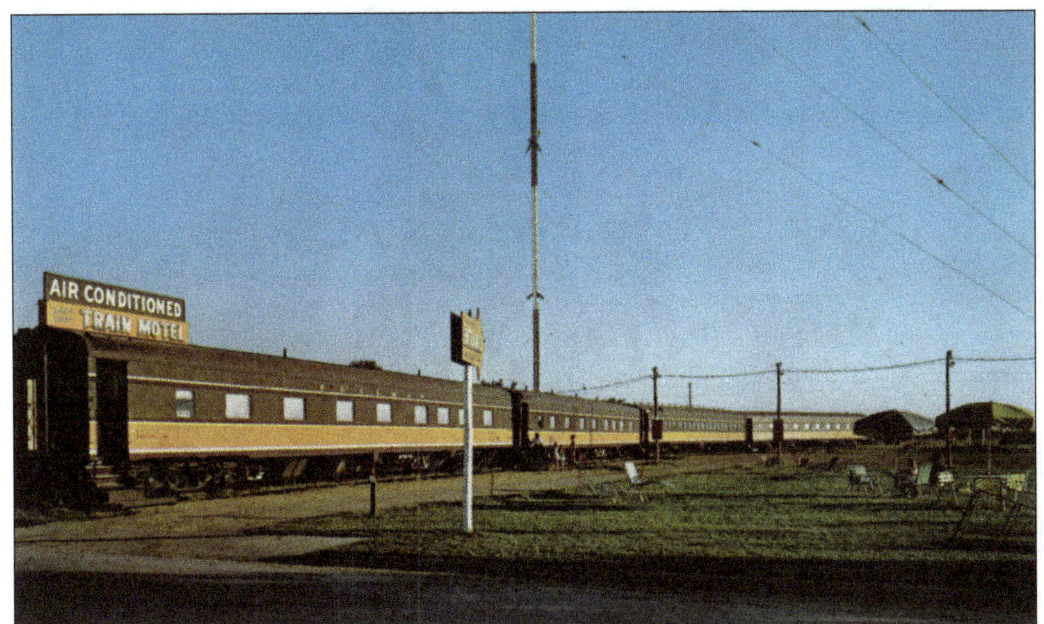

In mid-summer of 1963, Verl Thompson had the vision to convert train passenger cars from San Francisco into sleeping cars for a motel in Sioux Falls. The Sioux Chief Traintel (train motel) was located on the southwest corner of Twelfth Street and Interstate 29, where Tower Campground is now. The motel was in business until 1975. The train cars were repurposed and traveled back to the West Coast.

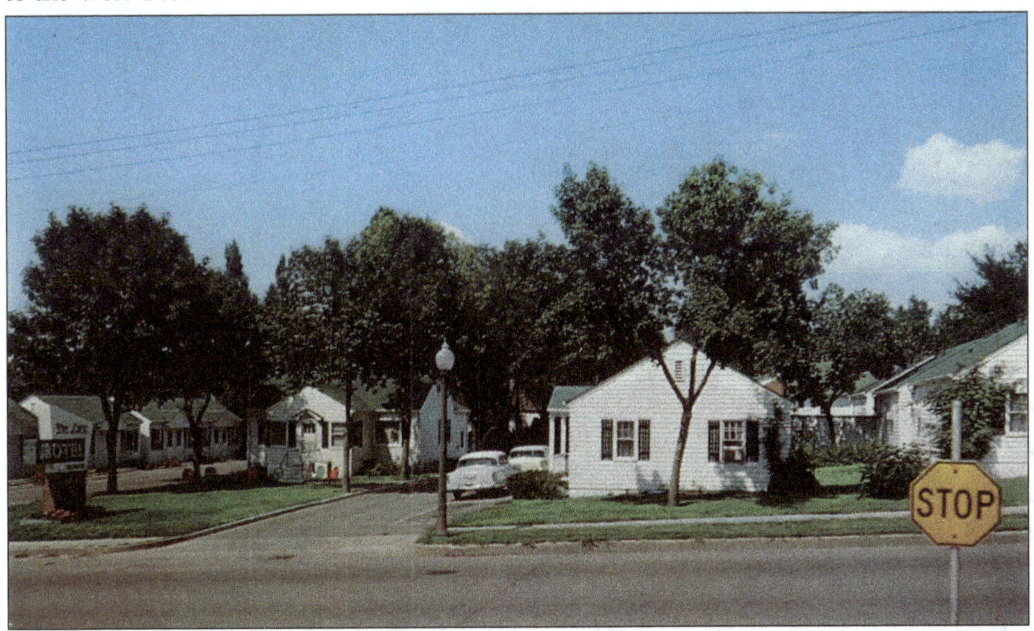

Originally built in the 1930s, the Delux Autocourt was home to many people when Highway 16 (Twelfth Street) was a major road for travelers heading from western South Dakota cities to Minnesota and Iowa. An autocourt was the precursor to a motel where one could stay in a little cabin and park right next door. Today, the grass areas between the buildings have been replaced with paved grounds.

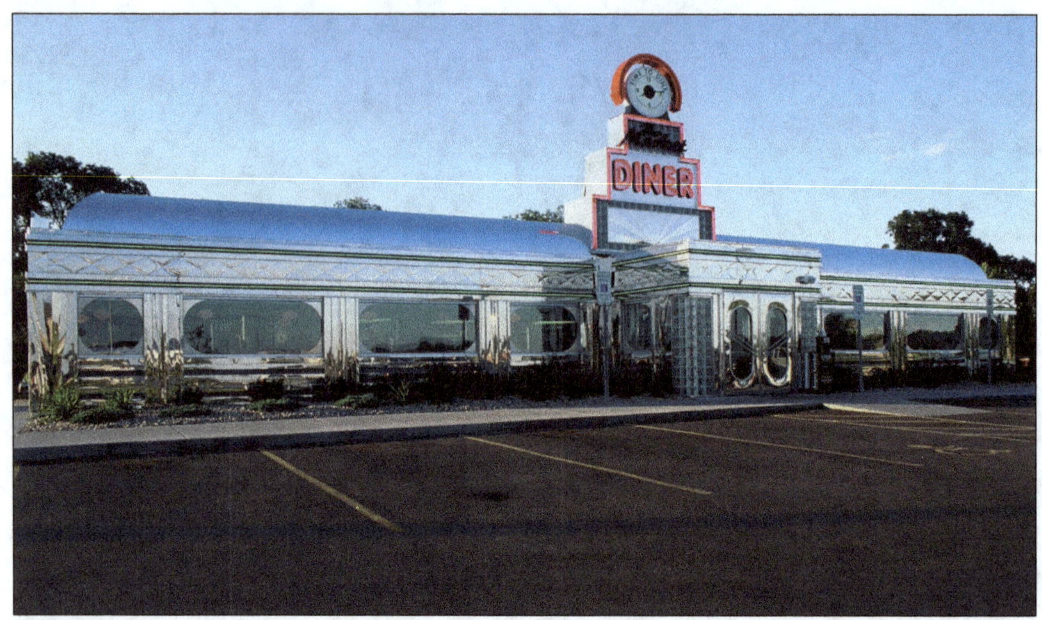

Pictured here is the Market Diner, which opened for business in 1998 at 2400 South Louise Avenue. From 2001 to 2004, the restaurant changed its menu and vibe from an old-fashioned malt and burger café to a Cajun-style restaurant called Dixie Bros. Grill. The building was then moved to 121 South Phillips Avenue and became the Phillips Avenue Diner, opening for business in 2005. (Courtesy Paul Van Bockern.)

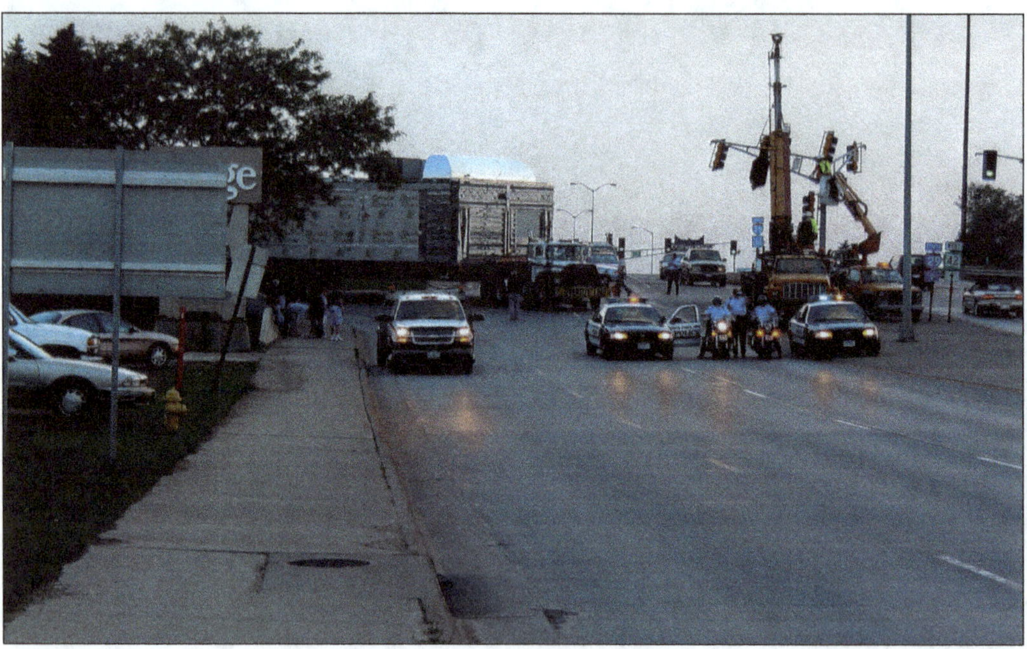

As the diner is making its way to its new home, it leaves Interstate 29 and enters Twelfth Street heading east. Note the caravan in front of Gage Bros. before Twelfth Street became an underpass; it was previously an overpass. (Courtesy Paul Van Bockern.)

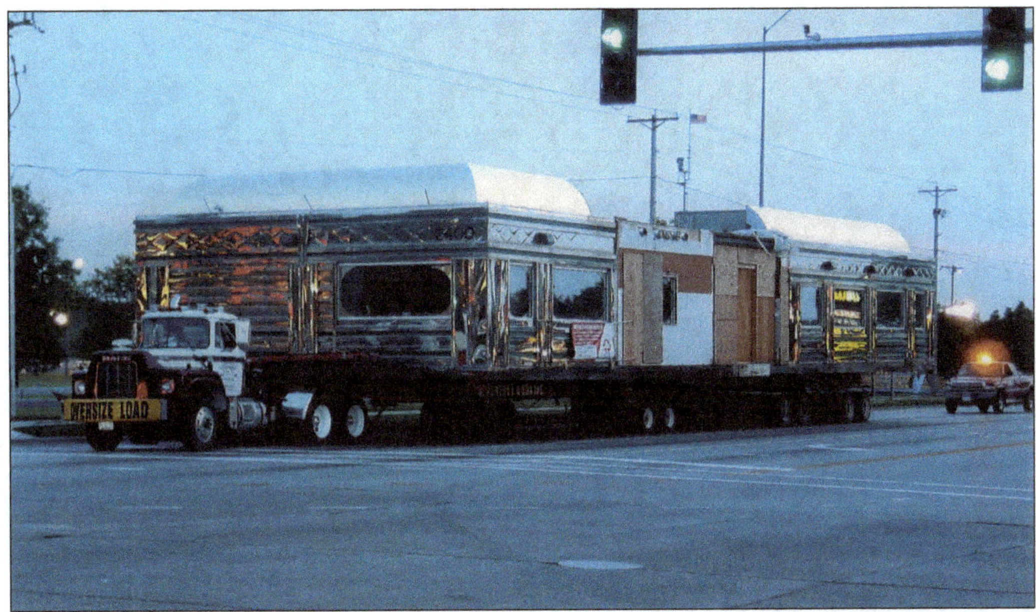

The Phillips Avenue Diner is pictured here not as a "drive-in," but a "drive-by," as it is being moved on June 1, 2005. The restaurant is heading east and has just passed the *South Dakota* battleship on Kiwanis Avenue and Twelfth Street. (Courtesy Paul Van Bockern.)

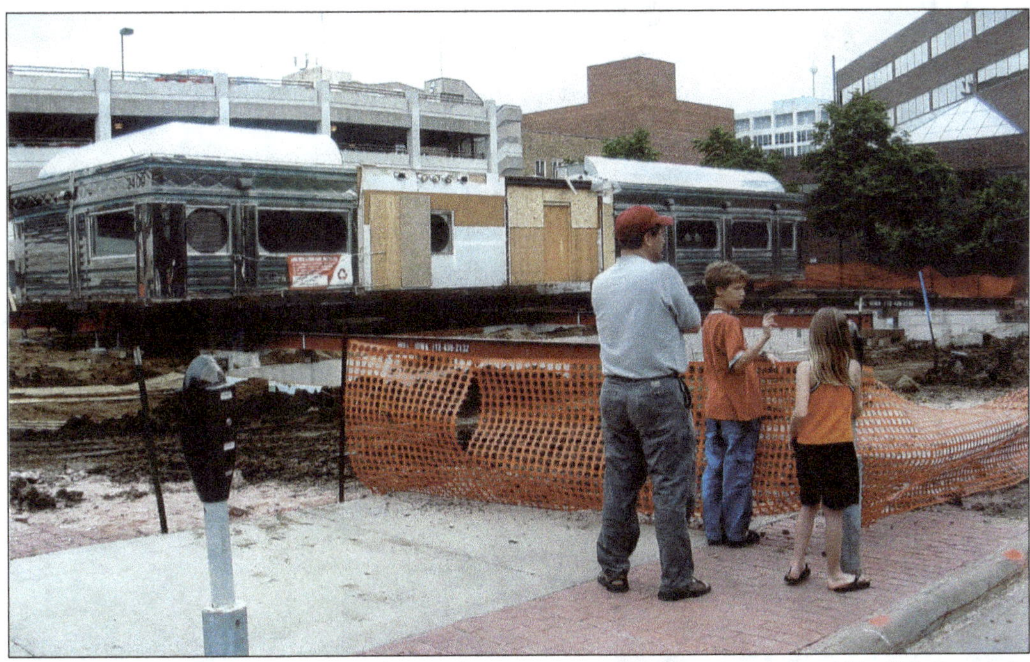

The Phillips Avenue Diner sits on the northwest corner of Phillips Avenue and Twelfth Street. In 1870, this was the location of the abandoned Fort Dakota Hospital, which C.K. Howard purchased and added onto to make C.K. Howard General Store. Then, the F.W. Woolworth Store was located here. Later, the Newberry's Store was located on this corner, but it was razed to become a parking lot until the Phillips Avenue Diner found its parking space. (Courtesy Paul Van Bockern.)

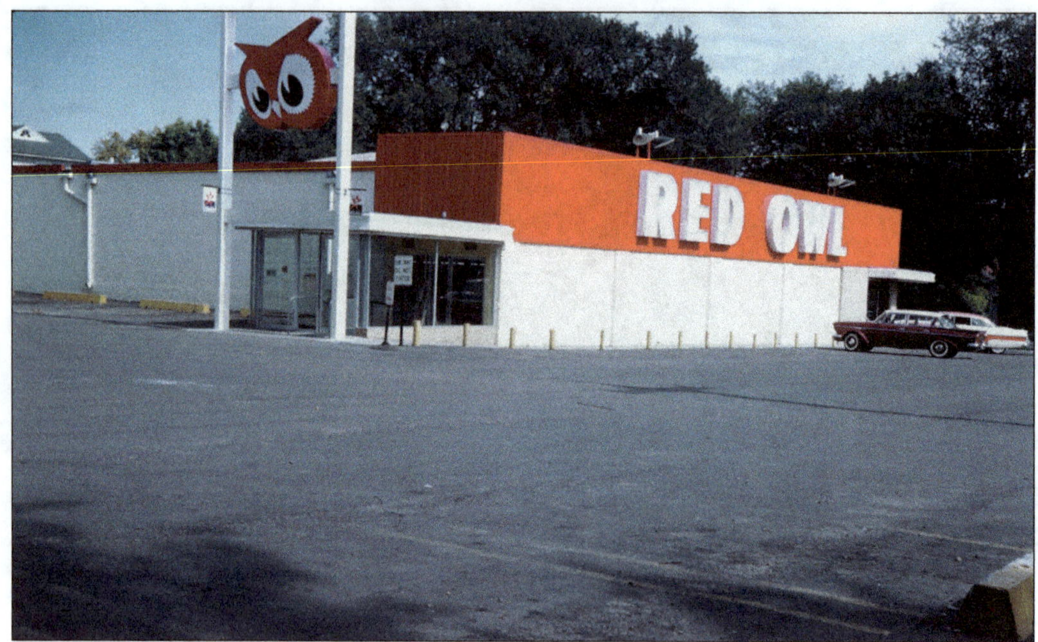

The building at 519 South Minnesota Avenue, on the northwest corner of Fourteenth Street and Minnesota Avenue, has gone through many changes. From the 1940s to the 1970s, the Red Owl Grocery Store and Golden Rule Bakery occupied the building. Getten's Friendly Food Store and Patty Cake Bake then took over the space. In the late 1970s, the building traded its shopping carts for bumper cars and became Granny's Ice-Cream Parlor and Fun Center. In the 1980s, the Circus Arcade and then Piccadilly Circus Arcade used the building. Beginning in the 1990s, Gigglebees Restaurant and Arcade occupied the space until 2008, when they closed their doors. Finally, the building took on a major renovation project and is now occupied by One American Bank. (Above, courtesy Olin Odland.)

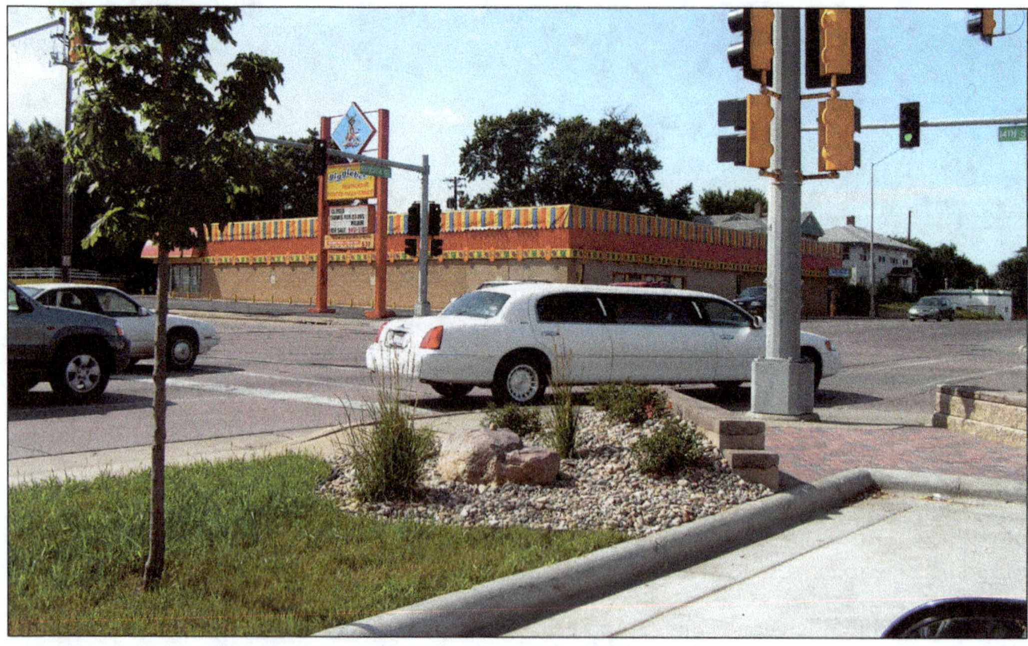

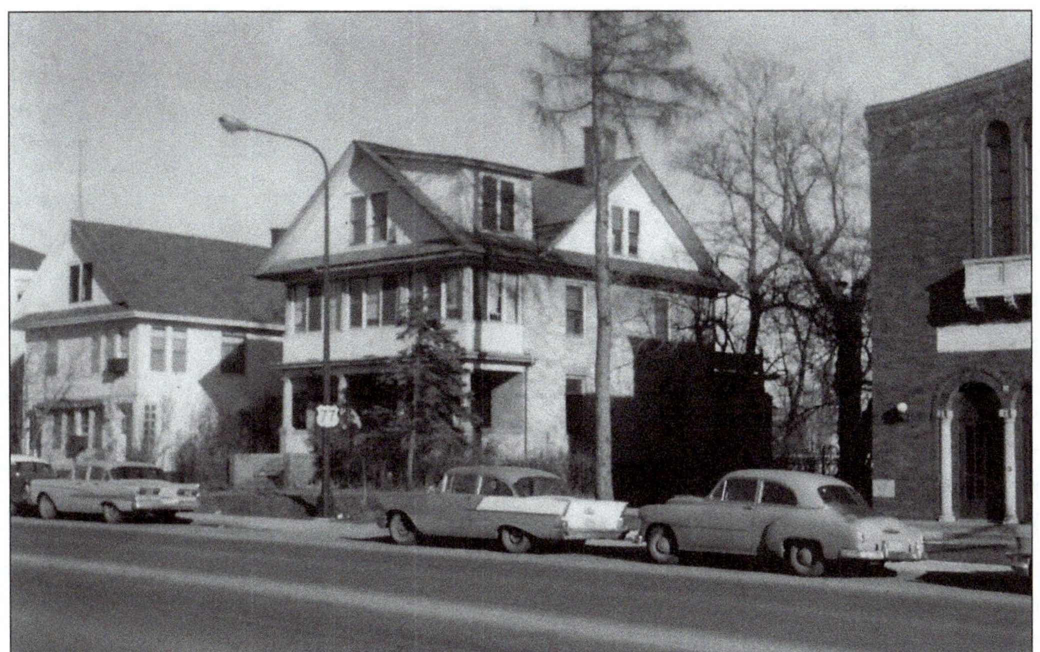

The above view is looking northeast from Fourteenth Street and Minnesota Avenue in 1962. The building at center was constructed in 1910 as a residence for the Ballard family. Ballard and Son Monument Company was an early Sioux Falls business that carved headstones out of marble. Their home was built with a marble block exterior and marble accents throughout. Wendell and Ken Hanson moved their realty business to this location and remodeled the house to appear as it does below. Former Sioux Falls mayor and current South Dakota public utilities commissioner Gary Hanson joined Hanson Realty in 1973. (Both, courtesy Gary Hanson.)

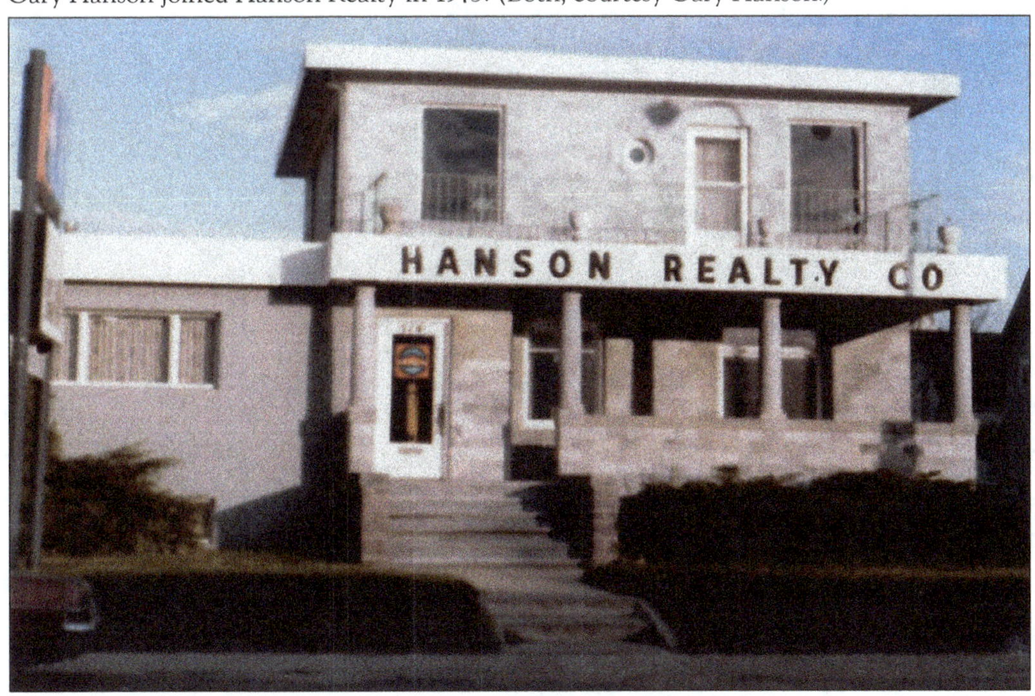

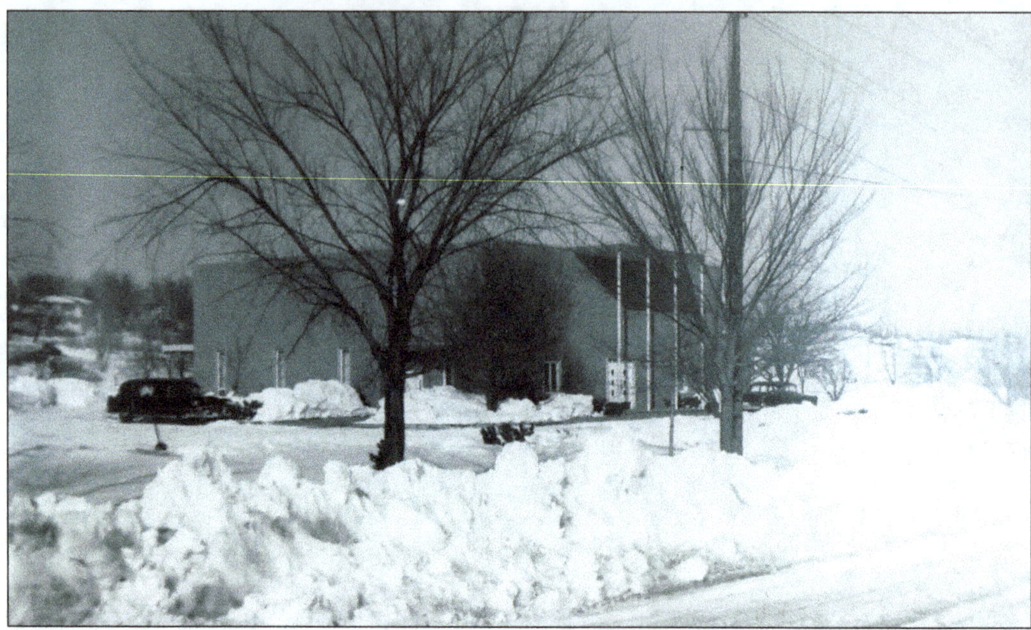

H.L. "Bud" Benz began his career in the funeral business working at the Banton Funeral Home at 400 West Eleventh Street. In 1952, Benz built the above funeral home at 420 West Thirty-Seventh Street, where Sioux Falls Fire Station No. 3 is now located. Benz continued in business until May 1972. The building was sold to and used by the Minnehaha County Extension Office before it was remodeled into the fire station. H.L. Benz was grandson to Hubert and Corlie Loonan, who owned Loonan Lumber Company, a longtime Sioux Falls lumber company. The picture below was taken in 1962 and shows the fleet of funeral cars parked on the west side of the Benz Funeral Home. The vehicle at far left is an ambulance. Up until the late 1960s, it was common for funeral homes to provide ambulance services, as they had vehicles long enough to transport an injured or sick person on a stretcher. (Both, courtesy Hubert "Skip" Benz.)

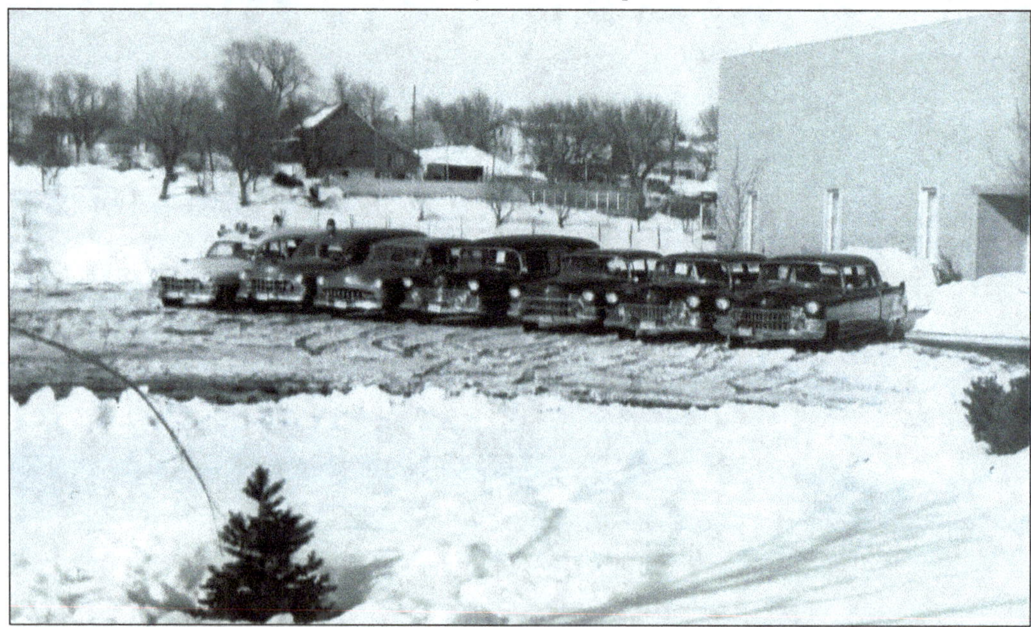

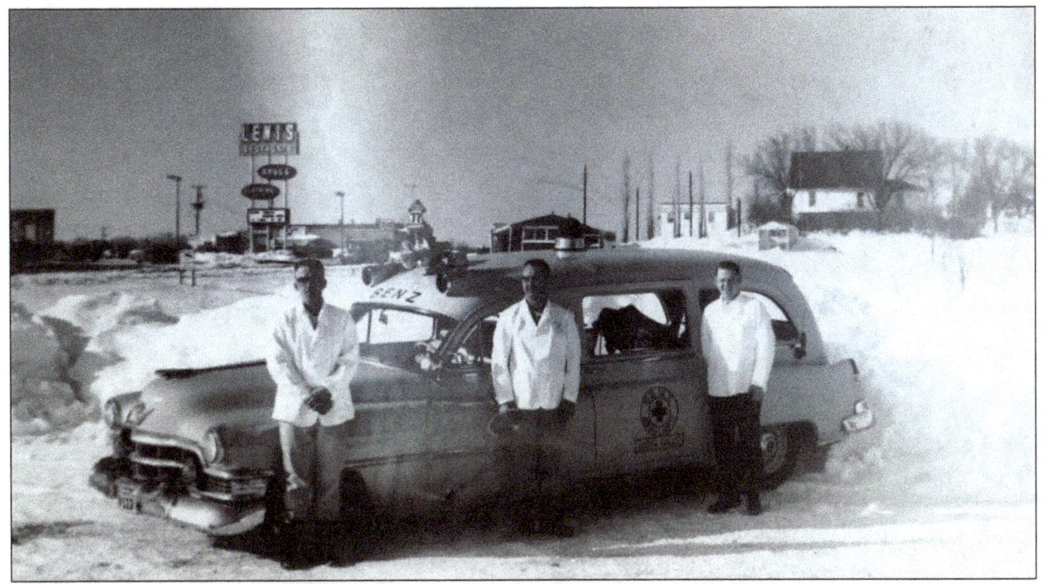

This view shows some young funeral directors in front of the Benz Funeral Home after a record snowfall. From left to right are Sherwood "Woody" Doggett, Jack Pepper, and Doug Noteboom. Lewis Southgate can be seen in the background, on Thirty-Fifth Street and Minnesota Avenue, its location at that time. Today, Poppadox Pub, Culvers Restaurant, and Famous Dave's Restaurant are in this once-open area to the north. (Courtesy Hubert "Skip" Benz.)

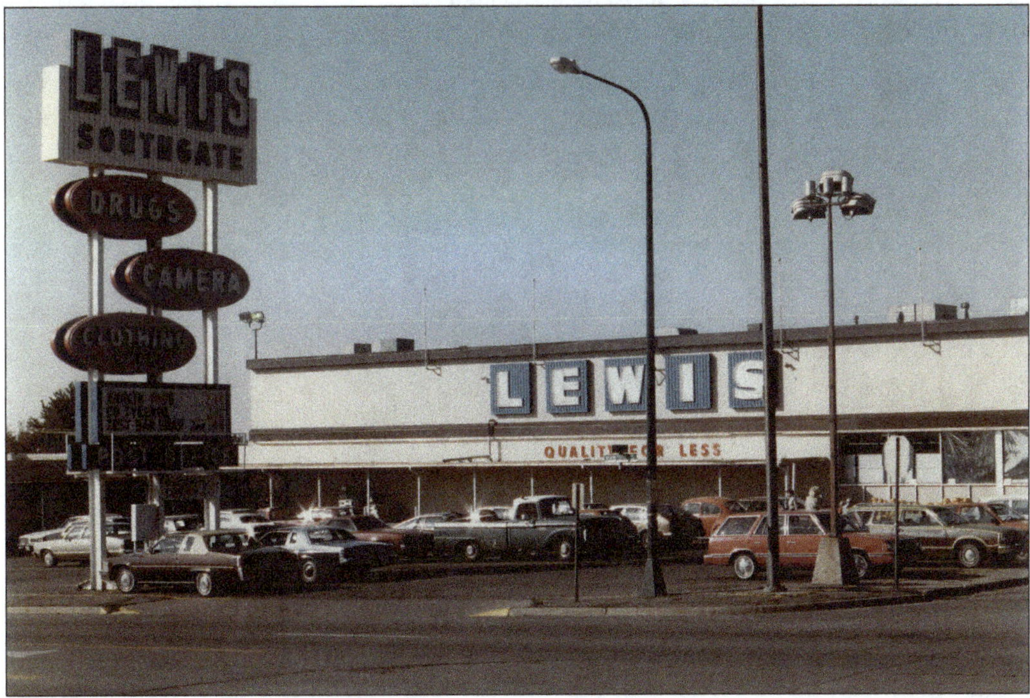

Lewis Drug Store was established on February 10, 1942, at 309 South Phillips Avenue and celebrates its 75th anniversary in 2017. In 1956, the store opened on the southwest corner of Thirty-Fifth Street and Minnesota Avenue. Today, this is the corporate headquarters for over 50 stores throughout South Dakota, Minnesota, and Iowa. (Courtesy Lewis Drug Store.)

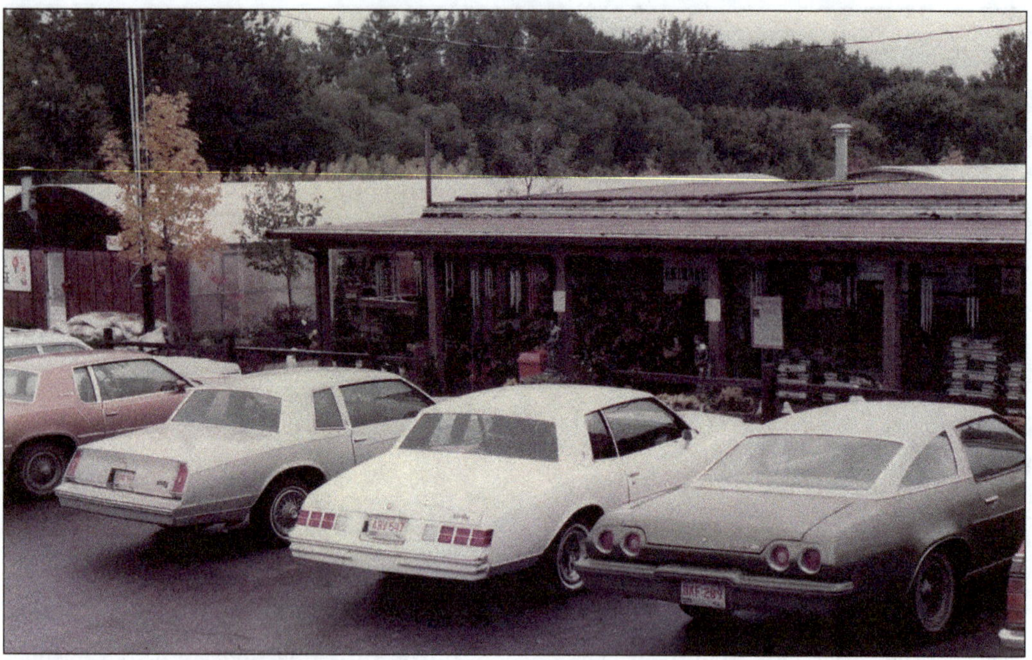

Cliff Avenue Greenhouse and Garden Center has kept the yards of Sioux Falls beautiful since the 1950s. Dick and Jane Bills bought the greenhouse from Daniel Grimsbo in 1971. The Bills family has owned and operated it since. Today, daughters Hayley (Bills) Zeigler and Heidi (Bills) Teal run the two locations. (Courtesy Bills family.)

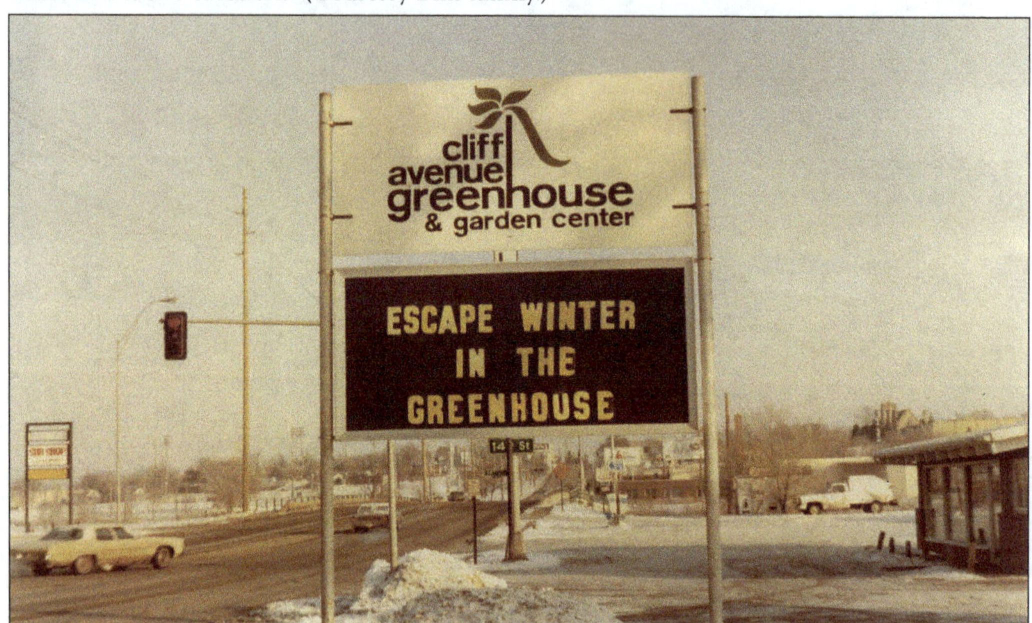

Originally, the Cliff Avenue Greenhouse was located at 600 South Cliff Avenue, where Fourteenth Street dead-ended. River Boulevard now runs through the original property of Cliff Avenue Greenhouse. In 1984, the greenhouse moved to its Twenty-Sixth Street location, next to Interstate 229. In 1992, a west side location sprouted on Forty-First Street, west of Sertoma Avenue. (Courtesy Bills family.)

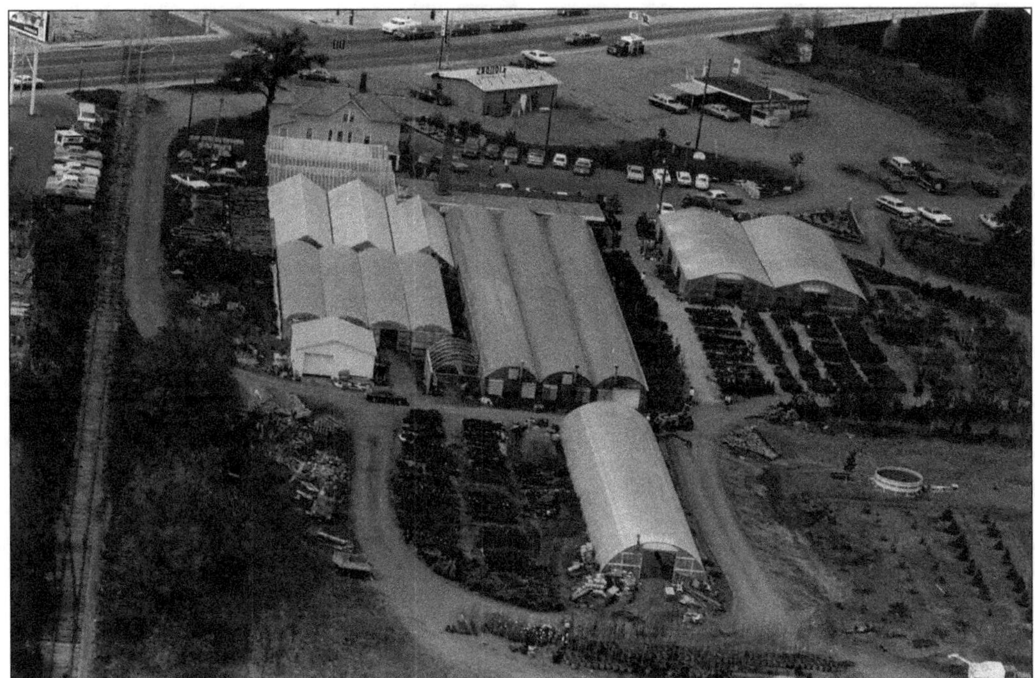

This is an aerial view of Cliff Avenue Greenhouse and Garden Center. The road at the top is Cliff Avenue. The street that dead-ends is Fourteenth Street. Today, Fourteenth Street continues east onto River Boulevard. To the right of the greenhouses are Cliff House Liquor and Thurman's Drive Inn. (Courtesy Bills family.)

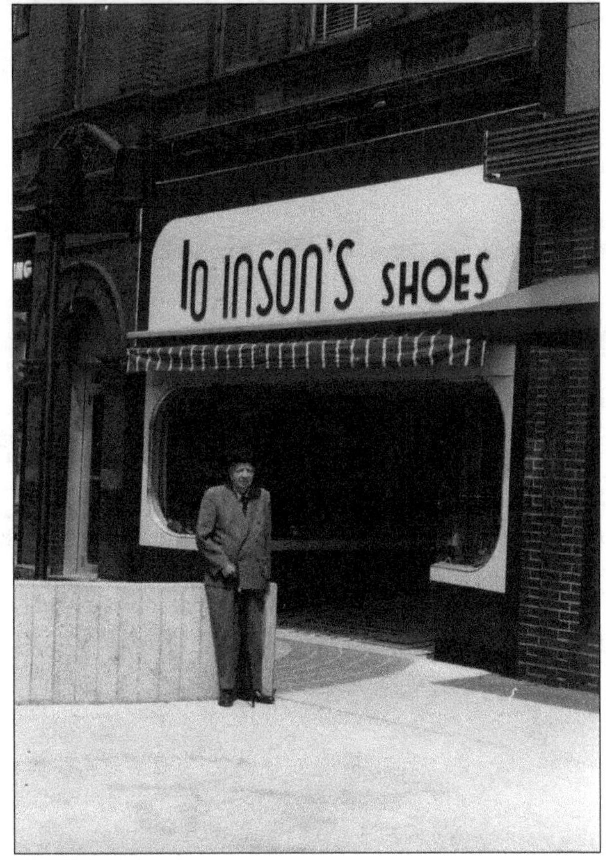

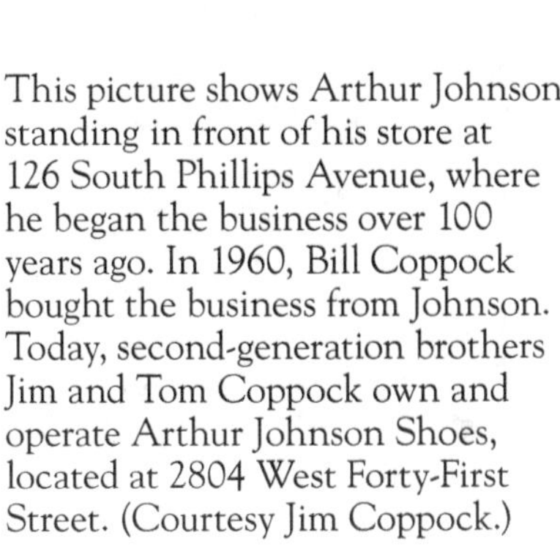

This picture shows Arthur Johnson standing in front of his store at 126 South Phillips Avenue, where he began the business over 100 years ago. In 1960, Bill Coppock bought the business from Johnson. Today, second-generation brothers Jim and Tom Coppock own and operate Arthur Johnson Shoes, located at 2804 West Forty-First Street. (Courtesy Jim Coppock.)

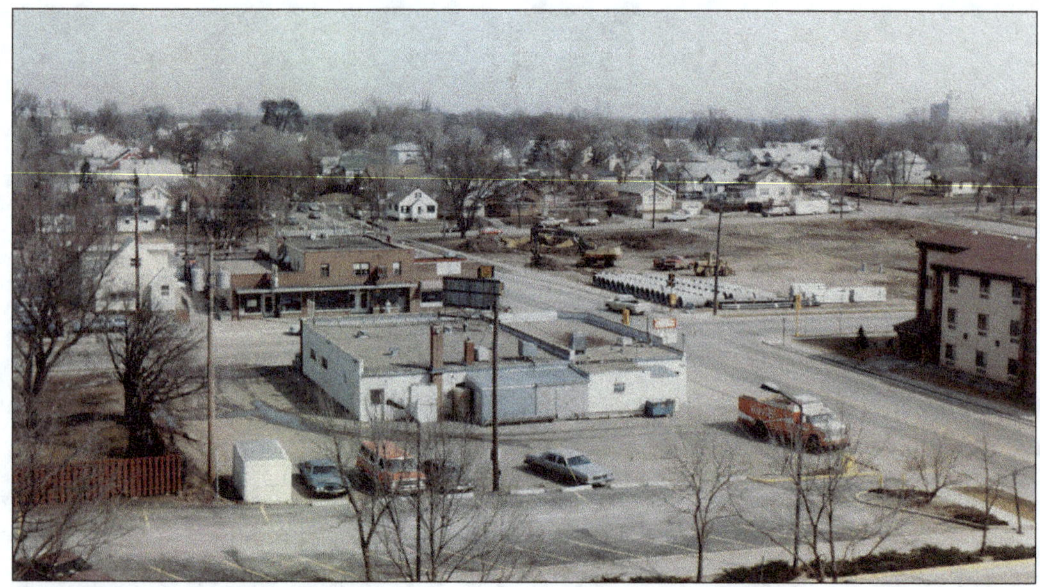

At some point, the Alick family has run a business or businesses on all four corners of Grange Avenue and Eighteenth Street. In 1928, Joe Alick Sr. began the family business, renting space in a building on the northwest corner of the intersection. Expanding his business, he bought land on the southwest corner of the intersection from the Hayward family and built a new grocery store in front of Sioux Valley Hospital, which was constructed in 1930. In 1984, the family built the Alick Valley Inn on the southeast corner of the intersection. The hotel provided housing for families of patients staying at Sioux Valley Hospital, an idea learned from the Mayo Clinic. In 1986, the Alick Valley Mall was built on the northeast corner of the intersection. Joe Alick Sr. and his wife, Mary, had four sons and one daughter. All the children, at some point, worked for their father and learned his impressive business skills. Sam, Joe Jr., and Rich eventually took over and greatly expanded the family businesses throughout the Sioux Falls community. (Both, courtesy Joe Alick Jr.)

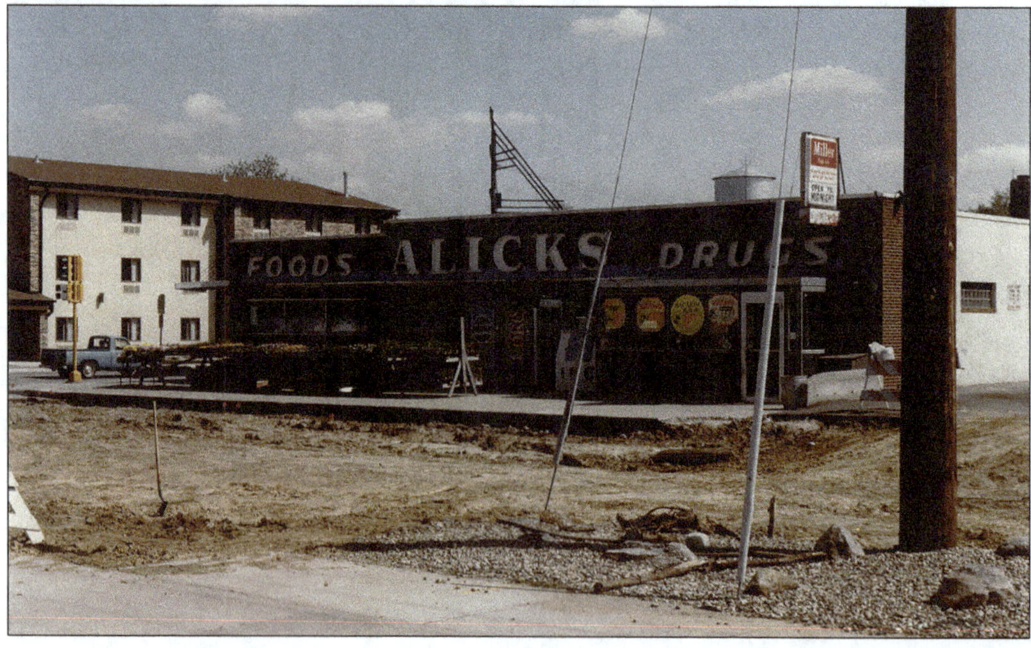

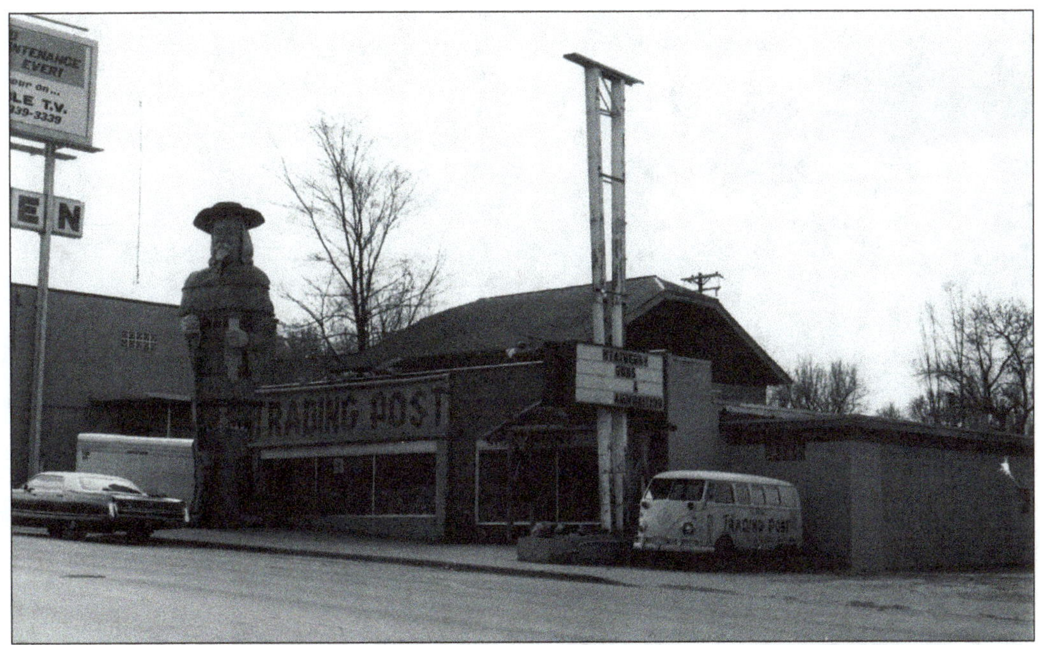

This view of 1711 West Twelfth St. was photographed in 1978. Note the Buffalo Bill figure standing at left in front of the Trading Post store. Buffalo Bill made his way around the city. Previously, he stood at Buffalo Bill's Wild West Family Restaurant on South Minnesota Avenue. He later was at Frontier Village on North Cliff Avenue. Today, he can be found resting on a trailer near the Sioux Falls Arena. (Courtesy Siouxland Heritage Museums, Sioux Falls, SD.)

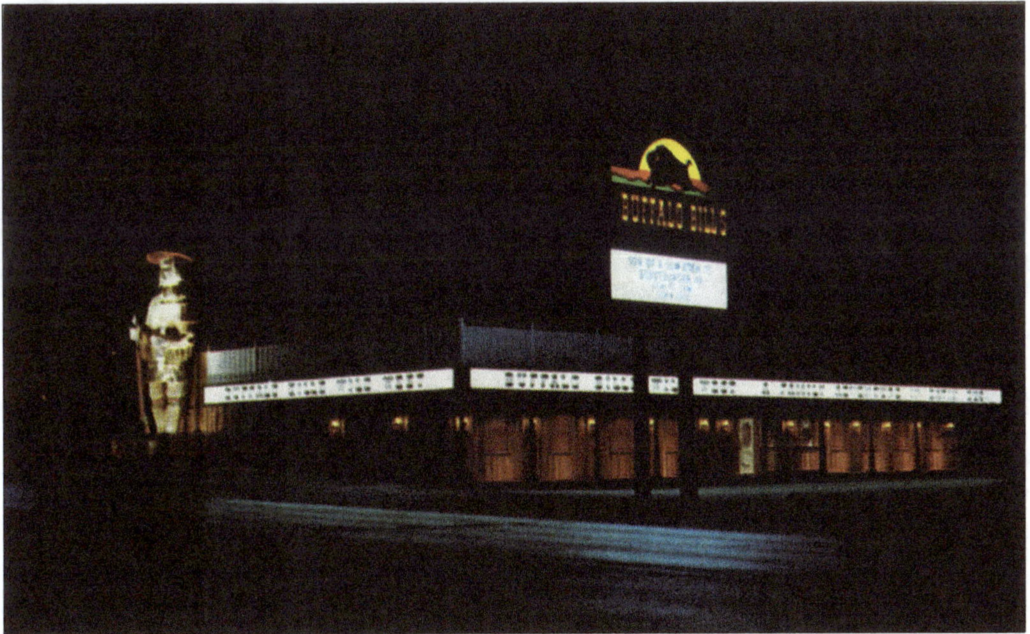

Buffalo Bill's Wild West Family Restaurant and Mr. Jiggs Steakhouse once occupied the Poppadox Pub building on South Minnesota Avenue. The neighbor to the north is Culvers Restaurant, and farther north is Famous Daves Bar-B-Que. King's Food Host, Crack'd Pot, and KCS restaurants were in the same building as Famous Daves.

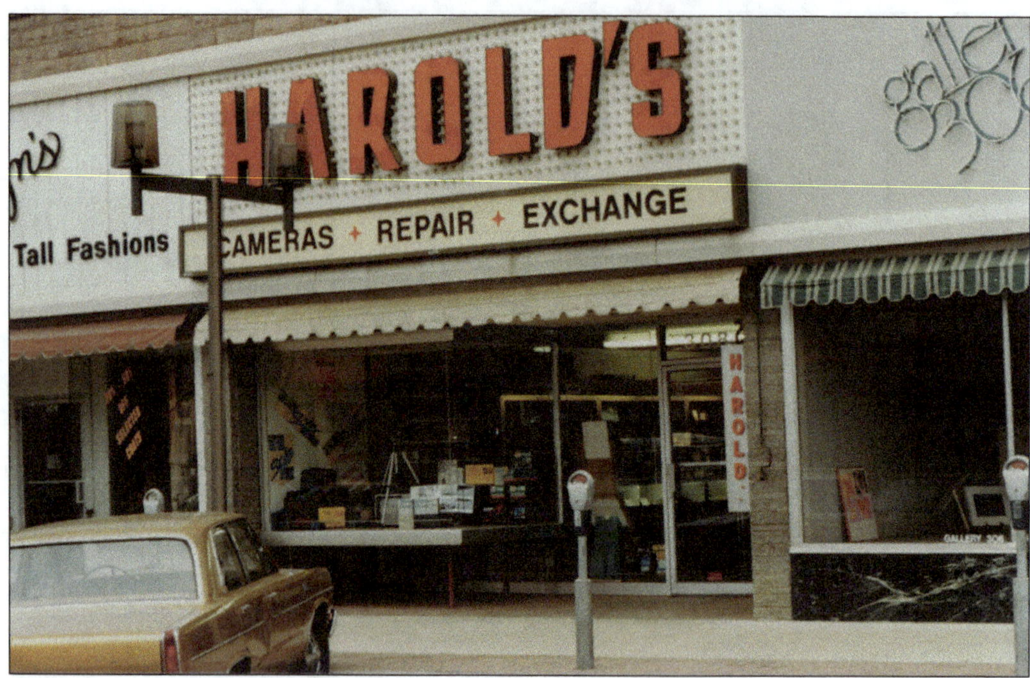

Since Sioux Falls began in 1856 with Fort Dakota, there have been incredible pictures taken over the years, but only one photography company has stood the test of time. Emil C. Hanson began a photography business in Sioux Falls after purchasing the portrait studio of George W. Fox in 1910. From 1912 through 1923, Hanson ran the business with his father-in-law, Charles Leigh, beginning a two-generation business. In 1938, the third generation began with Hanson's sons Howard and Harold joining at a new location under the name Harold's Photography, at 308 South Phillips Avenue. Howard and Harold's children joined in the late 1960s, making it a four-generation family business. Today, Howard's son Bob Hanson runs the Sioux Falls Harold's Photo Experts stores with his daughter Emily Erfman and sons Davis and Andrew, making it a five-generation business that has lasted over 116 years in Sioux Falls. (Both, courtesy Harold's Photo.)

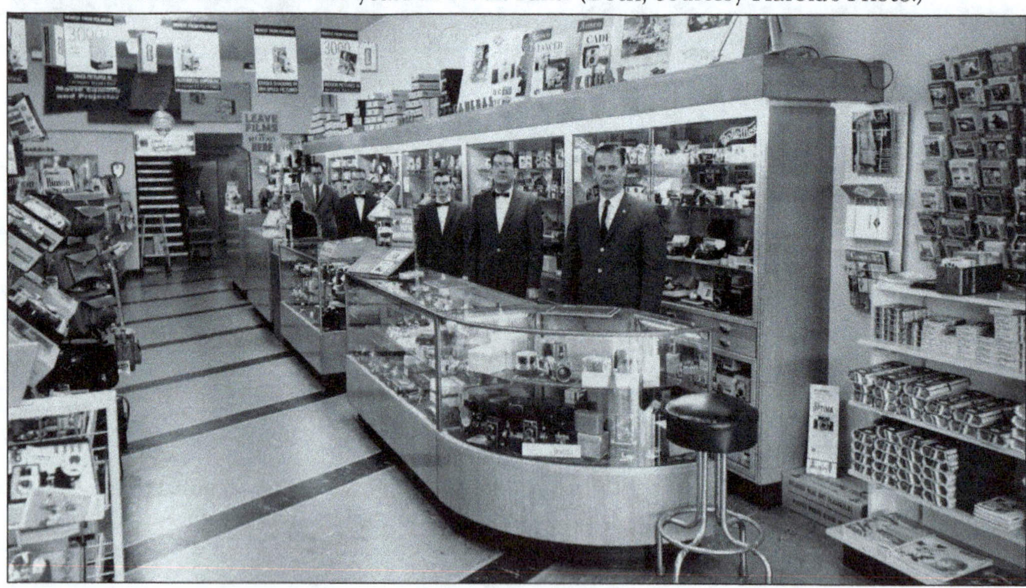

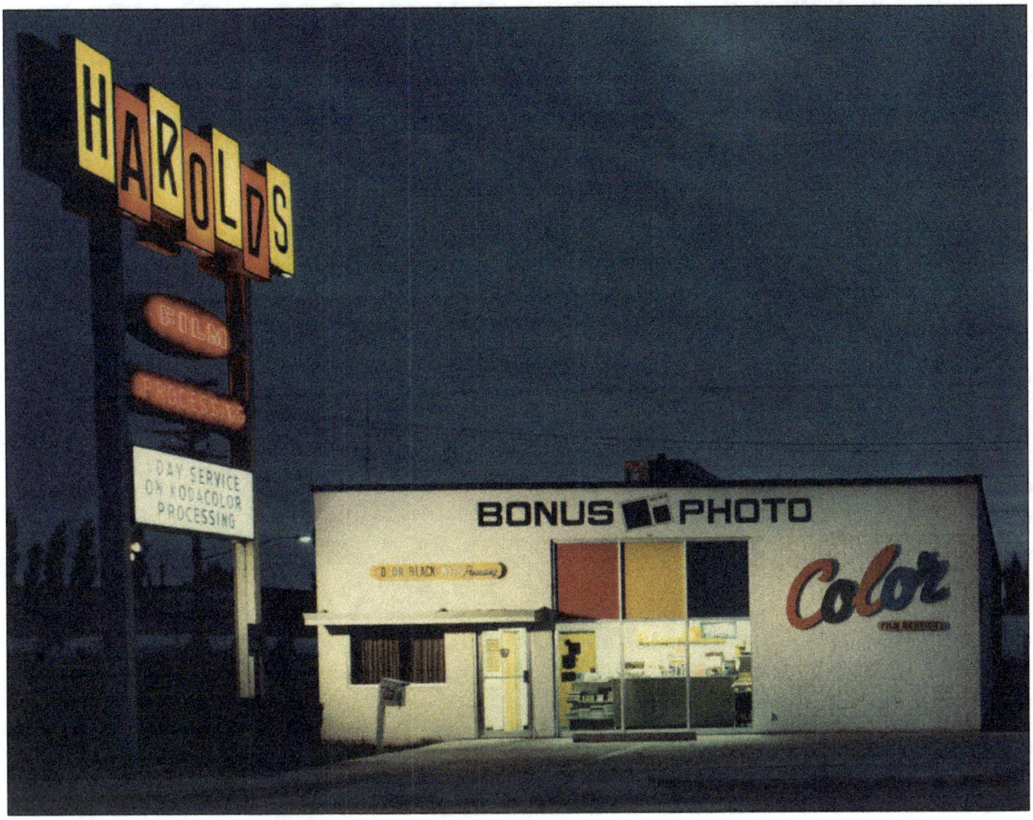

Harold's Photo has been in Sioux Falls for over 100 years. Above is a picture of the 912 West Forty-First Street store. This was originally on the edge of town and built for the C.M. Olsen paint warehouse, seen below. The paint delivery truck would enter the building and drive through the center. Above, the original entrance has been remodeled with three glass and colored panels. The current building has been beautifully remodeled since the above picture was taken, but a careful observer can still see where the trucks would have driven through. (Both, courtesy Harold's Photo.)

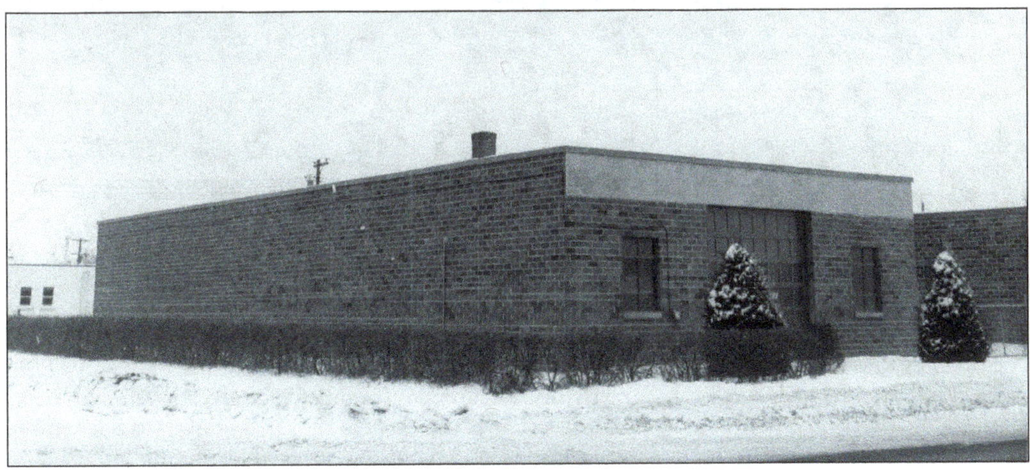

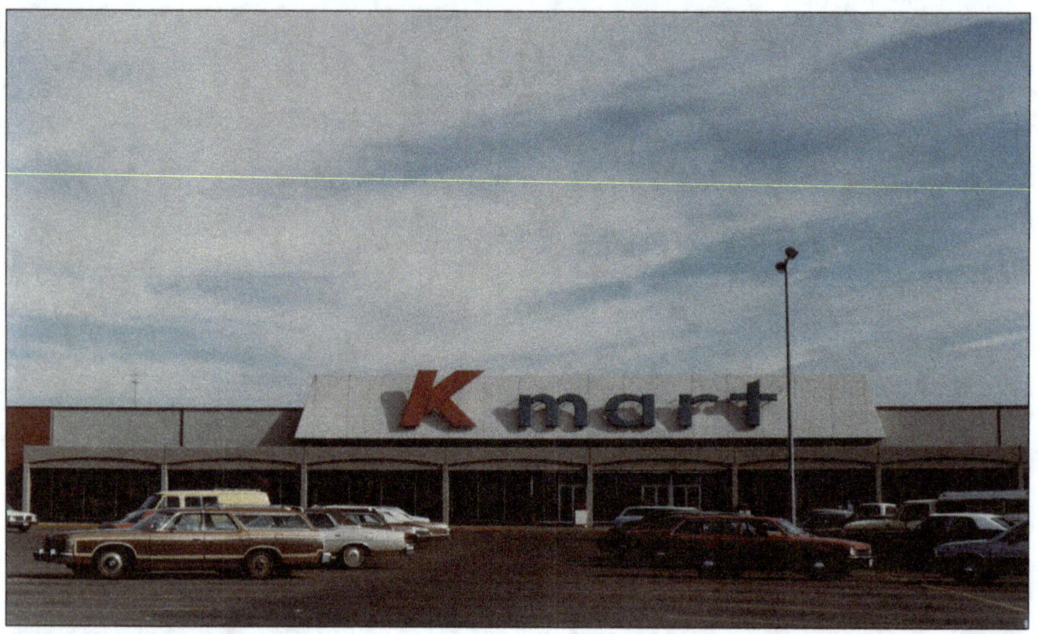

Kmart was built at 3000 South Minnesota Avenue. This was one of the first big stores to be built away from downtown Sioux Falls, in October 1963. This new concept offered many departments under one roof and all on one level compared to the stores downtown that had multiple floors. The store closed in 2006 and was torn down for a new Hy-Vee grocery store. (Courtesy Judy Eisenbraun.)

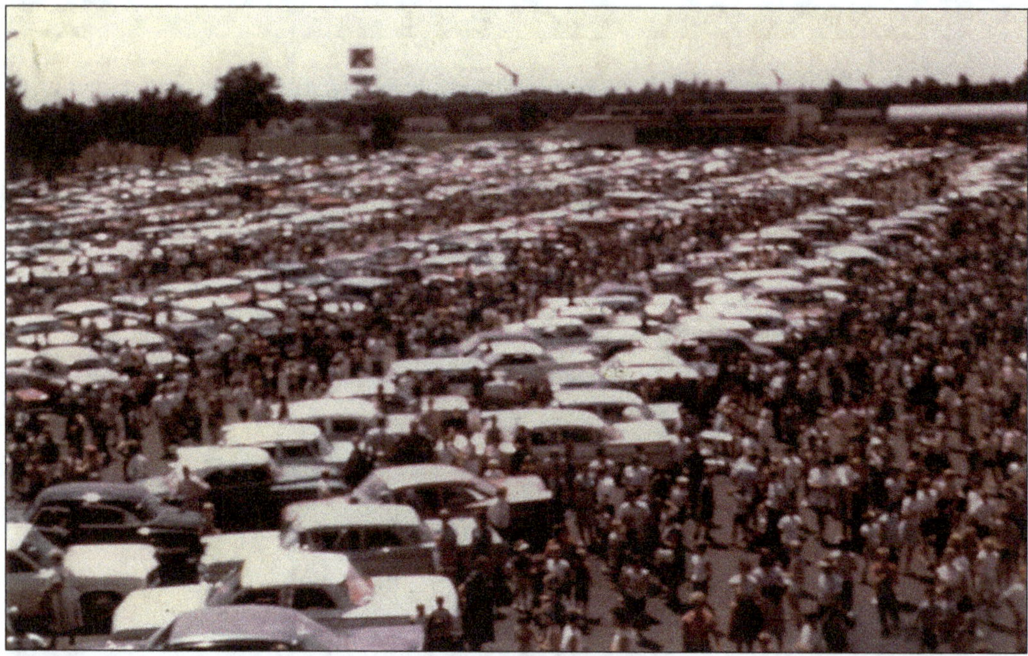

The opening day of Kmart on South Minnesota Avenue was a big event for many in the city. Part of the grand opening included an airplane flying over, dropping numbered ping pong balls for prizes. There were close to 10,000 people in the parking lot for the event. This photograph was taken from the roof of the Kmart looking west toward Minnesota Avenue. (Courtesy Judy Eisenbraun.)

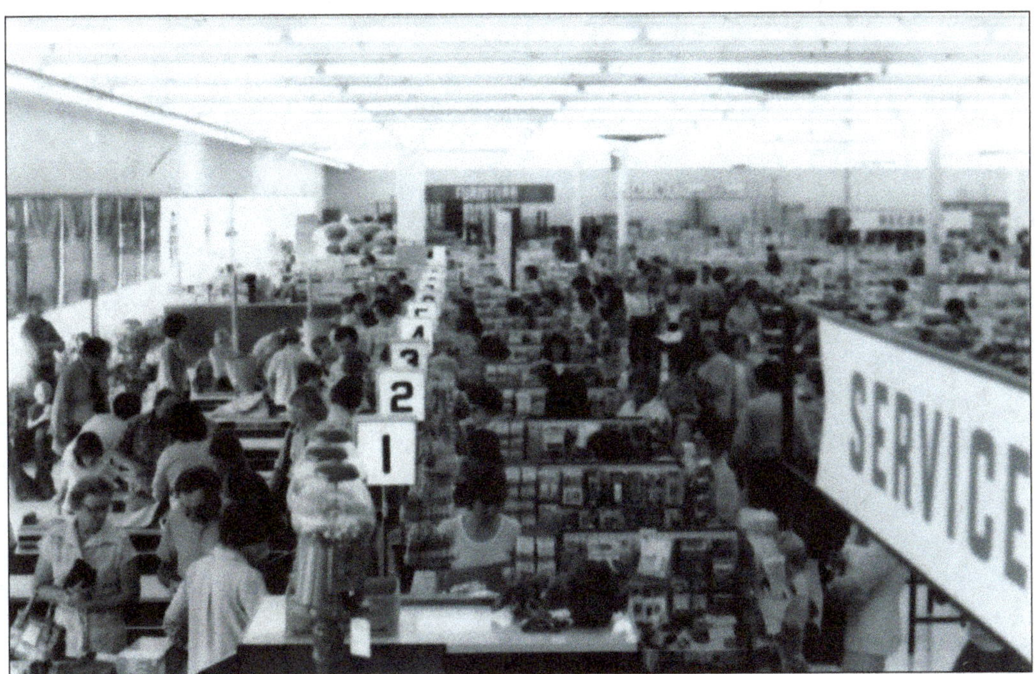

Two other Kmart stores opened in Sioux Falls in the early 1980s: one at 3709 East Tenth Street and another at 3020 West Twelfth Street. The West Twelfth Street location was the last survivor of the Kmart chain in Sioux Falls and closed in 2017. (Courtesy Judy Eisenbraun.)

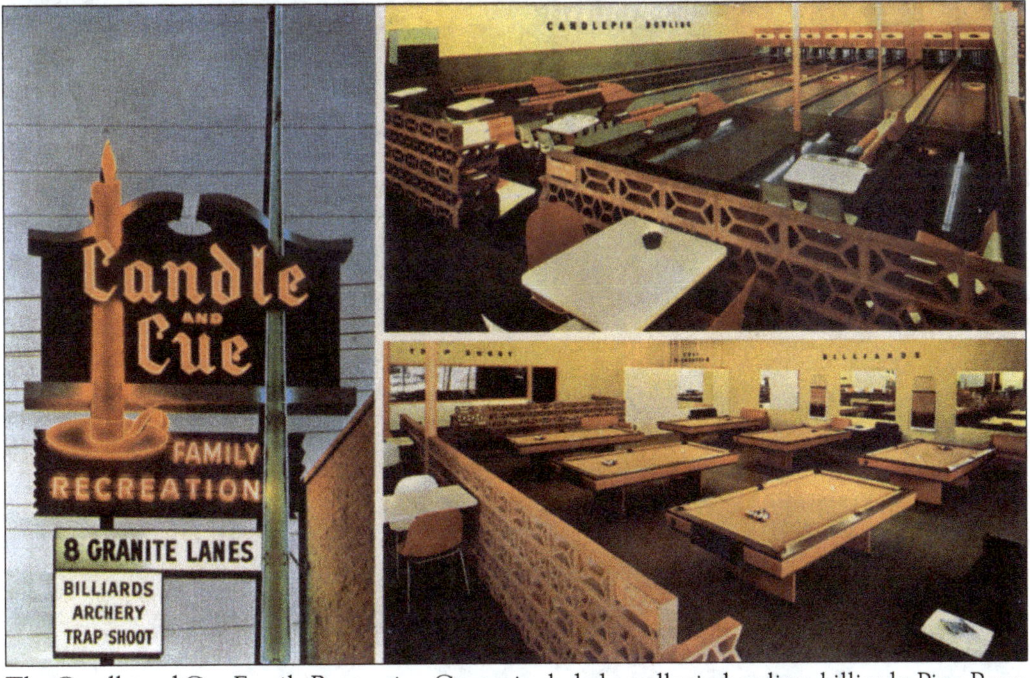

The Candle and Cue Family Recreation Center included candlepin bowling, billiards, Ping Pong, shuffleboard, and coin machines. Candlepins are shaped more like a cylinder instead of a common bowling pin. This business was promoted as the First Granite Candlepin Recreation Center and was located at 417 West Thirty-Third Street, slightly east of Minnesota Avenue.

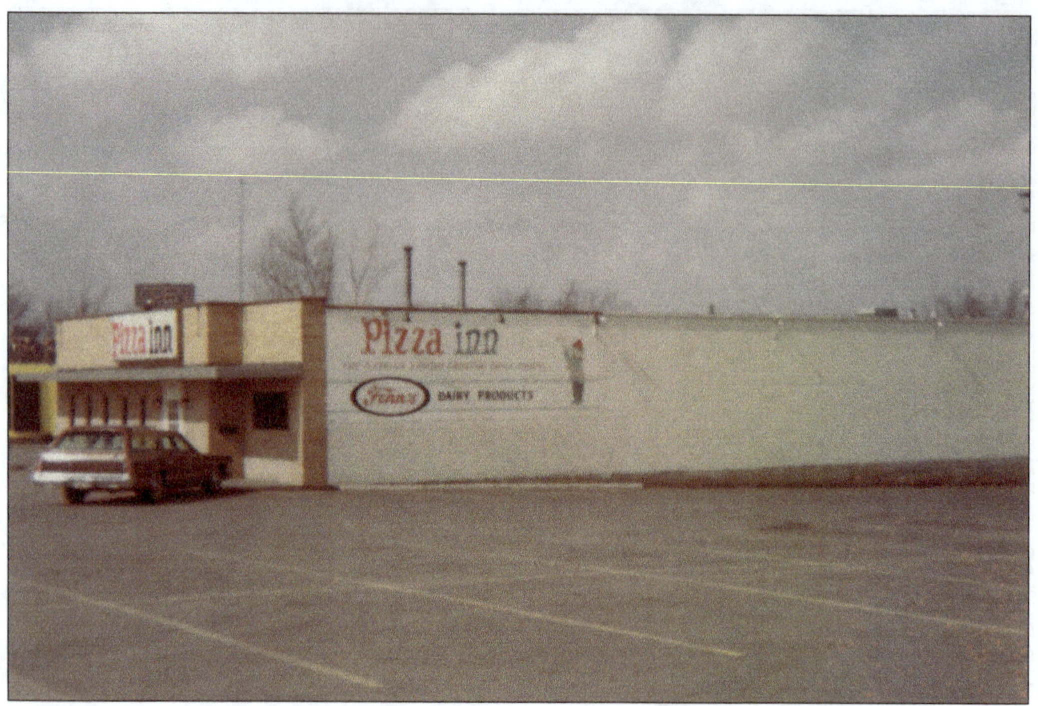

Pizza Inn opened in Sioux Falls in 1967 and continued in business until December 2015. The above picture shows the building where the restaurant was started, at 2208 East Tenth Street. It was originally a Piggly Wiggly grocery store. The picture below shows how the restaurant looked after remodeling, before it was torn down and rebuilt as a Popeye's restaurant. In the background, the South Dakota School for the Deaf can be seen. (Both, courtesy Wally and Doris Johnson.)

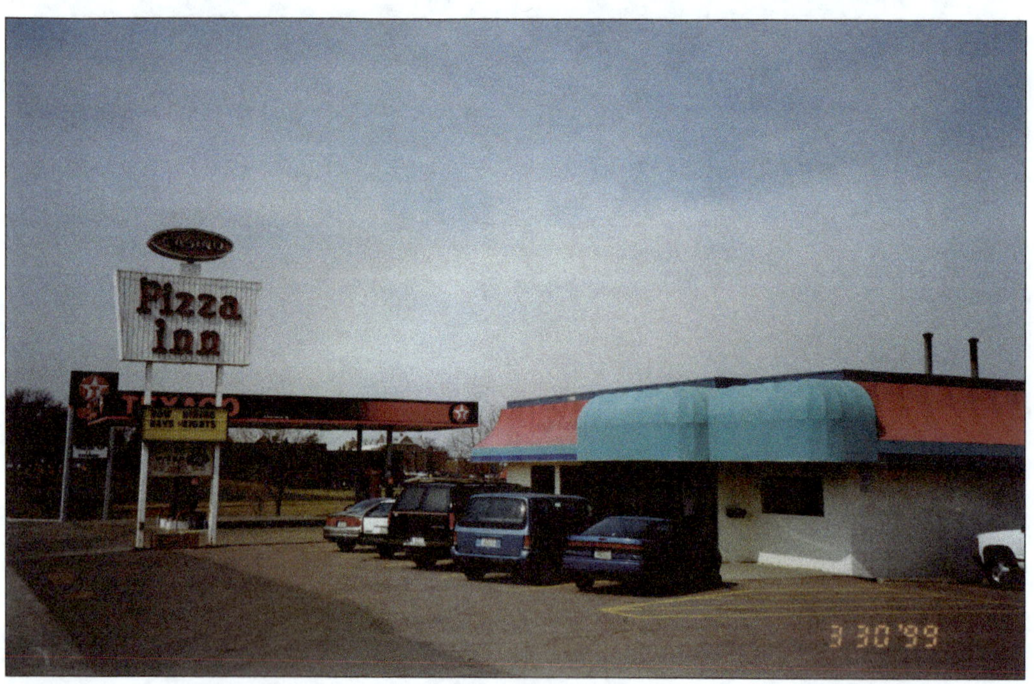

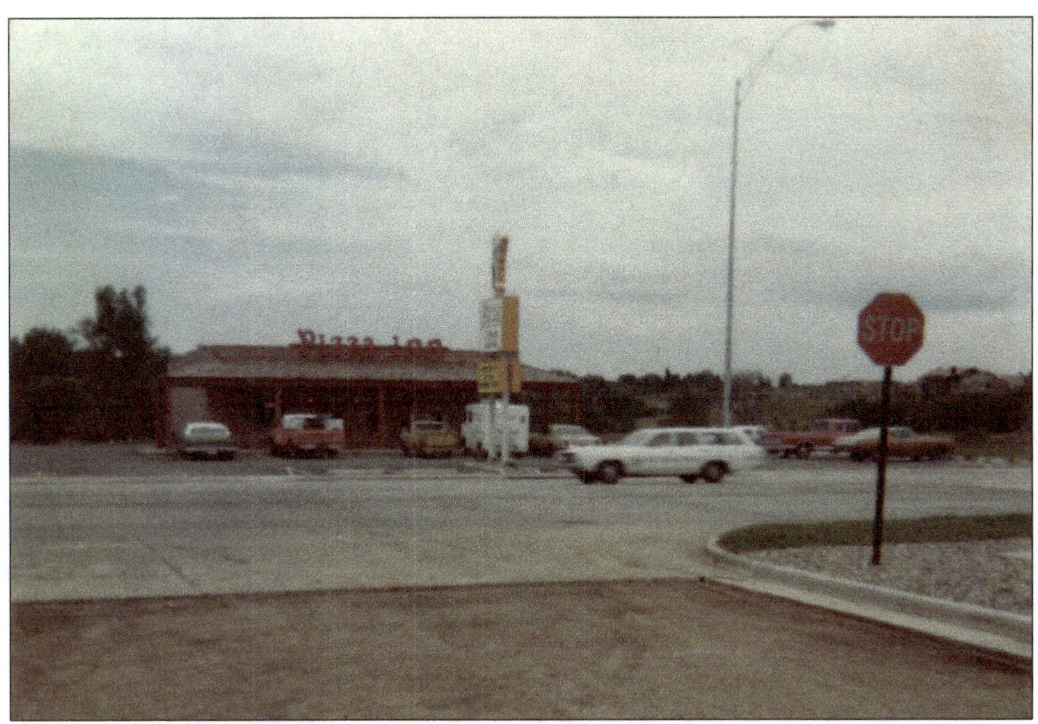

In February 1976, a second Pizza Inn was built at 3600 West Forty-First Street near Louise Avenue. Prior to Pizza Inn being built at this location, it was an open field. The location stayed in business until December 2013. The picture below shows what the restaurant looked like before its closing. Wally Johnson worked with his wife, Doris; son Mark; and grandsons Matthew and Allan in the business. During 49 years of business, they made over half a million pizzas. (Both, courtesy Wally and Doris Johnson.)

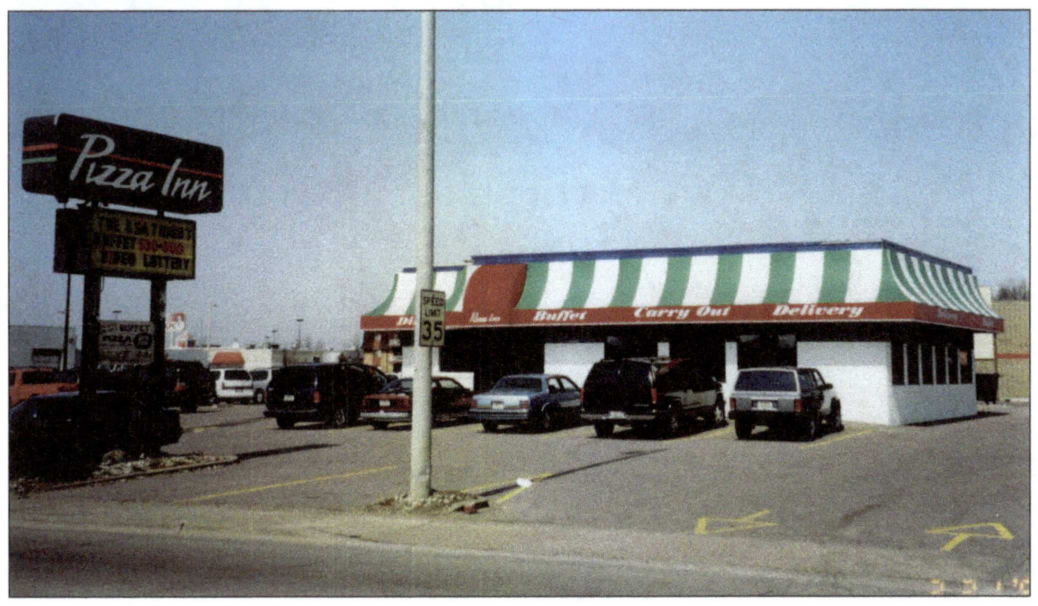

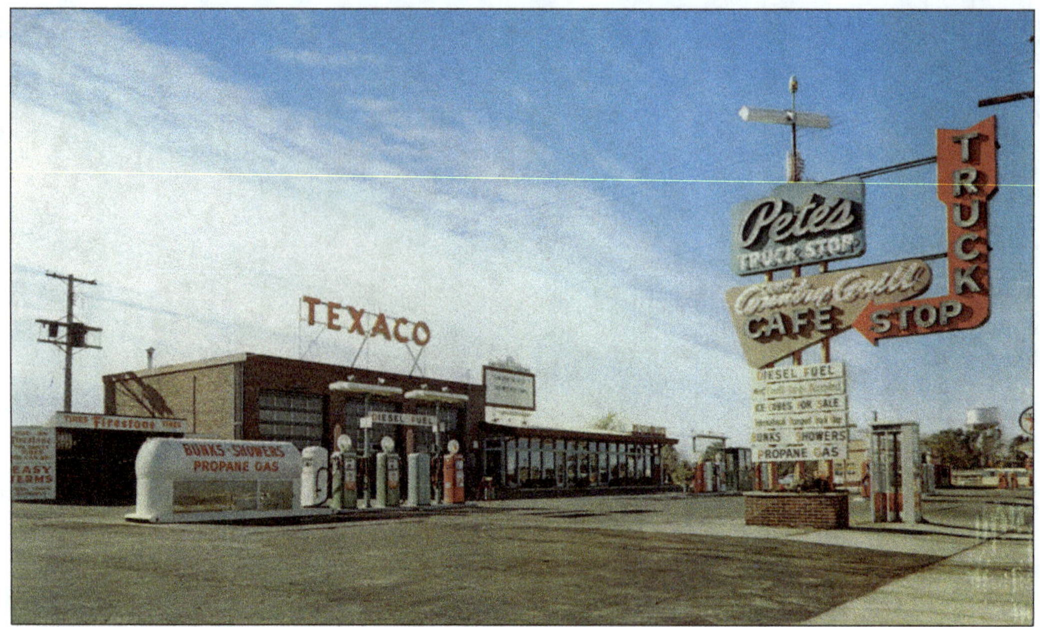

Pete's Texaco Super Service and Truck Stop was located at 2405 East Tenth Street near Interstate 229. Chris' Country Grill was in the west end of the building. For many years, this building was known as Cone's Corner. In 2011, fire destroyed the structure. The corner is now home to a strip mall.

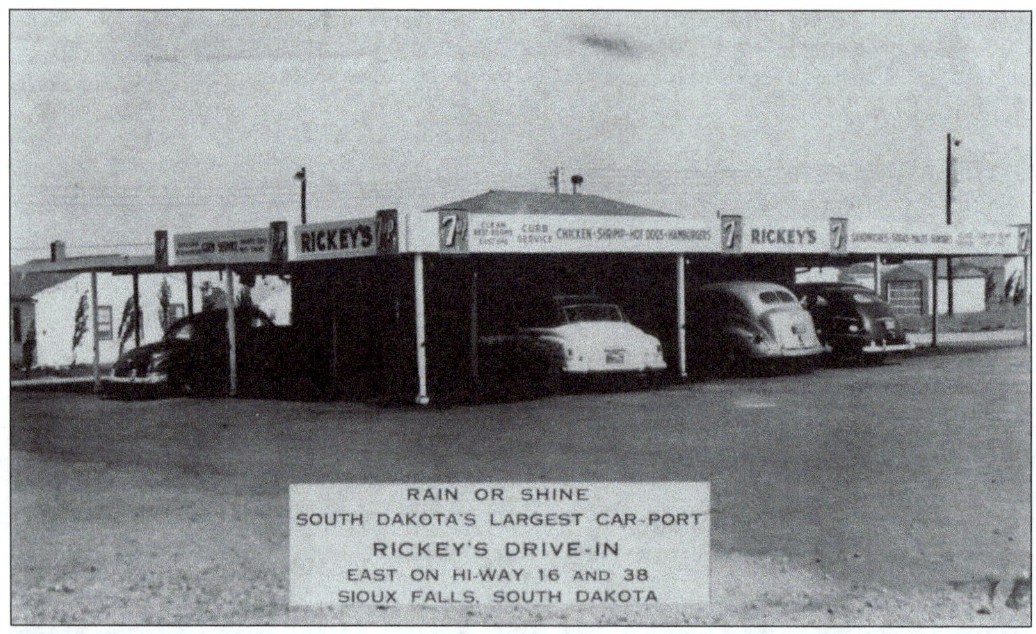

Rickey's Drive-In was located at 2212 East Tenth Street, across the street from Pete's Texaco Super Service and Truck Stop and to the east of Pizza Inn. Richard (Ricky) Haggar started the business in the early 1950s and continued it until the late 1960s. The restaurant was known for its Ricky's Quicky Chicky.

Crossroads has provided Christian books, music, church supplies, and gifts for nearly 50 years. Pictured is the first location on the south side of Ninth Street, between Phillips and Main Avenues. The business has seen the transition of music, beginning with eight tracks and vinyl LPs and now offering digital downloads. This building was constructed in 1883, as shown on the marker on top. (Courtesy Siouxland Heritage Museums, Sioux Falls, SD.)

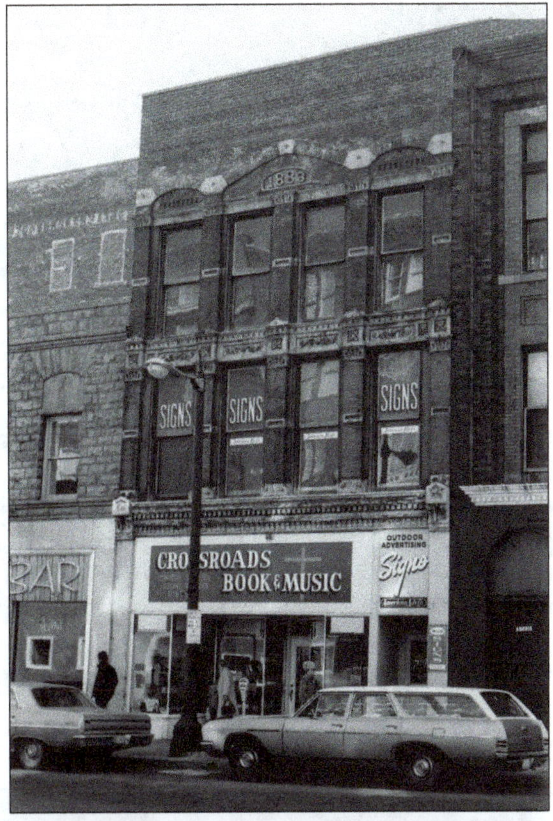

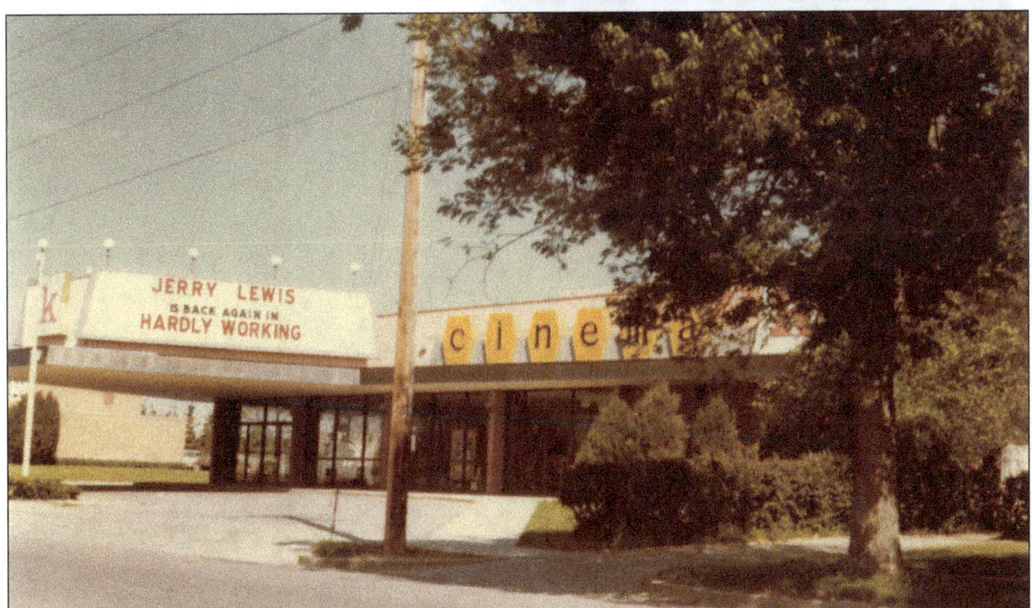

The K Cinema Theatre was built in 1968 on the north side of Thirty-Seventh Street, between Minnesota and Phillips Avenues. It was the vision of Sioux Falls radio and television pioneer Joe Floyd. The movie theater stayed open until 1983. Today, the Sioux Falls Lutheran School occupies the building. (Courtesy Siouxland Heritage Museums, Sioux Falls, SD.)

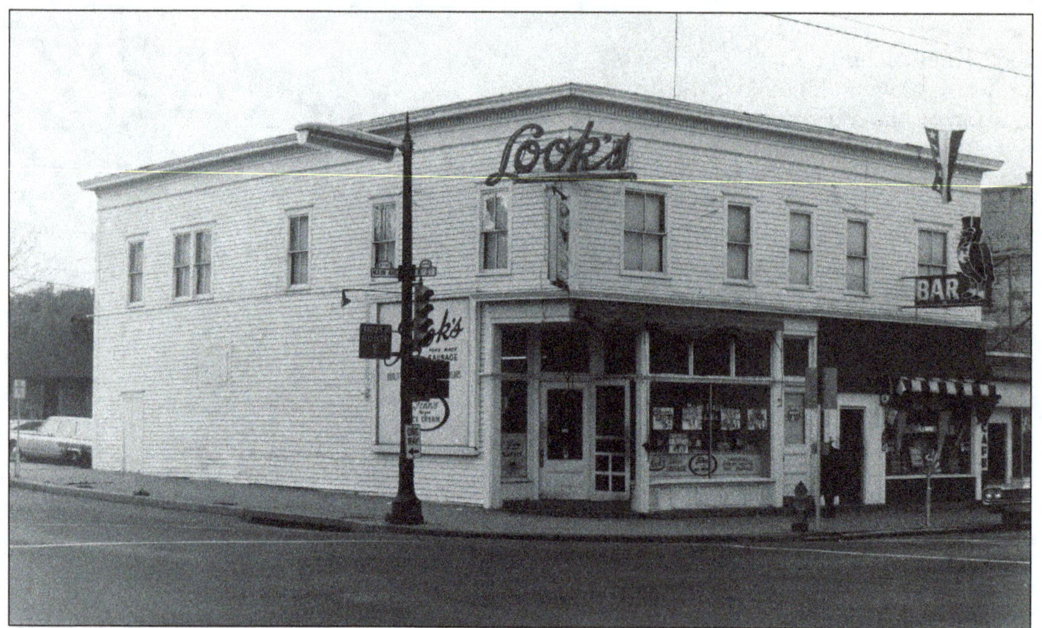

Beginning in 1883, Look's Market offered the area's finest meats. This picture shows the market's first location on the corner of Eighth Street and Main Avenue. Next door is the Crow Bar. Both businesses are in operation today at different locations. This building was torn down, and in 1973, the Sioux Falls Public Library was constructed in its place. (Courtesy Siouxland Heritage Museums, Sioux Falls, SD.)

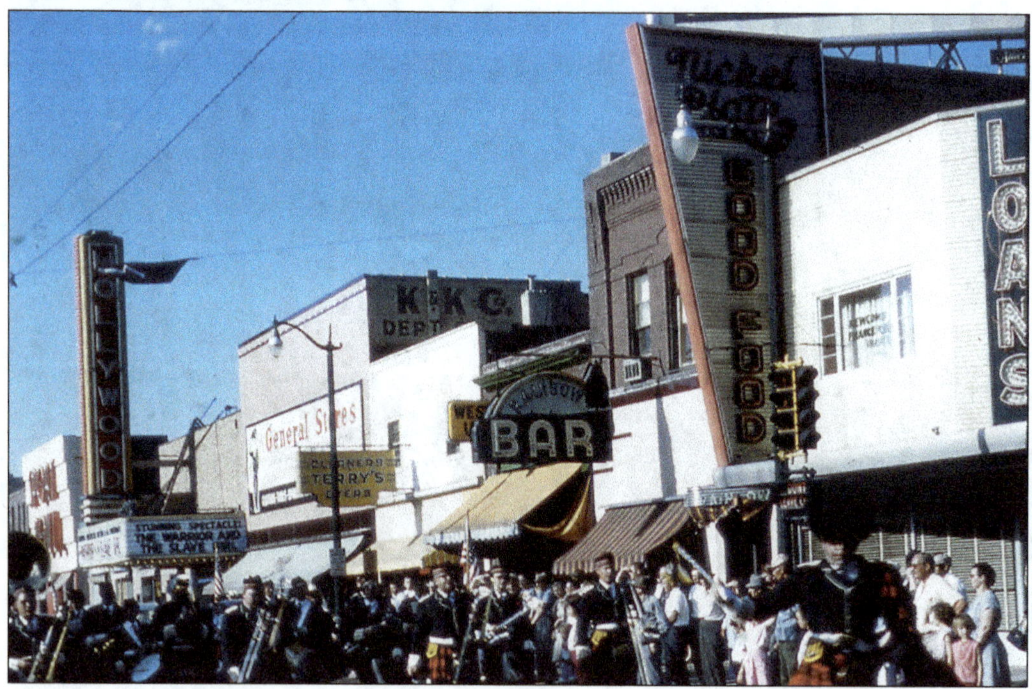

The Nickel Plate Cafe opened in 1940 in two different locations—Eighth Street and Phillips Avenue and Twelfth Street and Phillips Avenue. When the cafe opened, everything cost a nickel. The Twelfth Street location was the last to close, in 1995. (R. Kolbe Dakota collection.)

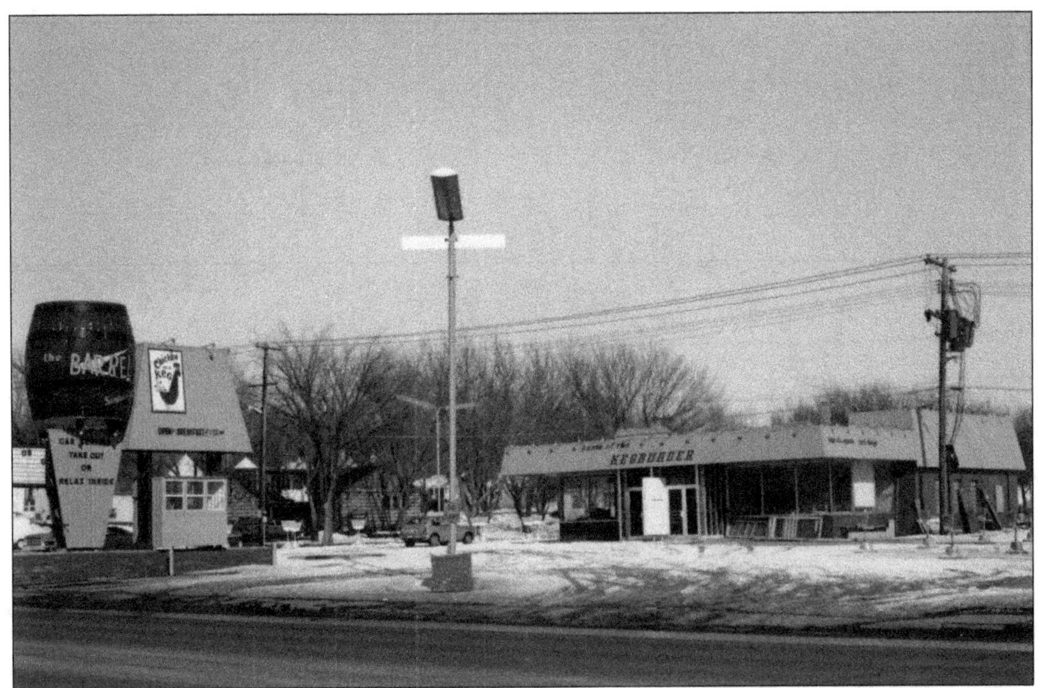

The Barrell Drive-In was located at Thirty-First Street and Minnesota Avenue. In 1939, Lloyd Eagan started the Barrell (misspelled due to a mistake when the sign was made) and continued running it until it closed in the mid-1970s. As fast-food chains became more popular, drive-ins began to close. (Courtesy Siouxland Heritage Museums, Sioux Falls, SD.)

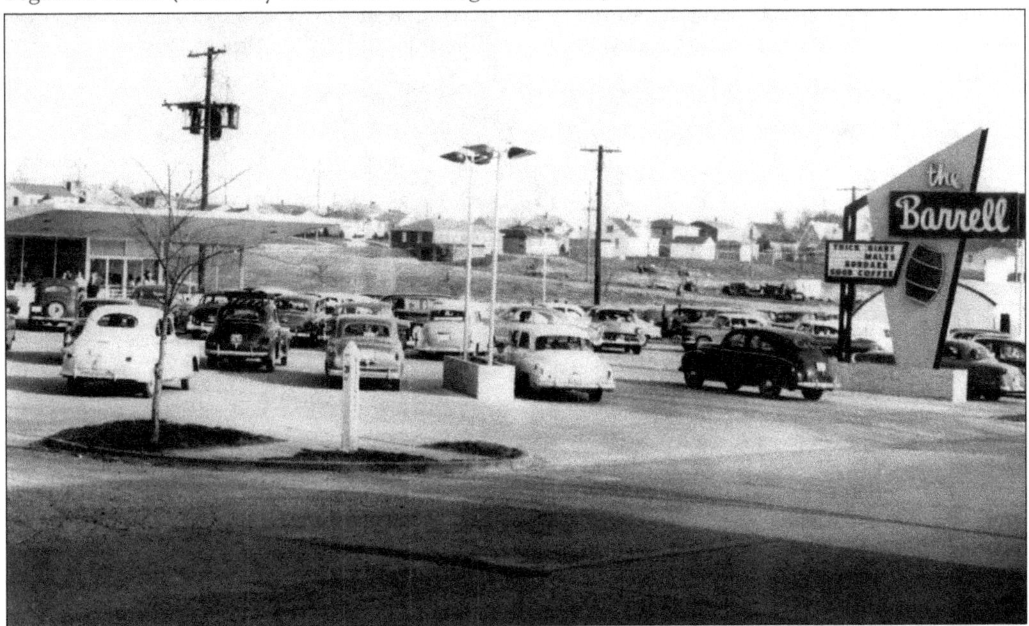

This view of the Barrell Drive-In is looking southeast from Minnesota Avenue. The excellent food and cute carhops made the Barrell a popular hangout for younger people. Maine Lobster and, more recently, Burger King both occupied the same spot. Today, the location is a strip mall. (Courtesy Tom Olsen.)

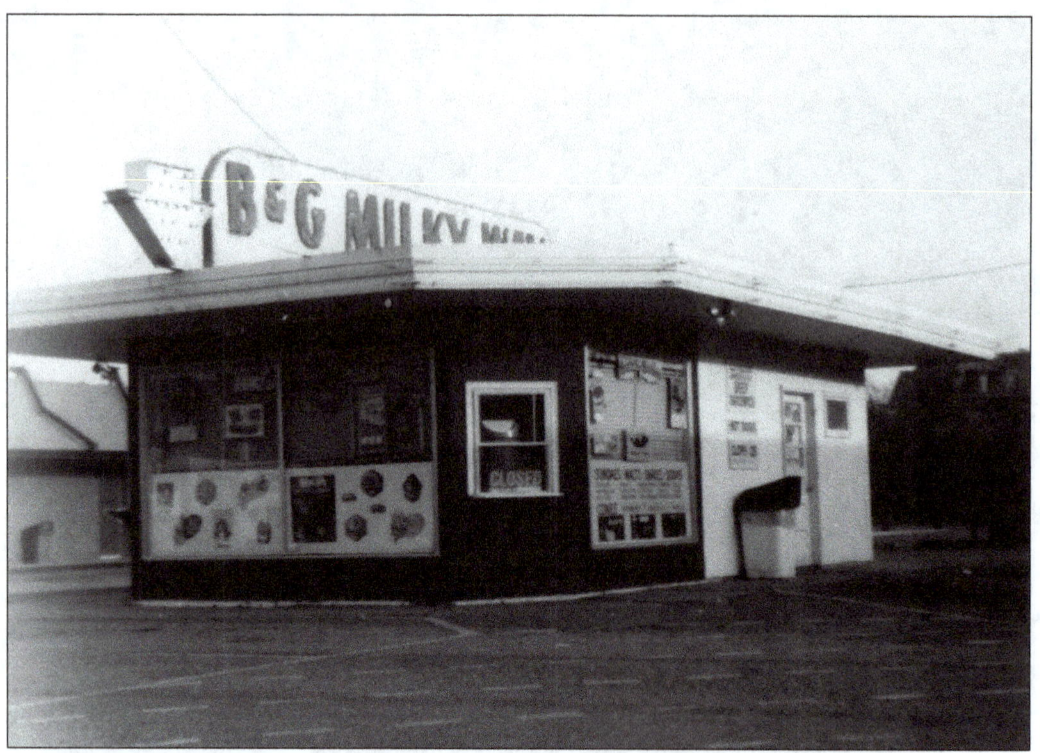

B&G Milky Way has been a Sioux Falls ice cream favorite for over 60 years. In 1954, Bertha and Guy Higgens (the B&G namesakes) opened a store at 2410 West Twelfth Street. In 1971, Gerald and Patricia Bruget purchased the business from Bertha, after Guy passed away. This original restaurant continues in operation today. (Courtesy Gerald and Patricia Bruget.)

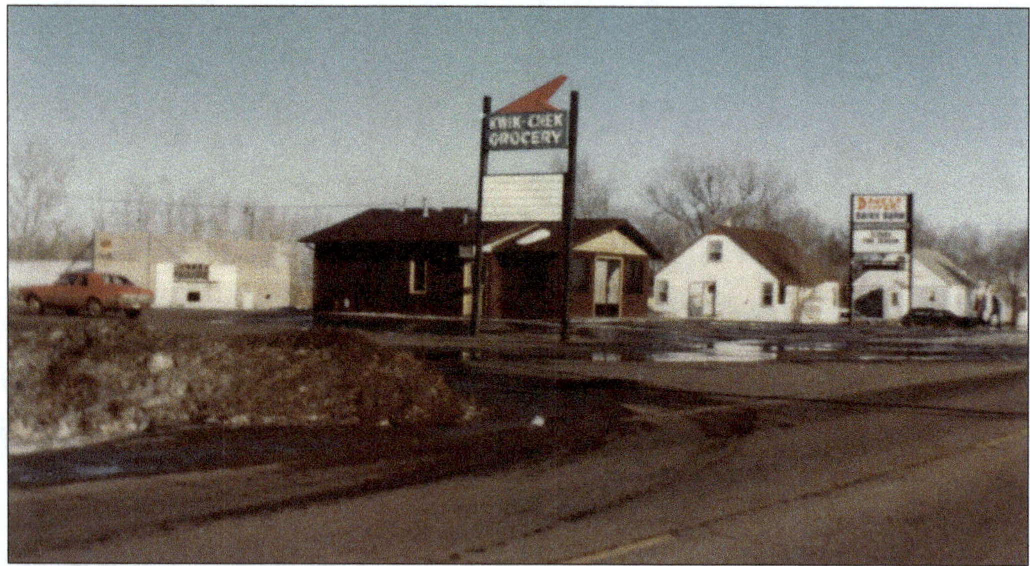

In 1976, Gerald and Patricia Bruget expanded B&G Milky Way by opening a second location at 5408 West Forty-First Street, where the Double Dipper Dairy Barn was previously located. In 1992, Bruce and Pam Bettmeng purchased the business and have continued to add more locations in the area. (Courtesy Gerald and Patricia Bruget.)

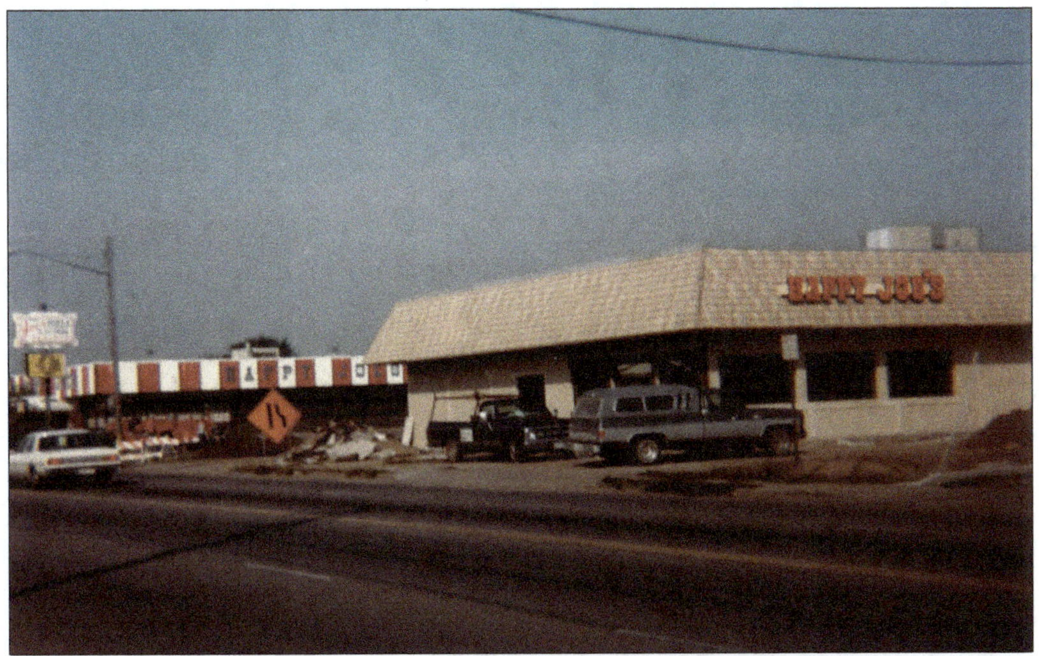

Happy Joe's was a favorite pizza and ice cream parlor for many years. Ed and Ellie Limke started the restaurant in 1975 at 2000 West Forty-First Street. In 1983, they moved east one block to a new building, where they continued until 1990. This picture shows the original building at left and the new structure near completion at right. (Courtesy Ed Limke.)

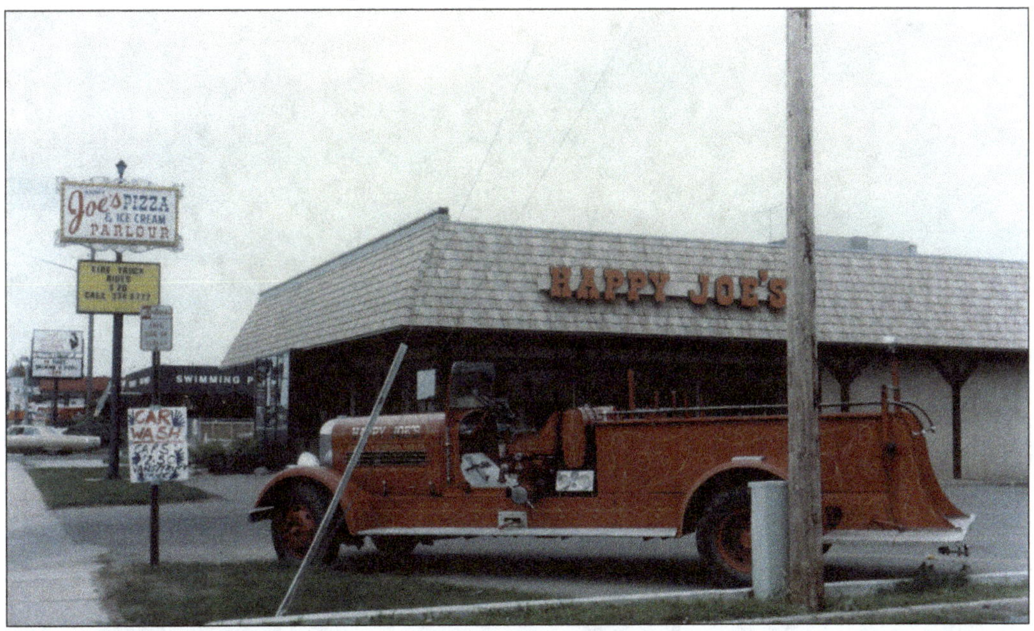

This is the second Happy Joe's, at 1912 West Forty-First Street. Inside the restaurant was a wonderland of pizza, pop, ice cream, and candy, and customers could watch their pizza being made through a window. Everyone was made to feel special on their birthday, but the "Birthday Whacker" might spank the person celebrating. The awesome fire truck out front was a 1936 Peter Pirsch. (Courtesy Ed Limke.)

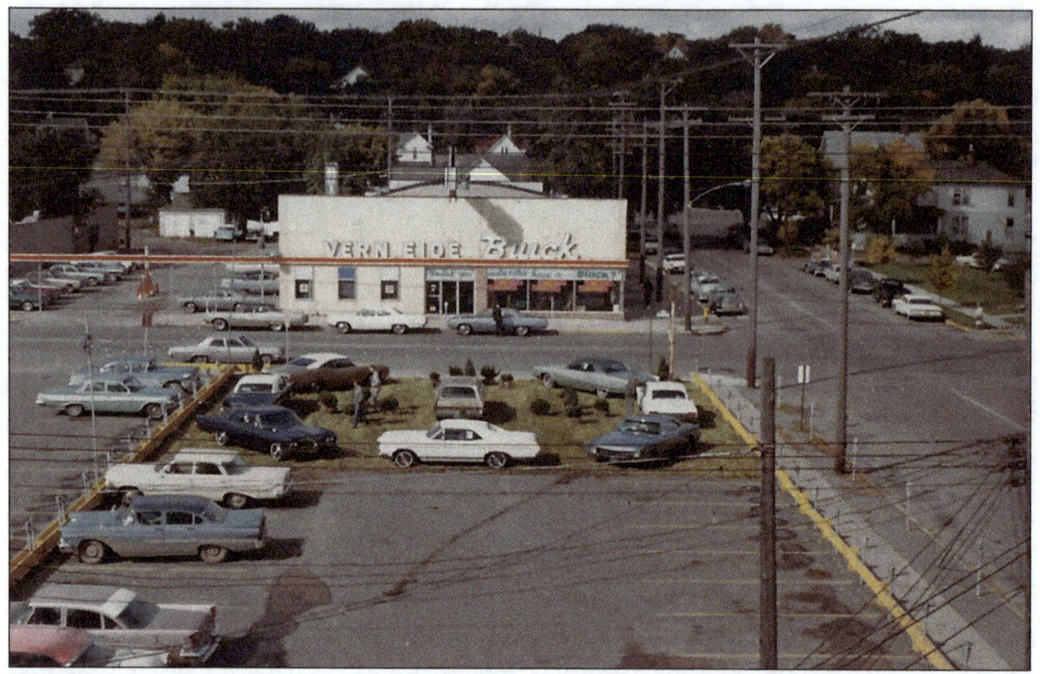

Beginning in 1965, Vern Eide purchased the Buick dealership in Sioux Falls at Sixth Street and Dakota Avenue, pictured here after Eide bought it. Three years later, he expanded and moved his business to the southeast corner of Thirty-Third Street and Minnesota Avenue. (Courtesy Vern Eide Motorcars.)

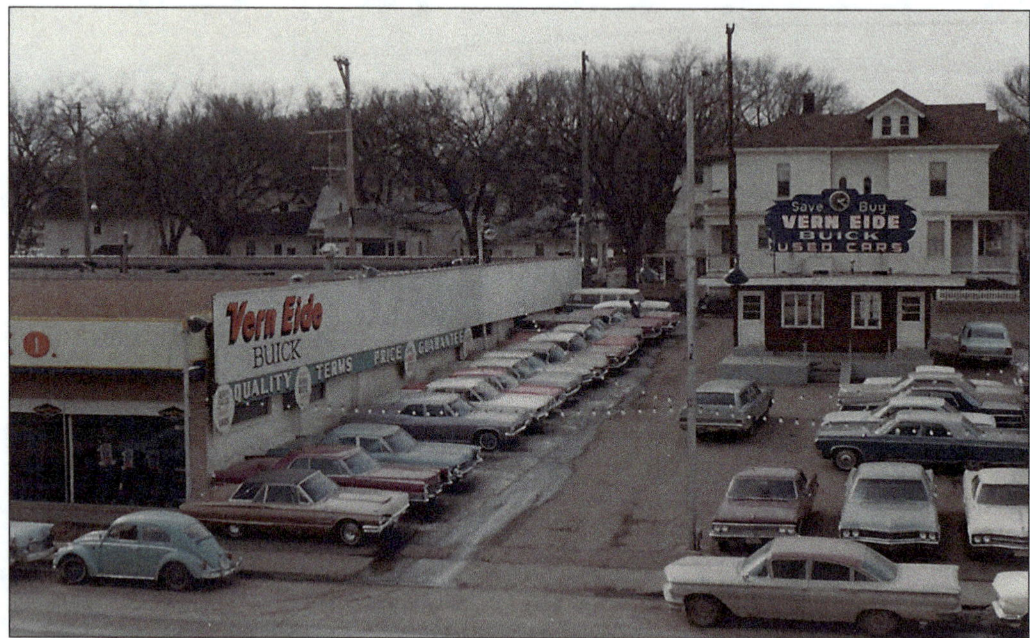

This picture shows the Vern Eide used car lot when it was located on the southwest corner of Ninth Street and Minnesota Avenue, to the north of Graham Goodyear and across from Central Fire Station. Over the years, the company has expanded the business into many dealerships both in Sioux Falls and in other communities. (Courtesy Vern Eide Motorcars.)

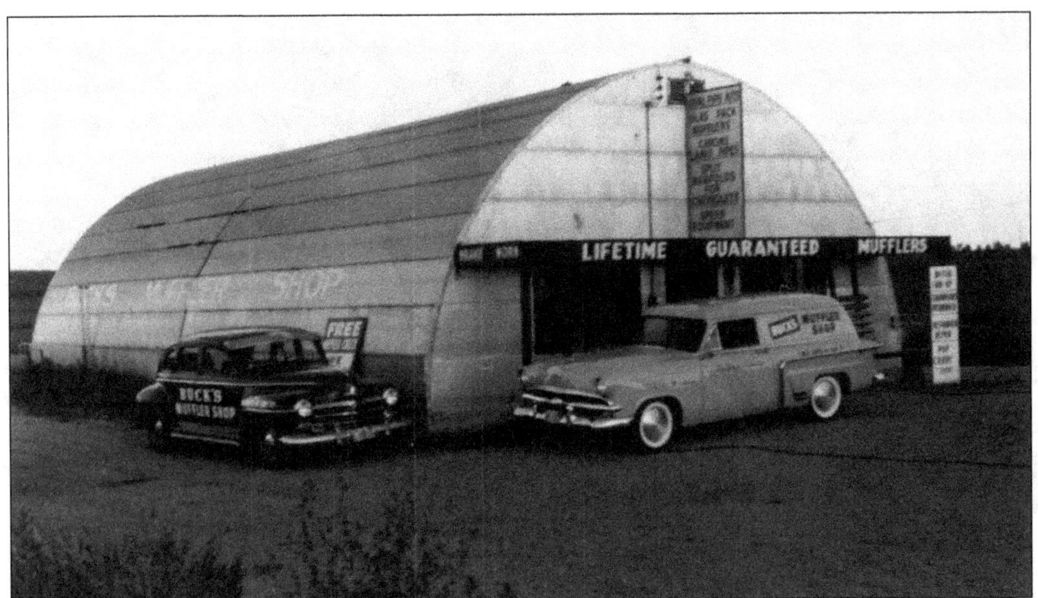

Mr. Bendo, the 18-foot-tall statue, has been keeping an eye on the city since 1963, but Darlo Buckwalter started Buck's Muffler Shop in 1957 on North Highway 77 (the Cliff Avenue portion of Highway 77). Prior to starting the muffler shop, Buckwalter had a gas station at 2101 East Tenth Street. The muffler shop moved to 500 South Phillips Avenue, north of the Shrine Temple. In 1967, the shop moved again to its present location at 500 South Cliff Avenue. The current owner, Jerry Wallenstein, began working at the muffler shop as a teenager in 1972 and later purchased the business. On St. Patrick's Day in 2010, Mr. Bendo was hit by a minivan and required an orthopedic procedure. After his repairs, his fashion changed from blue pants and white shirt to gray pants and a red shirt. (Both, courtesy Jerry Wallenstein.)

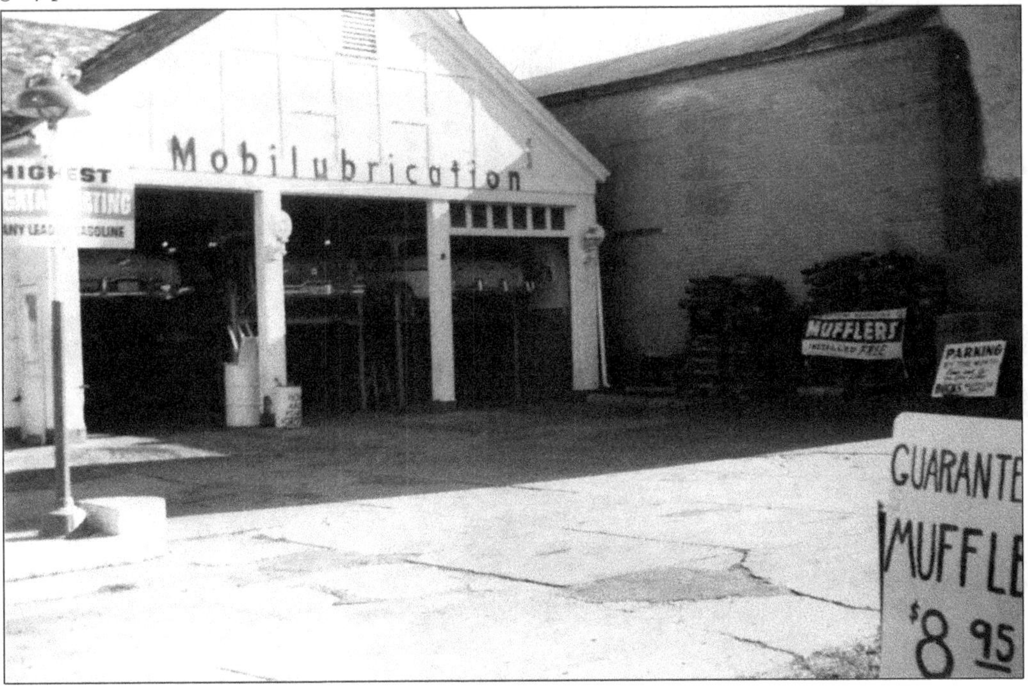

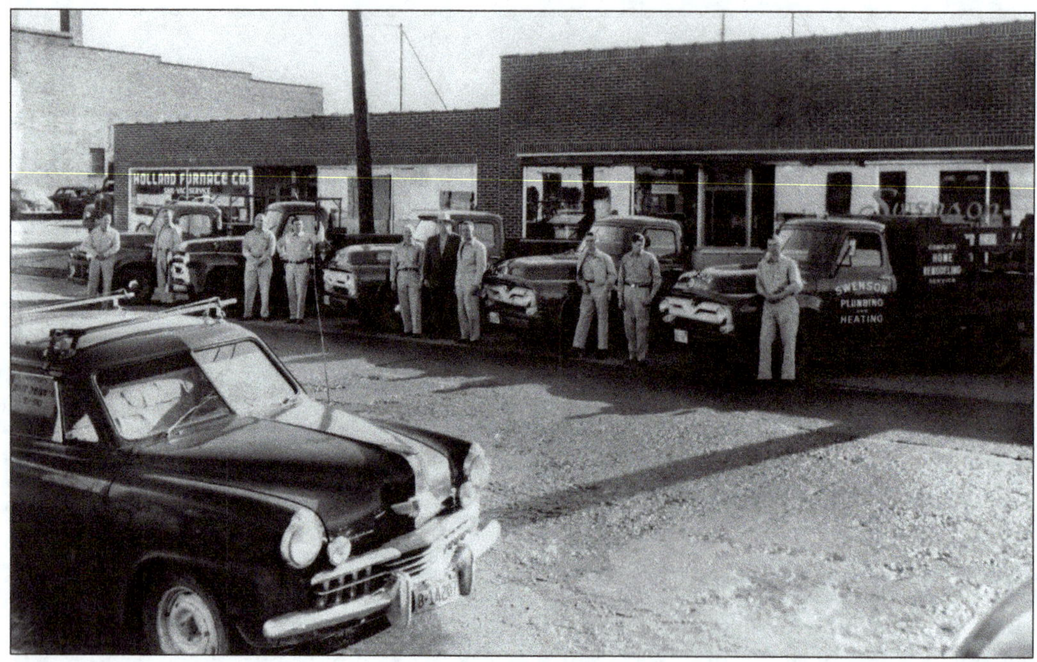

Selmer G. Swenson started Swenson Plumbing & Heating in Sioux Falls in 1946 with his son Mark and son-in-law Chuck Connor. Seventy years later, S.G. Swenson and Sons continues with the fourth generation, a different name, and various locations. Selmer's grandsons Joe, Ted, Steve, and Matt Swenson run the company today, and the fourth generation, Stacia McGrann, serves as director of marketing. In 1970, the company started doing business as Handy Man Home Remolding Center and Dakota Wholesale Plumbing and Electric Company. The location changed from the original spot at 204 North Weber Avenue (just across from the old Stockman's Bar) to 1101 South Cliff Avenue in 1959, to the current location at 910 East Tenth Street in 1994. In addition to the Sioux Falls Handy Man plumbing showroom, the company has locations in Sioux City, Iowa, and Lincoln, Nebraska. (Both, courtesy Joe Swenson.)

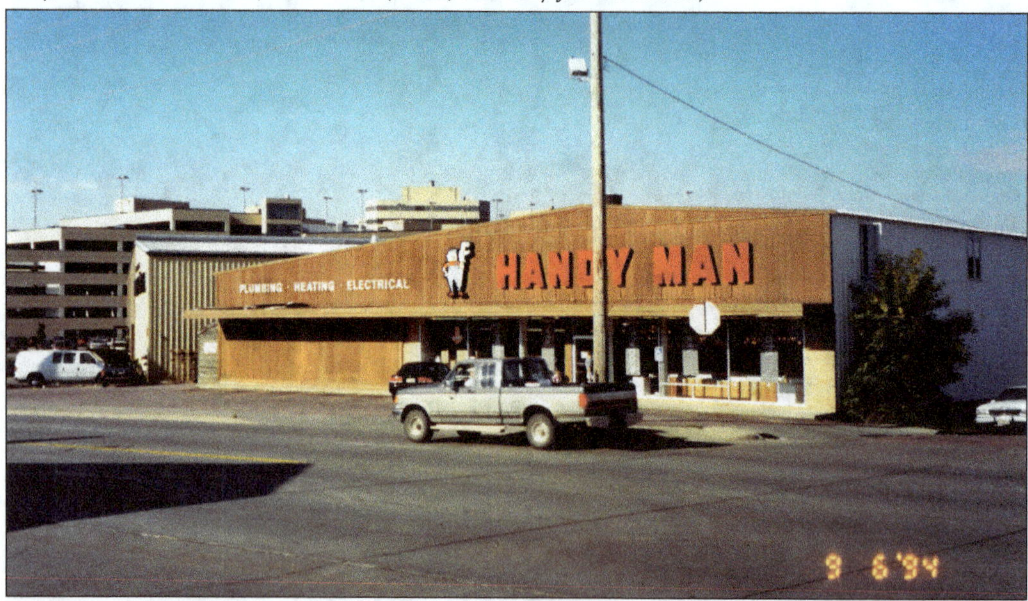

Three

Street Views

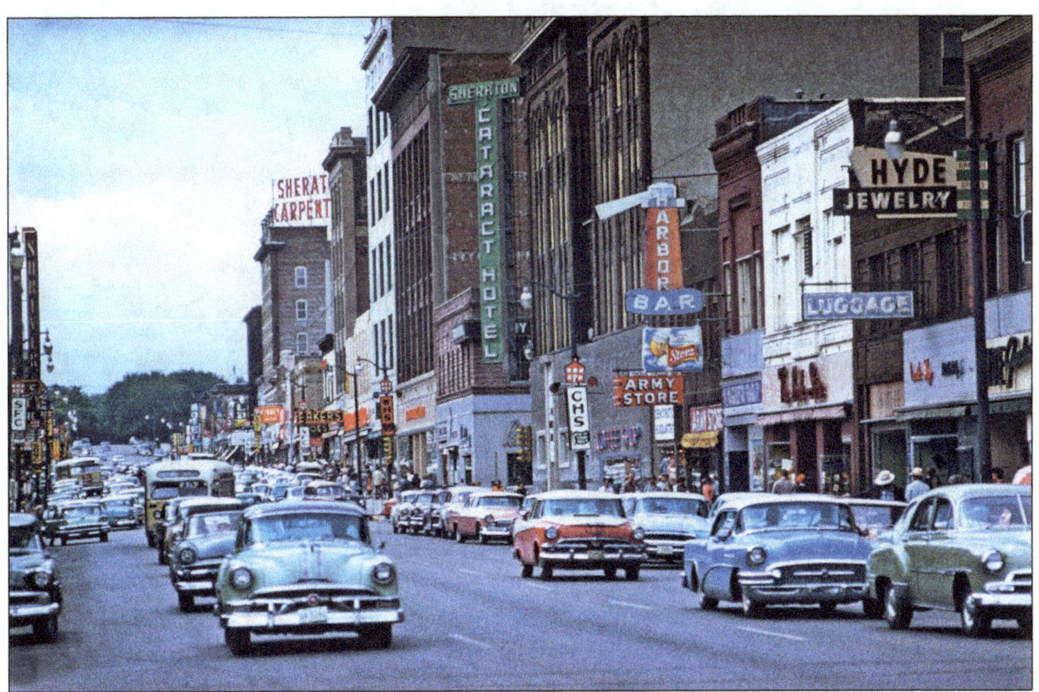

This great view of Phillips Avenue was photographed on August 30, 1958, by Charles W. Cushman. It shows a busy street with three lanes of one-way traffic. This would have been one of the busiest intersections in the city at the time. (Courtesy Charles Cushman Collection, Indiana University Archives, P10228.)

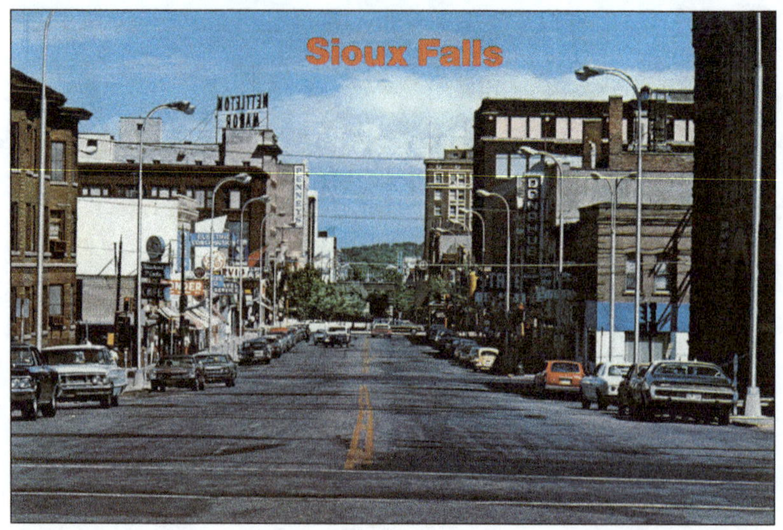

This view of Phillips Avenue is looking north from Thirteenth Street around 1974. In the distance, the recent addition of the walking mall that interrupted traffic on Phillips Avenue between Ninth and Eleventh Streets can be seen. By the late 1980s, the walking mall was removed, and Phillips Avenue was again a through street.

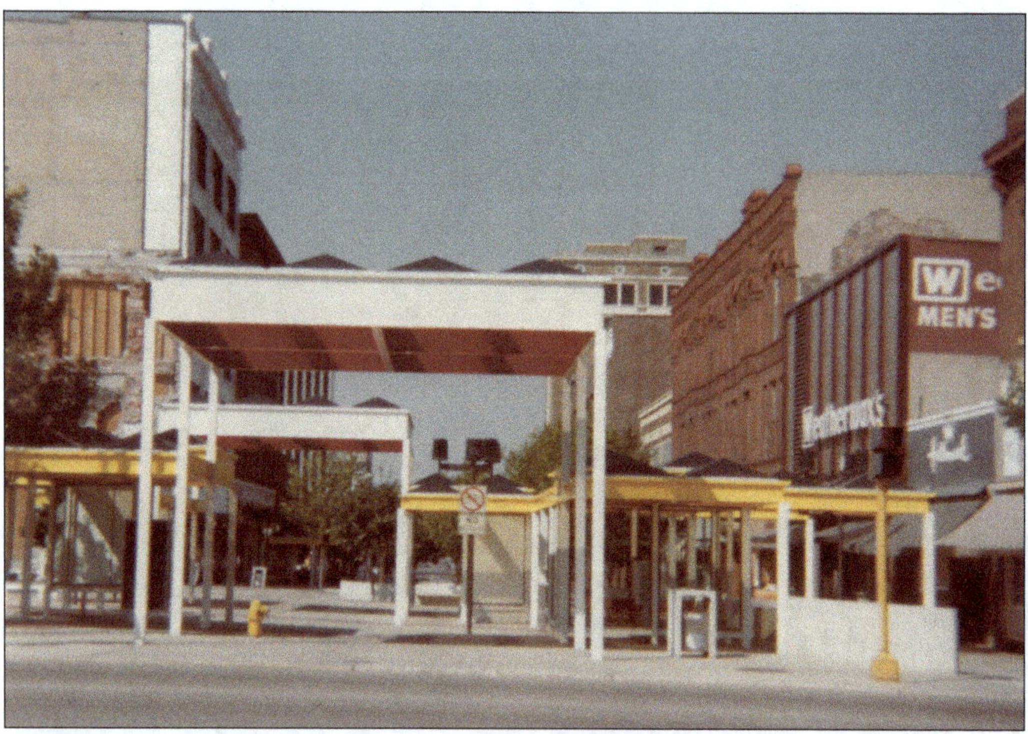

As the city grew away from downtown and many of the stores in that area moved to the edges of town, the city made many attempts to draw shoppers back. The pedestrian mall was one of the not-so-successful attempts to make downtown shopping more attractive. The walking mall was on Phillips Avenue between Ninth and Eleventh Streets from 1973 until 1986. (Courtesy Siouxland Heritage Museums, Sioux Falls, SD.)

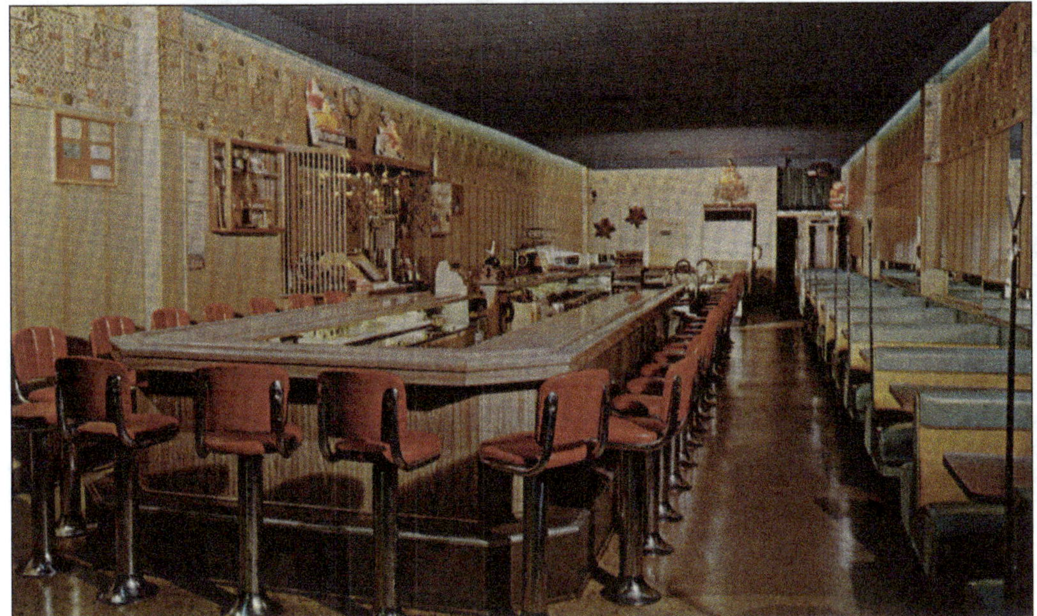

This is the inside of the Rainbow Bar when it was located at 202 North Phillips Avenue, before moving to its better-known location at 303 North Phillips, south of the Orpheum Theater. The Rainbow Bar was established in the 1940s and was in business until the early 1990s, when it became the Limelight Lounge.

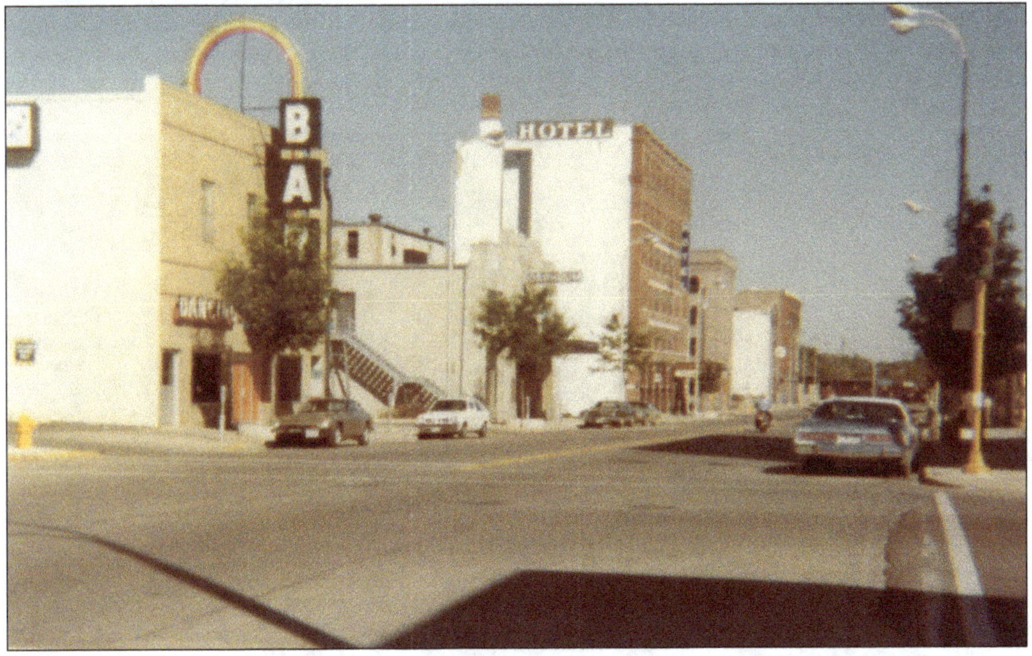

This view is looking north on Phillips Avenue from Seventh Street. The Rainbow Bar was in business for approximately 50 years, first near Eighth Street and Phillips Avenue and then at this location. In 1994, this building was purchased by the city and sold to the owners of the Orpheum Theater. In 1995, the two buildings were connected by a new structure. (Courtesy Siouxland Heritage Museums, Sioux Falls, SD.)

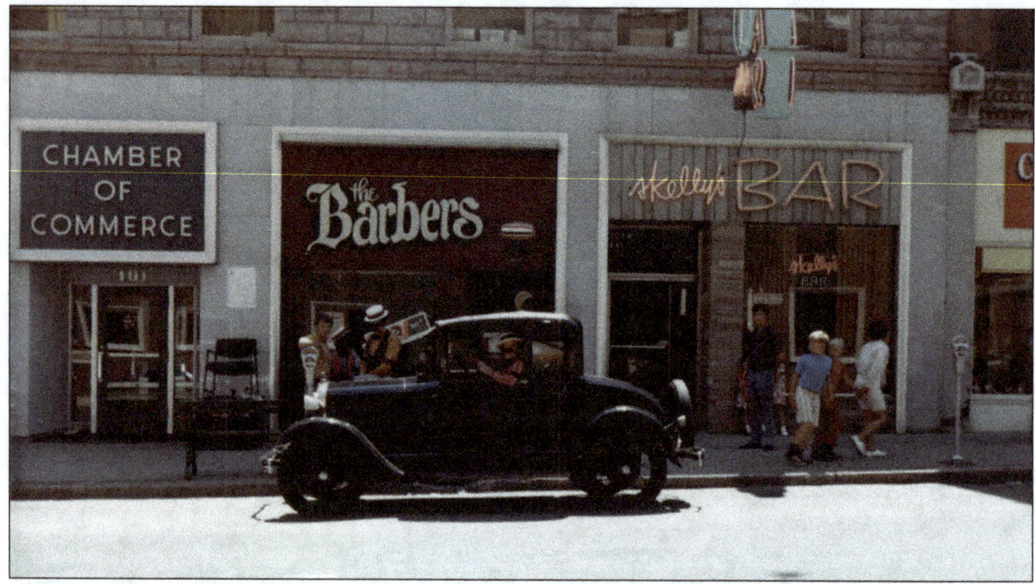

These barbers are having fun during a 1970 Crazy Days event in front of their shop in the Minnehaha Building (once known as the Edmison-Jamison Building). Above, note the first location of Skelly's Pub and Grill before it moved to the 132 South Phillips Avenue spot. The picture below was taken at the intersection of Phillips Avenue and Ninth Street looking west and shows many buildings that would soon meet the wrecking ball. From left to right are the Kindler Pontiac dealership (brown building), city hall (cream), Lincoln Hotel (the pink quartzite structure, once known as the Chicago House), the Elks Club (white), and the famous Cataract Hotel (gray and tan). Except for city hall, the rest of the buildings have all been destroyed. A careful look reveals a sign showing parking for Fantle's, which was across the street to the south. (Both, courtesy "Clipper" Jim Dresch.)

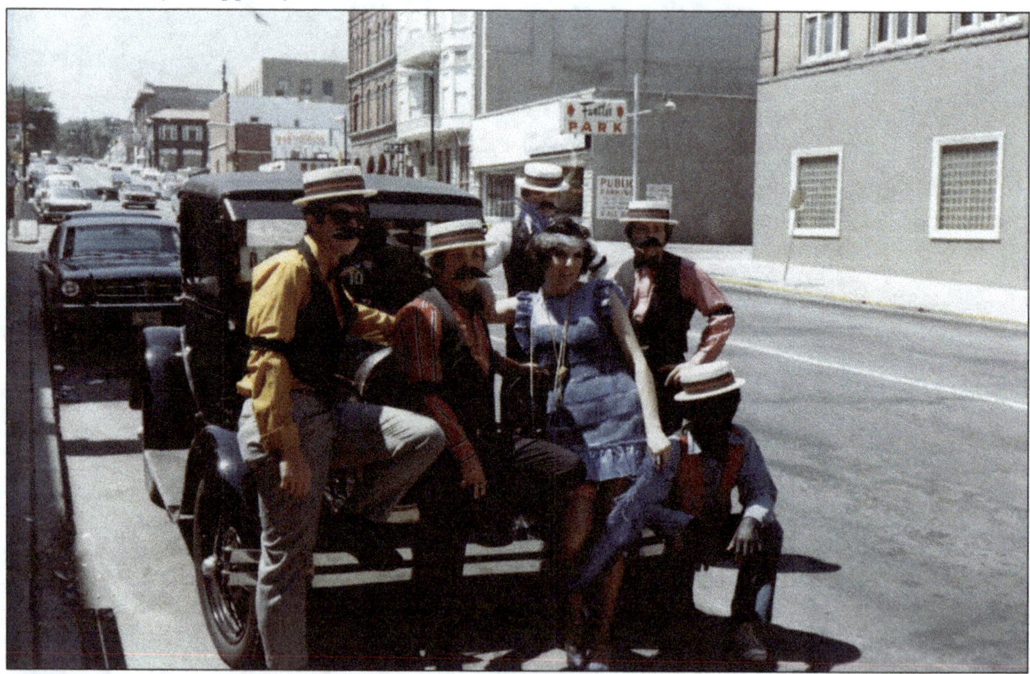

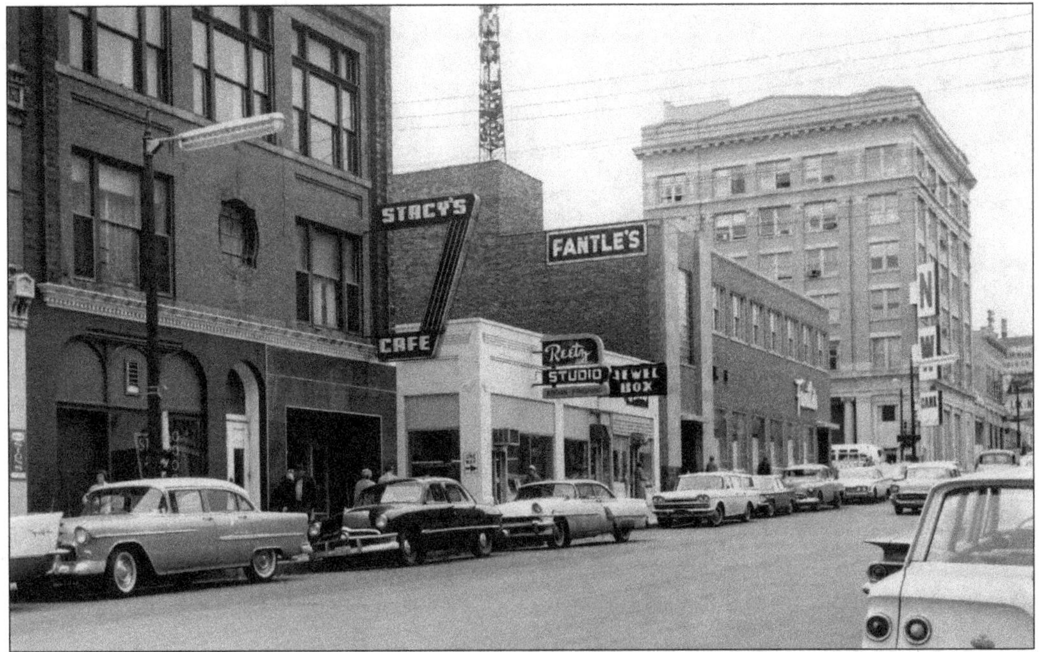

This is a view of the south side of Ninth Street looking west from Phillips Avenue toward Main Avenue. On the corner, the famous downtown department store Fantle's can be seen. To the right of Fantle's is the Security Bank that was shot up and robbed in 1934. The John Dillinger gang are the most likely suspects. (Courtesy Harold's Photo.)

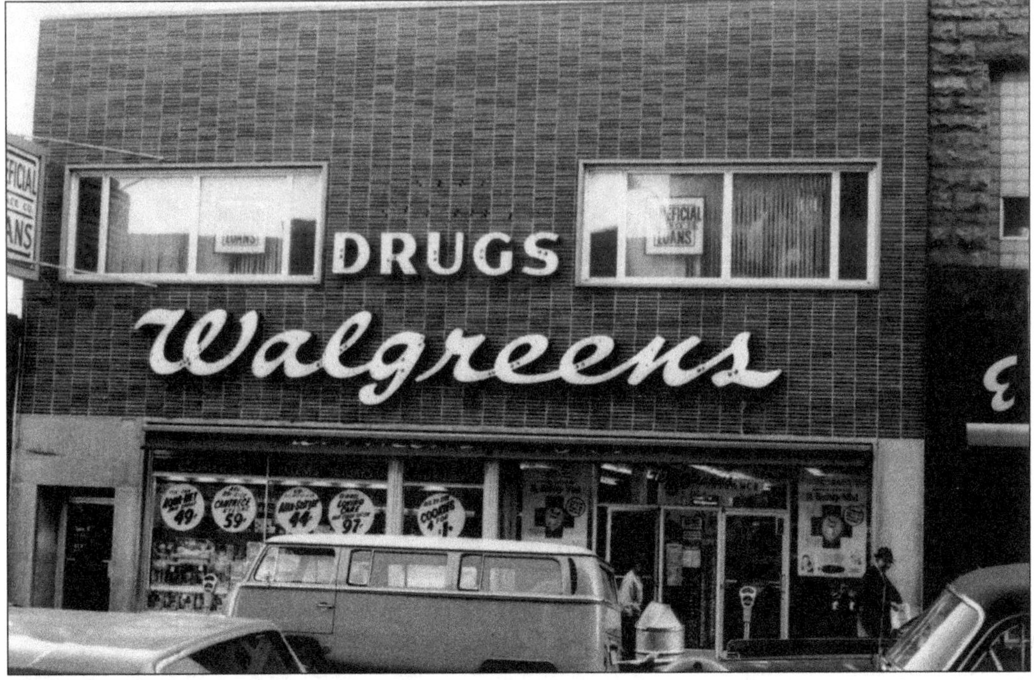

Walgreens drugstore was located on the east side of Phillips Avenue, between Ninth and Tenth Streets. This structure was razed in the early 1970s to make room for the First National Bank building. (Courtesy Siouxland Heritage Museums, Sioux Falls, SD.)

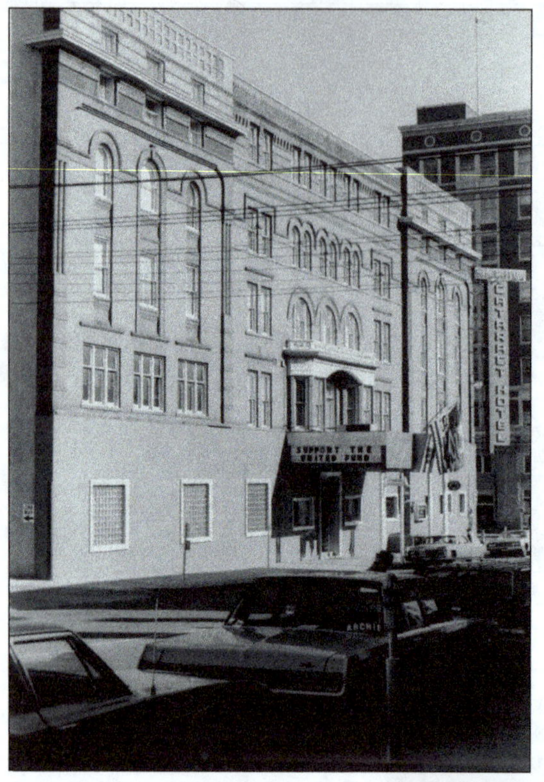

The Cataract Hotel had been a landmark in Sioux Falls since 1871, lasting more than 100 years. Located on the northwest corner of Ninth Street and Phillips Avenue, this hotel was the place for important meetings and events, as well as the premier location for people to stay and eat. The intersection of Ninth and Phillips was considered the center of the city and defined the grid for the city streets. (Courtesy Siouxland Heritage Museums, Sioux Falls, SD.)

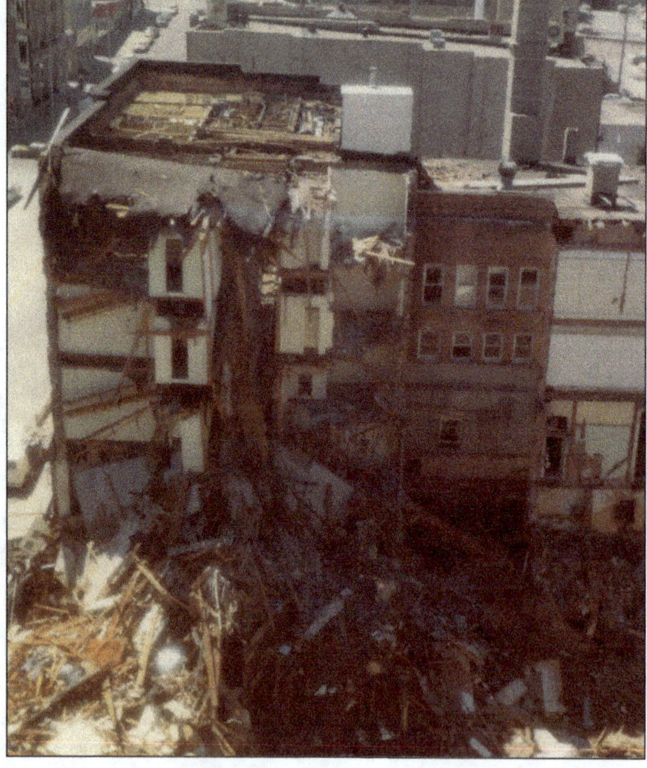

The Cataract Hotel was a symbol of downtown. It was a social center for many locals and visitors. Three different Cataract Hotel buildings stood on the northwest corner of Phillips Avenue and Ninth Street between 1871 and 1973. This picture shows the demolition of the last one. Urban renewal was a federally funded program with the goal to help cities rebuild or renovate dilapidated buildings and neighborhoods. Sioux Falls razed many historic buildings and some entire city blocks in hopes of slowing the progression of businesses leaving downtown for new shopping centers and office structures. At the time, urban renewal made sense, but many are thankful that more historic buildings were not torn down. (Courtesy Siouxland Heritage Museums, Sioux Falls, SD.)

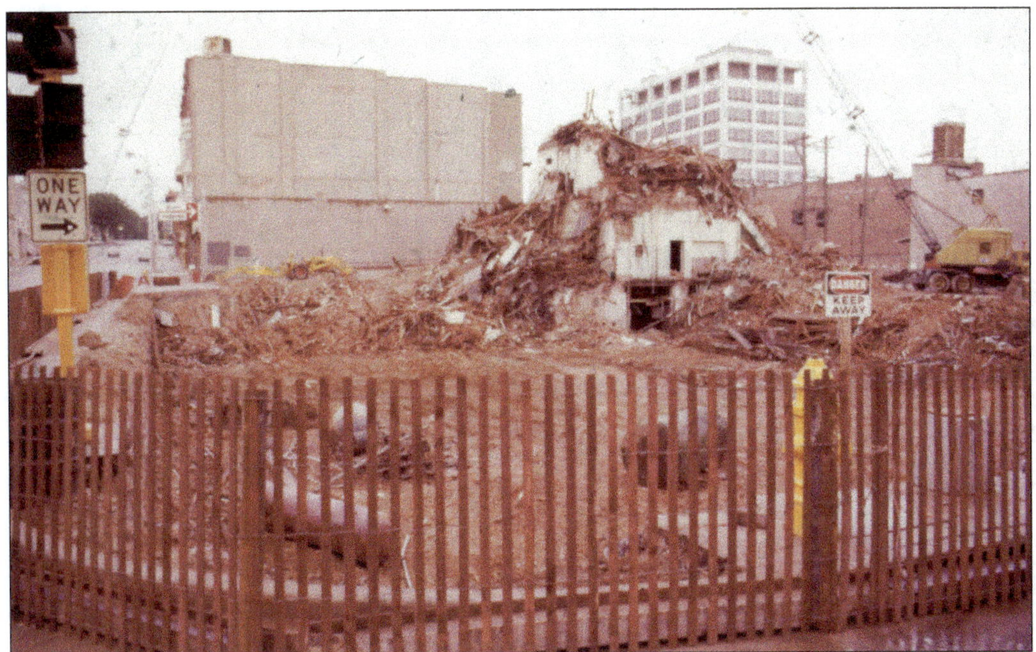

This is a view of the Cataract Hotel as it was being razed as a part of urban renewal. Looking west, the Elks Club can be seen at left, soon to be razed as well. From Phillips Avenue to Minnesota Avenue on the north side of Ninth Street, the only remaining building is city hall. (Courtesy Siouxland Heritage Museums, Sioux Falls, SD.)

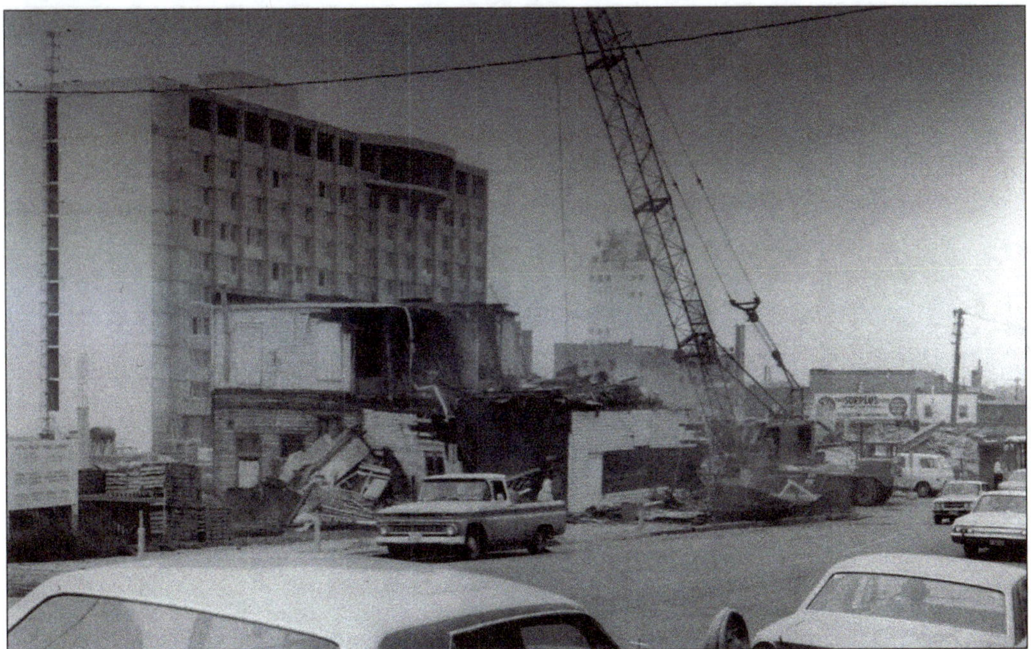

This is the intersection of Main Avenue and Eighth Street looking northeast. The downtown Holiday Inn is being built and was completed in 1972. The crane sitting on Main Avenue was tearing down Looks Meat Market, which was on the northwest corner where the Sioux Falls Public Library now stands. The Zip Feed Mill is in the background. (Courtesy William Pay.)

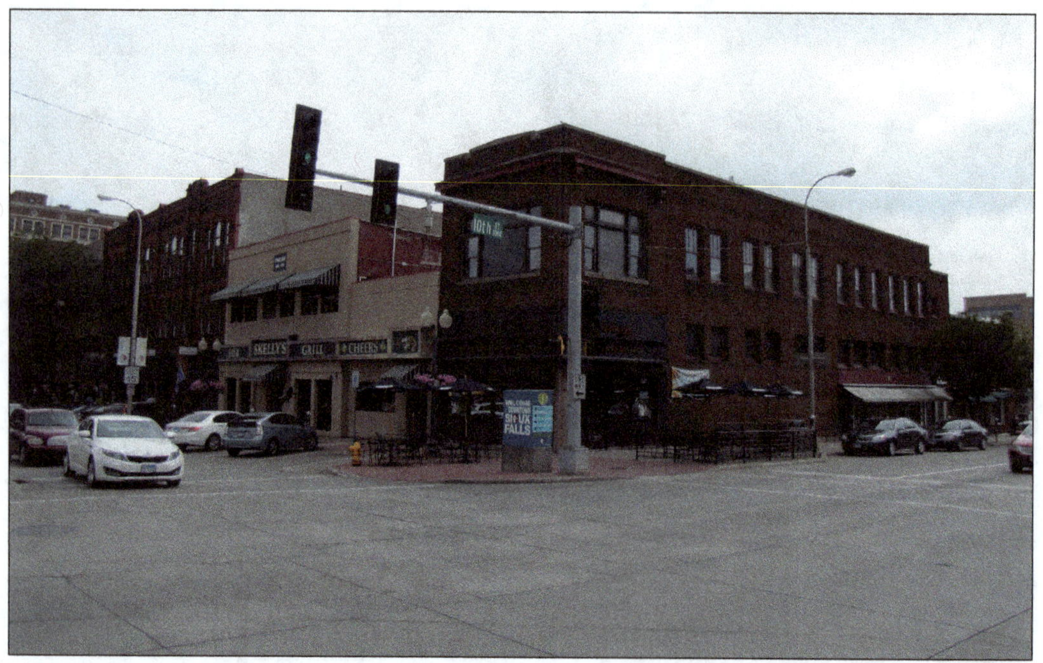

This picture was taken during the summer of 2015 and shows the northeast corner of Phillips Avenue and Tenth Street before the renovations began to the Copper Lounge and Skelly's Pub and Grill. Skelly's had been a pub in Sioux Falls since the 1950s and was first located at 105 West Ninth Street. The restaurant PAve took Skelly's place. PAve is short for Phillips Avenue.

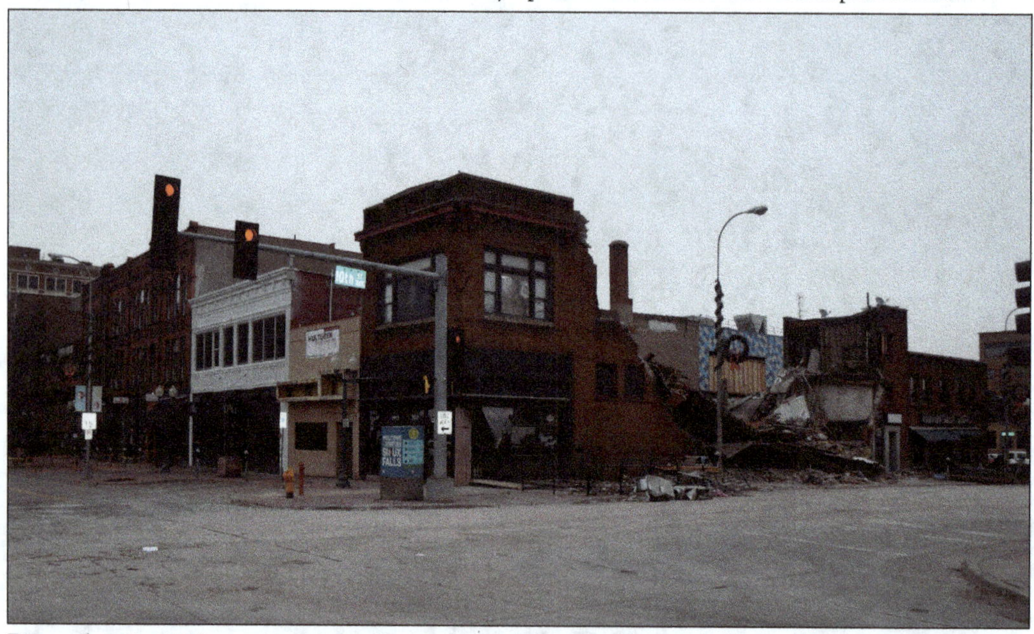

December 2, 2016, was a sad day for the community of Sioux Falls. A 100-year-old building collapsed, trapping two people and three dogs inside the rubble. The dogs and one person were rescued. Tragically, the second person died in the collapsed structure. The building was in the process of a major renovation project converting the Copper Lounge and neighboring part of Skelly's Pub and Grill into a Lewis Drug Store.

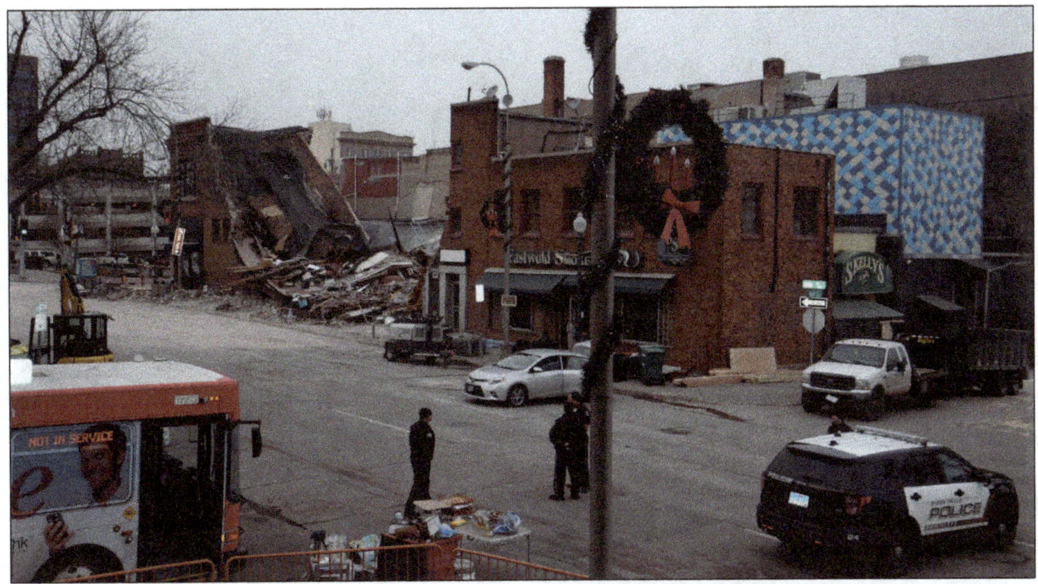

This view is looking west on Tenth Street. The picture was taken the day after the Copper Lounge building collapsed. The brick building in the middle, Eastwold's Smoke Shop, was torn down soon after the photograph was taken.

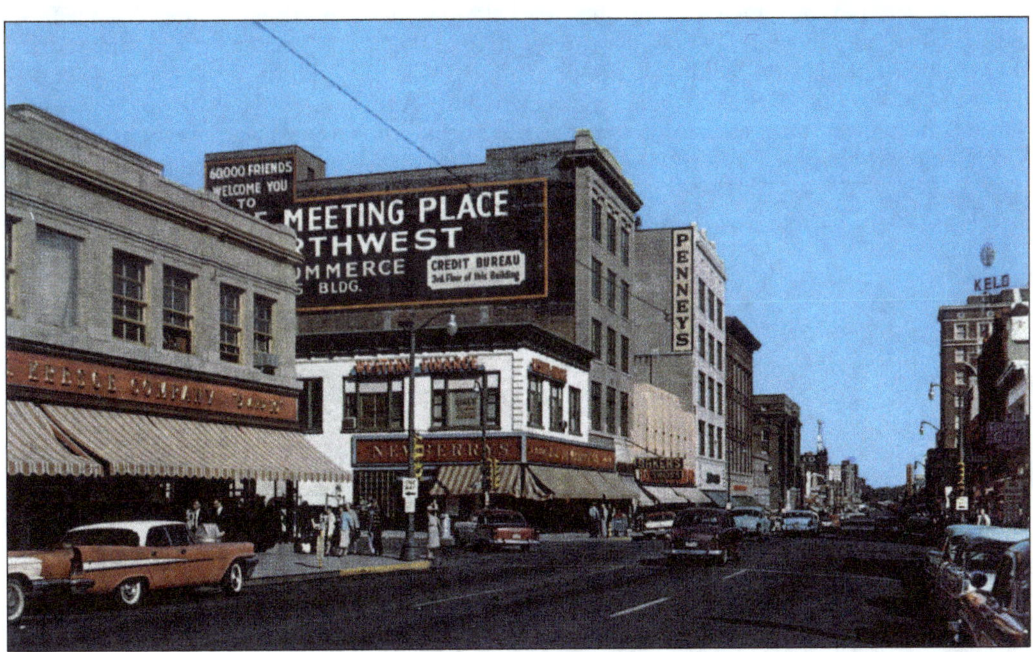

This is the intersection of Phillips Avenue and Tenth Street looking north on Phillips Avenue. At left is the Kresge Building, constructed in 1928. In the last 10 years, it has undergone significant restoration. At center is the Newberry Store where the Phillips Avenue Diner is now located. The buildings on the west side of Phillips Avenue from Tenth to Eighth Streets were all eventually razed.

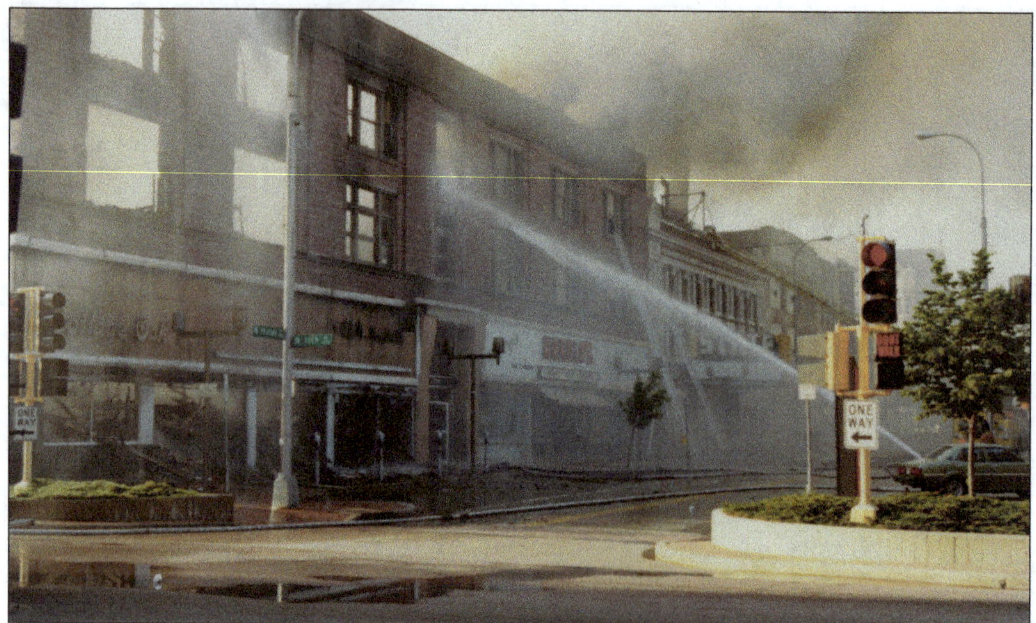

On May 25, 1991, fire destroyed the Hanson Building. Originally constructed in 1906 as the Paulton Building, this majestic structure stood on the southeast corner of Eleventh Street and Phillips Avenue. The Hanson family, which owns Harold's Photography, owned the building. Their business had been located on ground level since 1938. The Phillips Centre office building was constructed in the same location. The view below is looking north on Phillips Avenue from Twelfth Street and shows firefighters continuing to fight the fire at the Hanson Building the day after the fire. The Hanson Building has smoke rising from the top. The State Theatre had closed the previous year but was saved from the fire. Donahue's Furniture, Shredder Skate Boards, and Music Mansion were businesses located on the east side of Phillips Avenue at the time of the fire. (Both, courtesy Harold's Photo.)

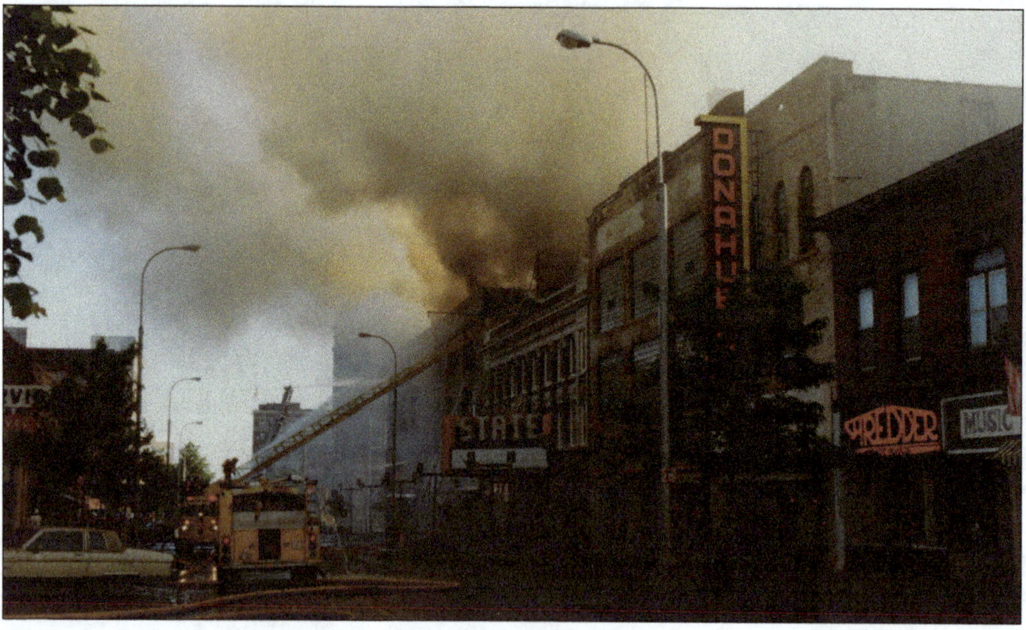

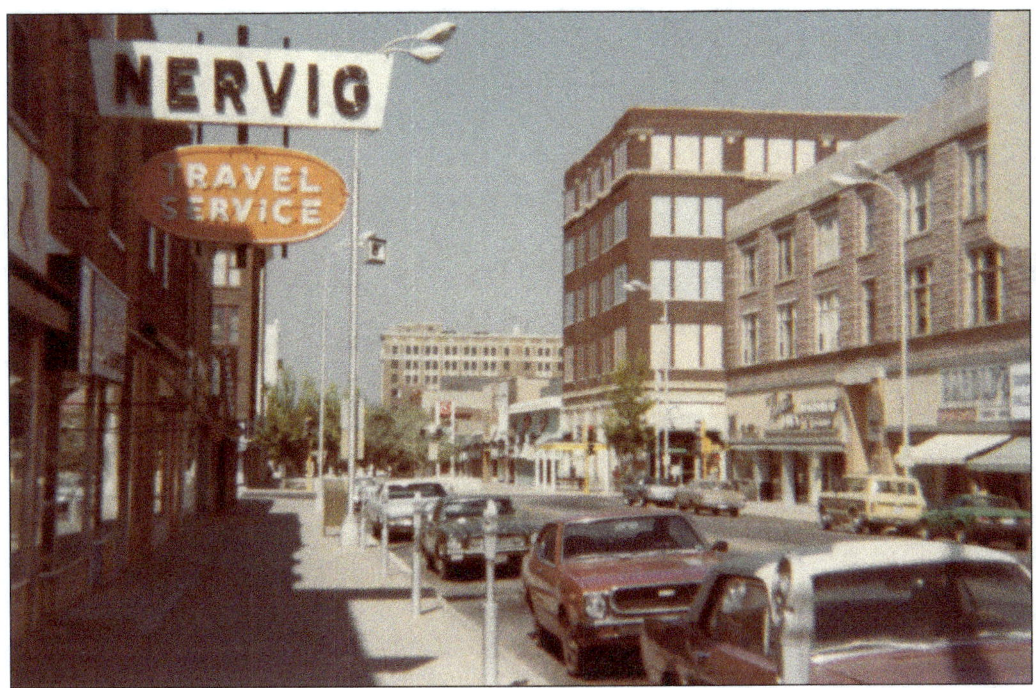

Both photographs were taken looking north on Phillips Avenue. The above picture shows a beautiful summer day in 1978. Below is a 65-degree March day in 2017. There are almost 40 years between the views, but they are similar. The biggest difference would be the loss of the Hanson Building, above at right, which was destroyed by fire in 1991. It is also apparent how much more vibrant the downtown area is today compared to 1978. After the mid-1960s, stores were quickly leaving the downtown area for the edges of the city. In recent years, more stores are opening and more people are living in downtown, making it a popular place to be. (Above, Courtesy Siouxland Heritage Museums, Sioux Falls, SD.)

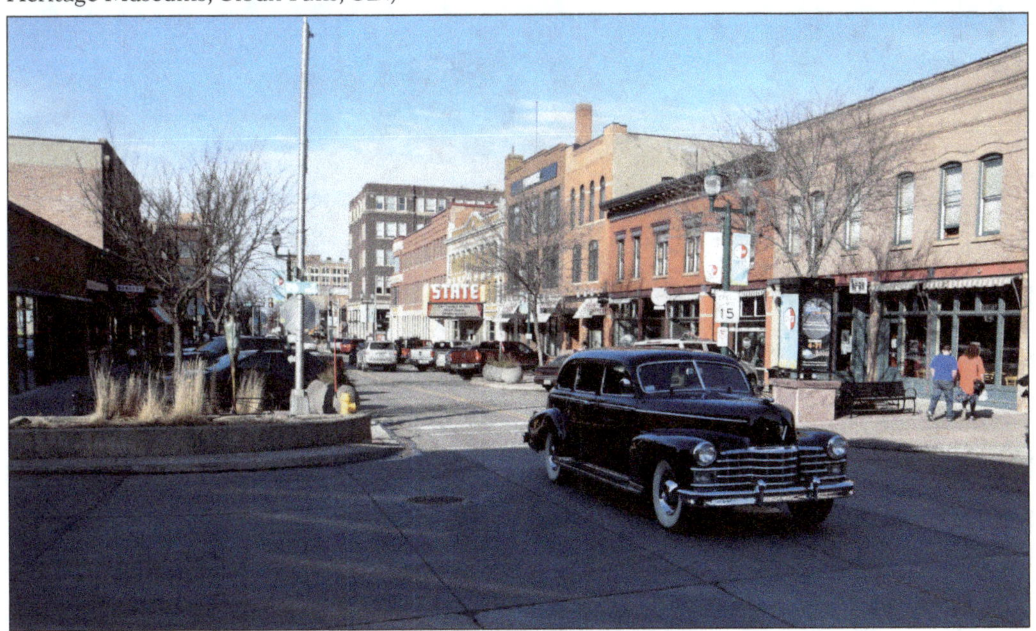

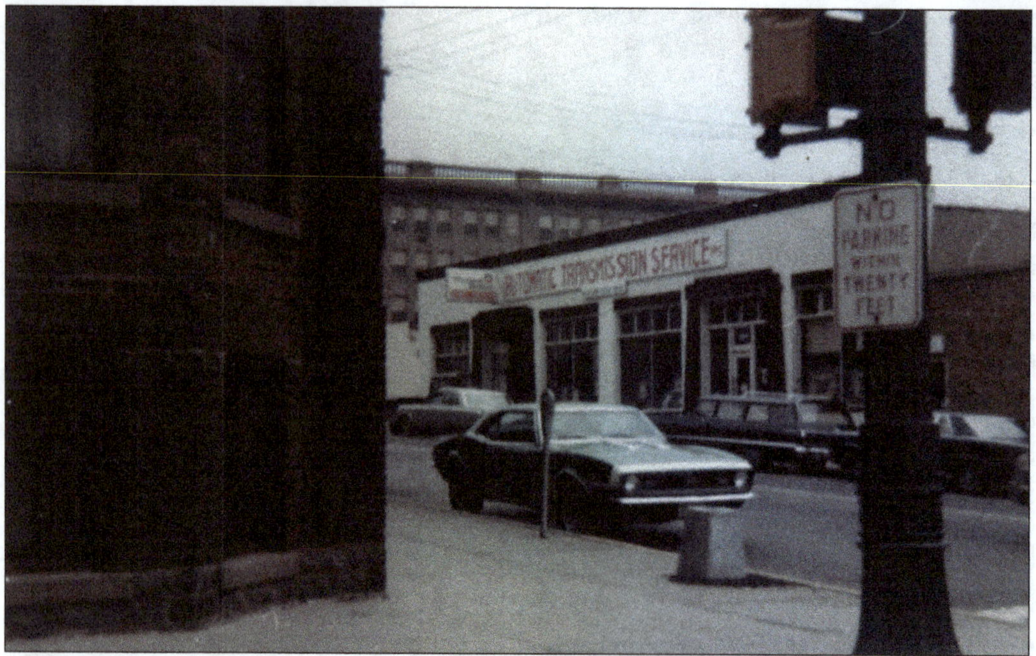

Many things have changed over the years. Both the above and below pictures were taken looking west on Twelfth Street and Phillips Avenue. The above photograph was taken in the early 1970s, and the image below was taken in 2017. Both show the Brownstone apartment building at left and the transmission shop at right. In the distance is Washington High School, which was later remodeled into the Washington Pavilion. The newest addition is the eight-story Washington Square building, which was being constructed on the northeast corner of Main Avenue and Twelfth Street. Washington Square plans call for luxury living and office and retail spaces, with two floors designated for parking. (Above, courtesy Tom Olsen.)

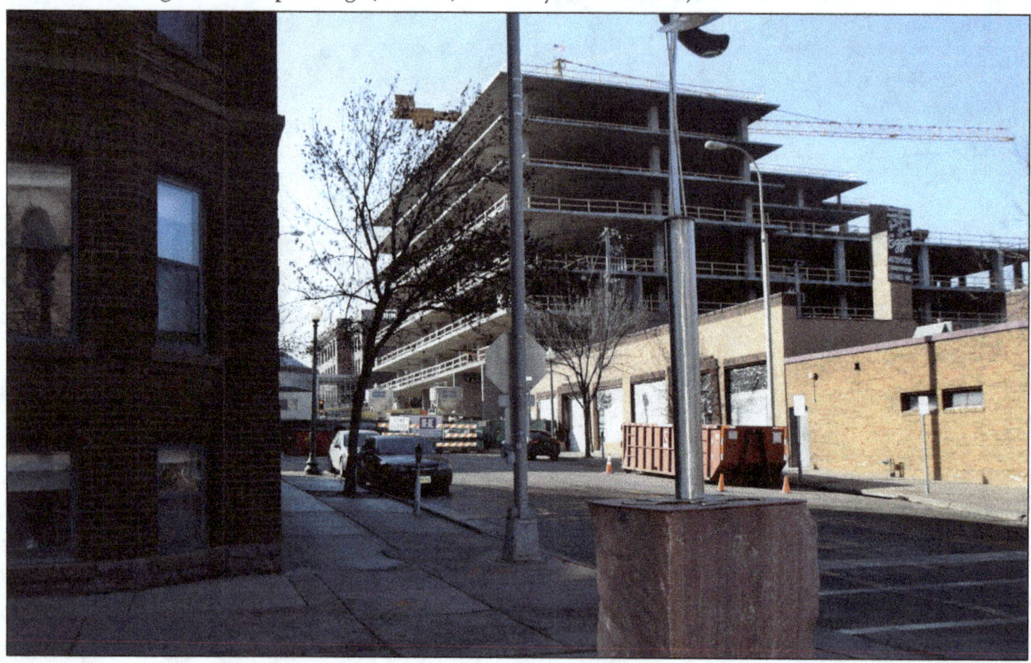

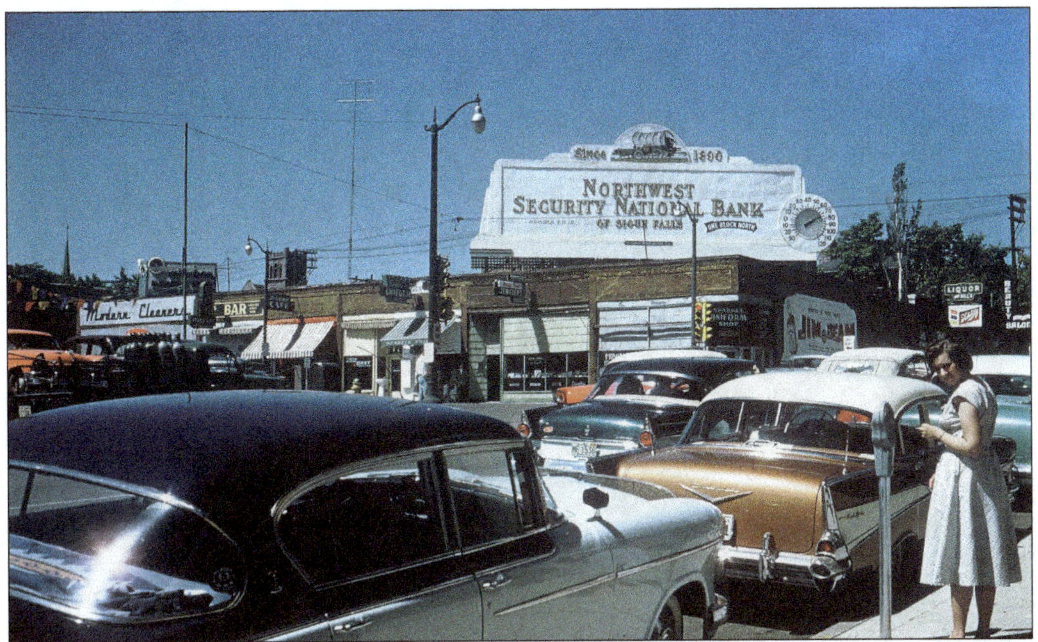

This photograph shows the southwest corner of Tenth Street and Main Avenue as it appeared in the late 1950s. To the left of center is the tower of First Congregational Church, and farther left is the steeple of First Lutheran Church. Today, this corner is a parking lot.

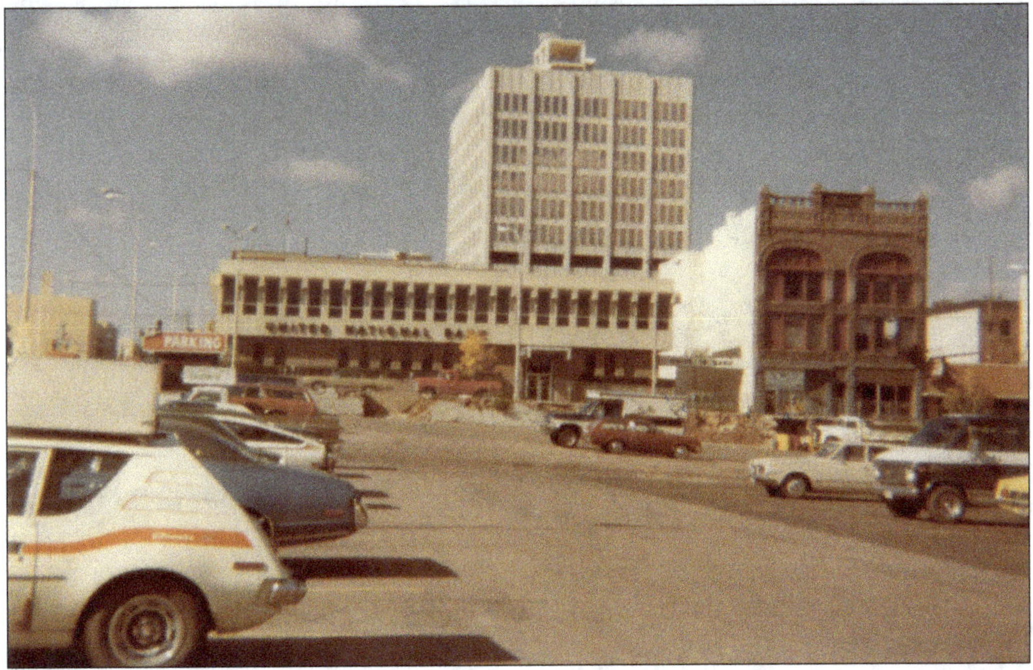

This view is looking toward Main Avenue and Tenth Street in 1978. Within a few years, a multilevel parking ramp was built on the northeast corner. The red quartzite building on the right is the Odd Fellows Hall, constructed in 1889. The large structure in the center background was the Northwestern Bell Telephone Building, constructed in 1971. (Courtesy Siouxland Heritage Museums, Sioux Falls, SD.)

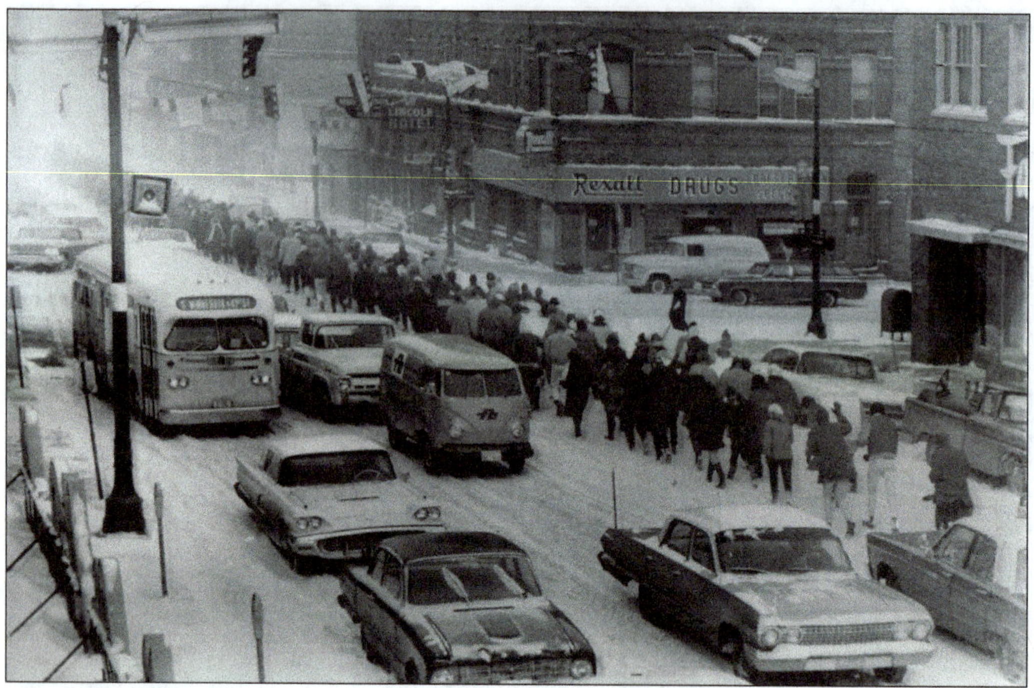

Here, a sympathy march of over 300 students, ministers, and local members of the NAACP walk north on Main Avenue through Ninth Street. The local sympathy march was one of many protests held nationwide in mourning of Rev. James Reeb. Reeb was a white American civil rights activist taking part in a protest in Selma, Alabama. After the protest, Reeb was beaten and died two days later on March 11, 1965. Reverend Reeb's death was pivotal in Pres. Lyndon B. Johnson drawing up and finally signing the Voting Rights Act of 1965.

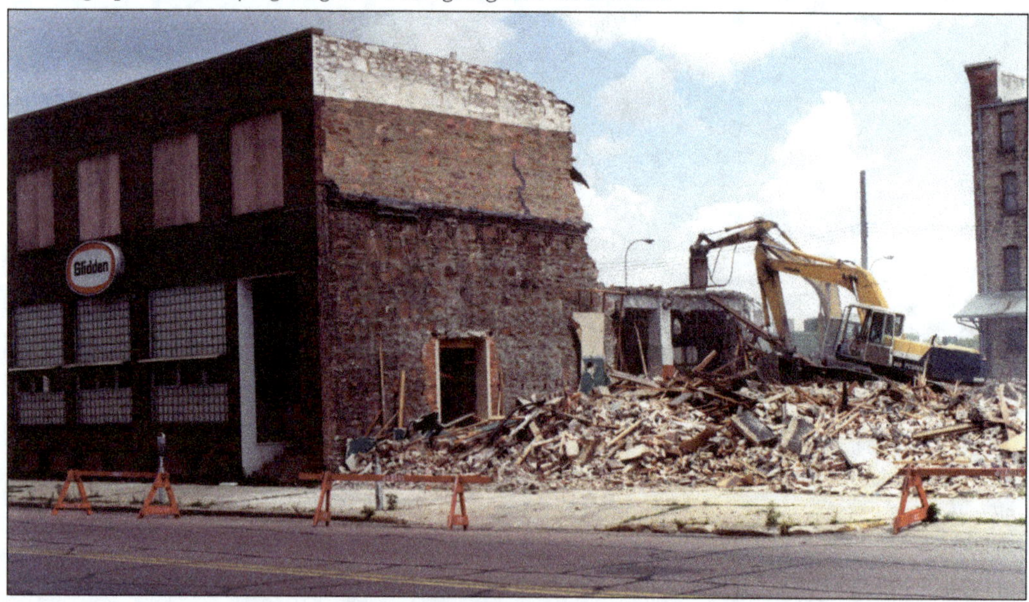

Kitty-corner from the Coliseum was the Glidden Building. Today, this same location is a parking lot, north of the Icon Lounge. At right is a large stone and brick building constructed in 1899 for Jewett Brothers Wholesale Grocery. (Courtesy Siouxland Heritage Museums, Sioux Falls, SD.)

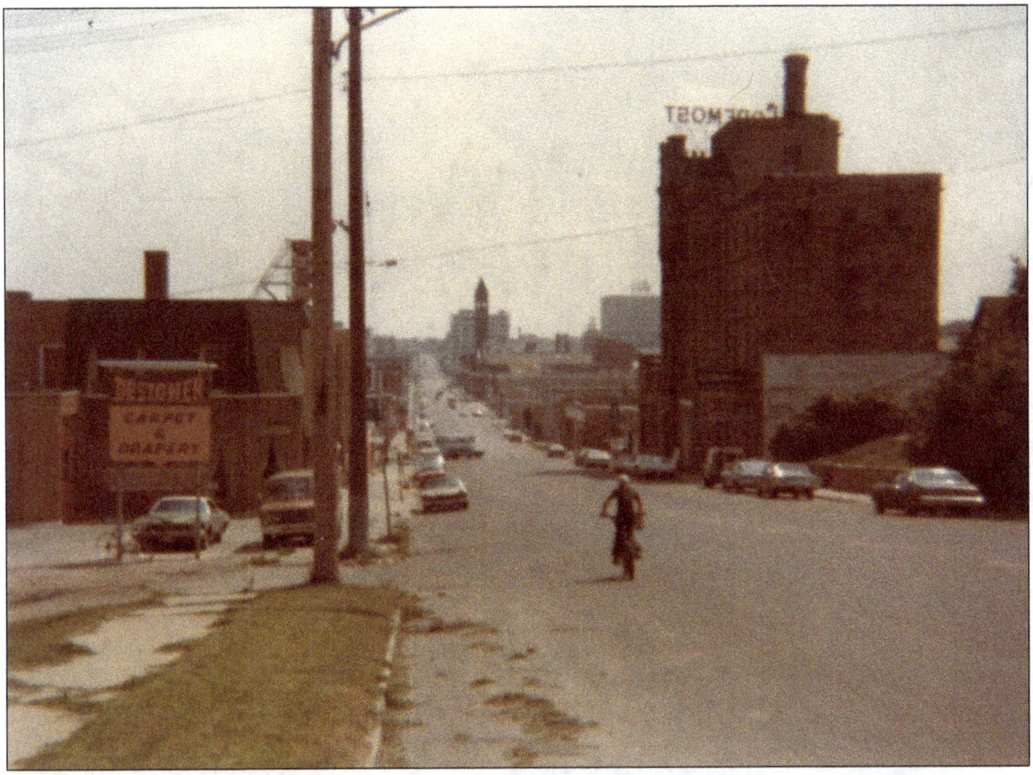

This is a view looking south on Main Avenue. The large building at right was originally the Sioux Falls Brewery, constructed in 1904 and in business until Prohibition. In 1919, Crescent Creamery took over the building until 1953, when Foremost Dairy was established. The dairy was in business until 1974, and the building sat vacant until destroyed by a fire on October 10, 1987. (Courtesy Siouxland Heritage Museums, Sioux Falls, SD.)

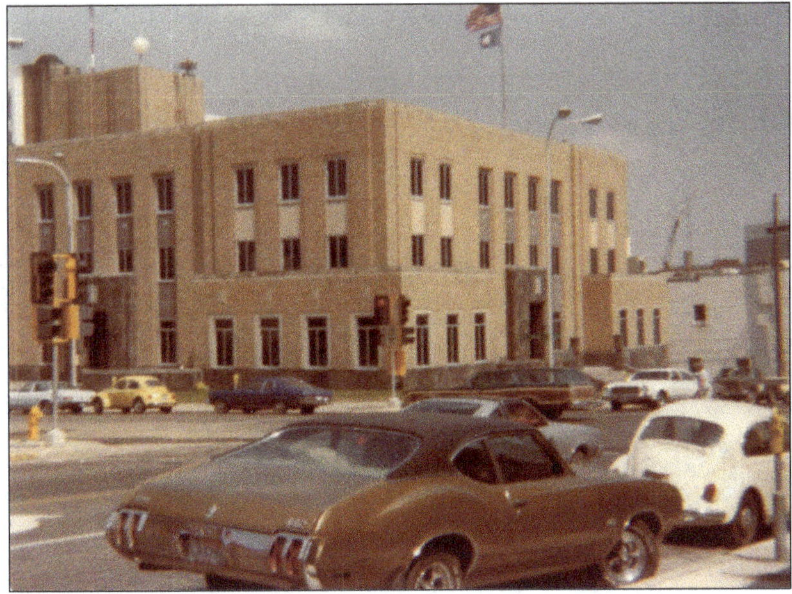

Pictured here in 1978 is city hall, located on the northeast corner of Ninth Street and Dakota Avenue. City hall was built in 1936 in the Art Deco style. The modern style was a drastic contrast to the architecture of the surrounding buildings in the downtown neighborhood. (Courtesy Siouxland Heritage Museums, Sioux Falls, SD.)

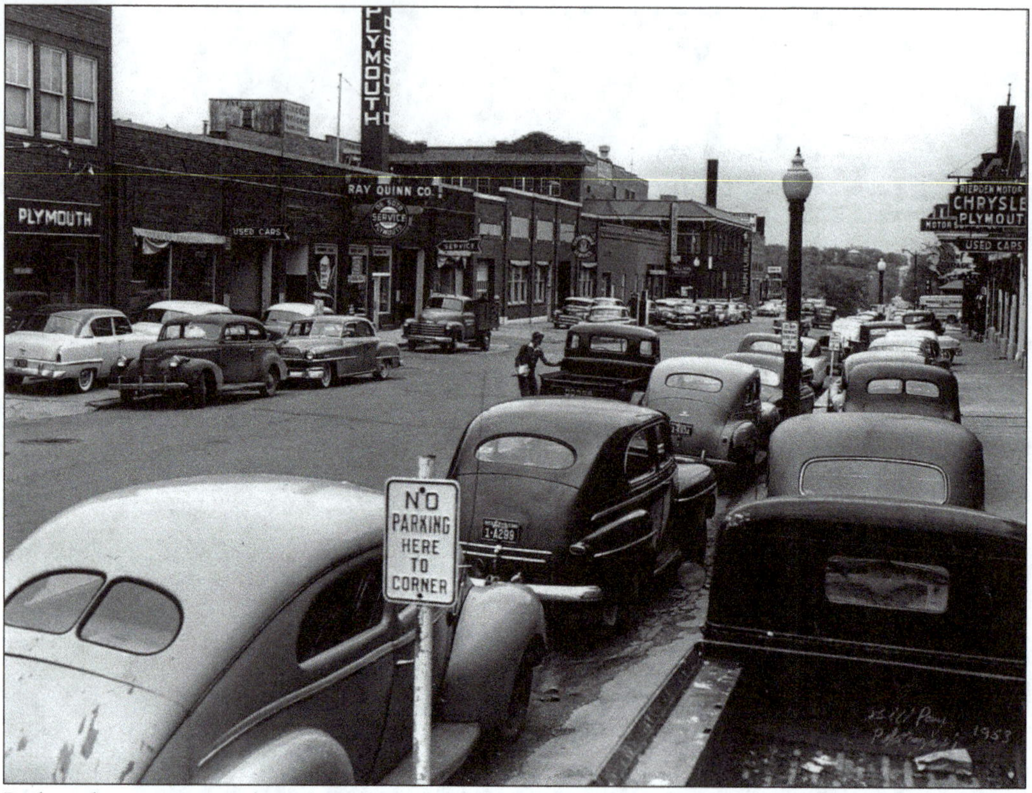

Parking lots were rare when the auto dealerships were located downtown. Note how the cars were parked parallel on the sidewalks instead of having a large parking lot to show them. This view of Dakota Avenue is looking north from Tenth Street. This photograph was taken by William Pay in 1953. (Courtesy Tom Olsen.)

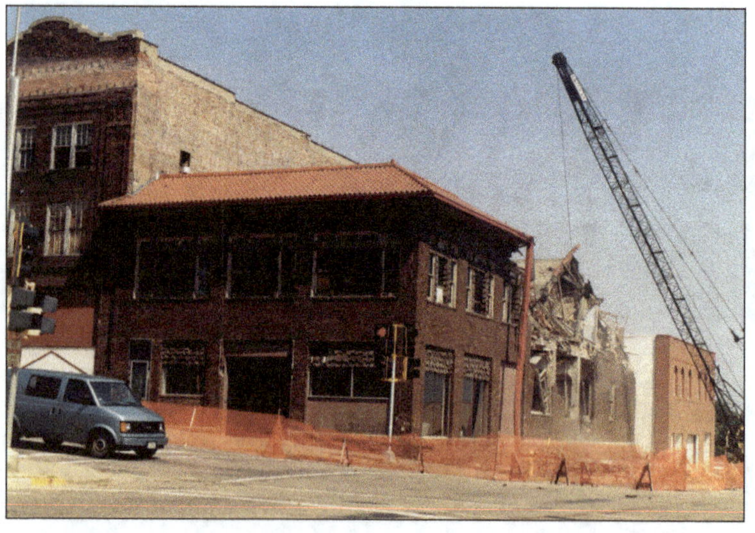

This view is looking north on Dakota Avenue from Ninth Street as the Knapp building is being torn down. From Dakota Avenue west to Minnesota Avenue on the north side of Tenth Street were most of the automobile dealers until they started to move away to the edges of the city. (Courtesy Siouxland Heritage Museums, Sioux Falls, SD.)

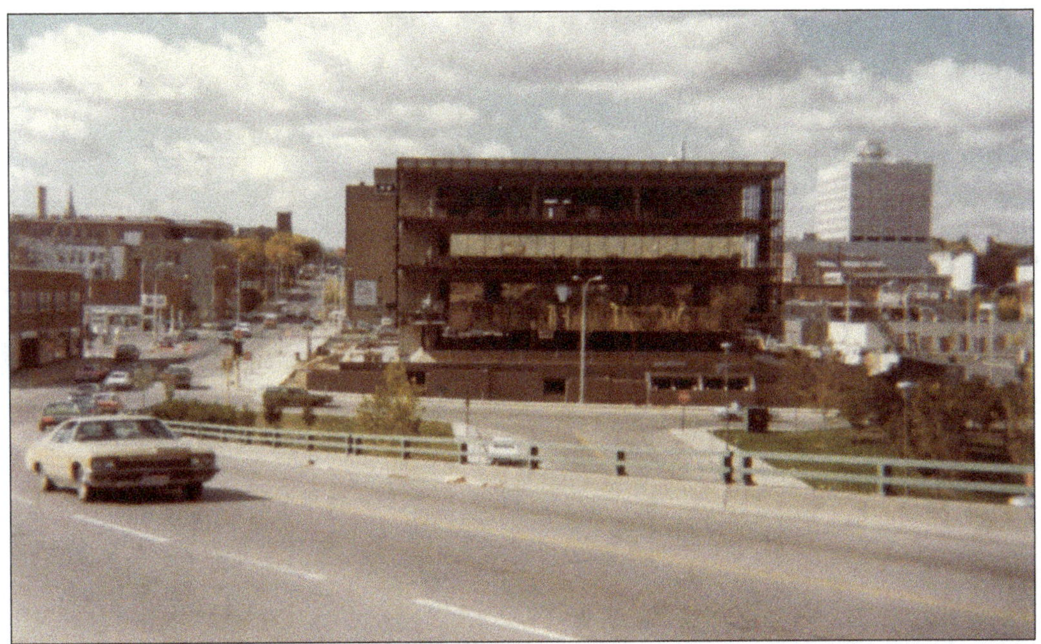

This image shows Midland National Life Insurance Company as it was being built. The large white structure at right is the Northwestern Bell Telephone Company building. The brown building to the left is Stewarts School of Hairstyling. The square-topped structure farther west on Eleventh Street is the First Congregational Church. (Courtesy Siouxland Heritage Museums, Sioux Falls, SD.)

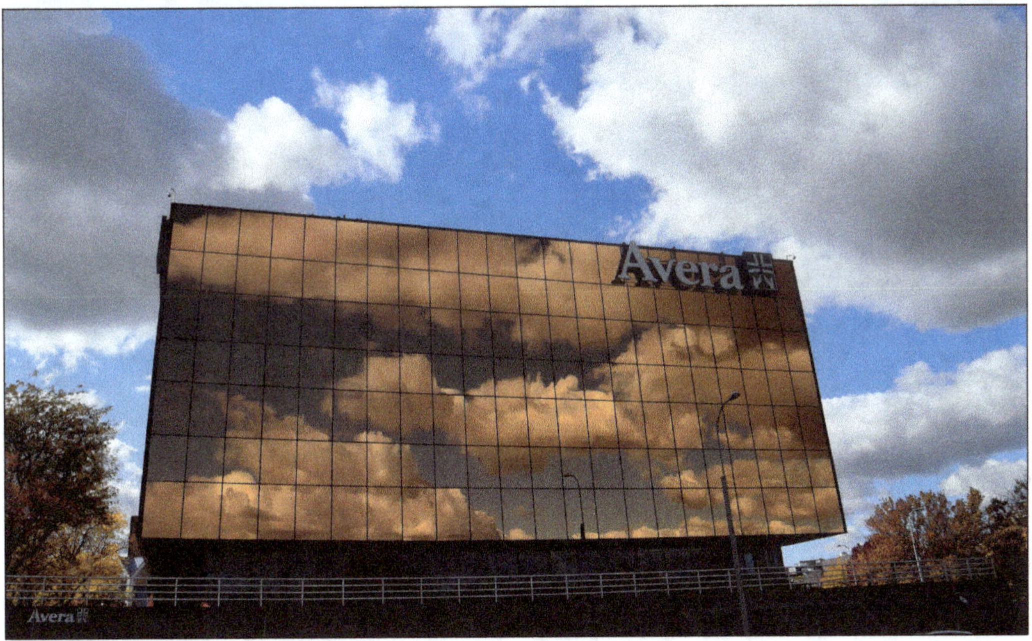

This building with all the mirrored windows was constructed in 1979 for the Midland National Life Insurance Company. It was designed to be energy efficient, allowing heat from the sun to warm it during the winter while reflecting heat during the summer. The insurance company later moved to a new office area south of Fifty-Seventh Street, east of Interstate 29. Today, Avera Health Foundation occupies this building.

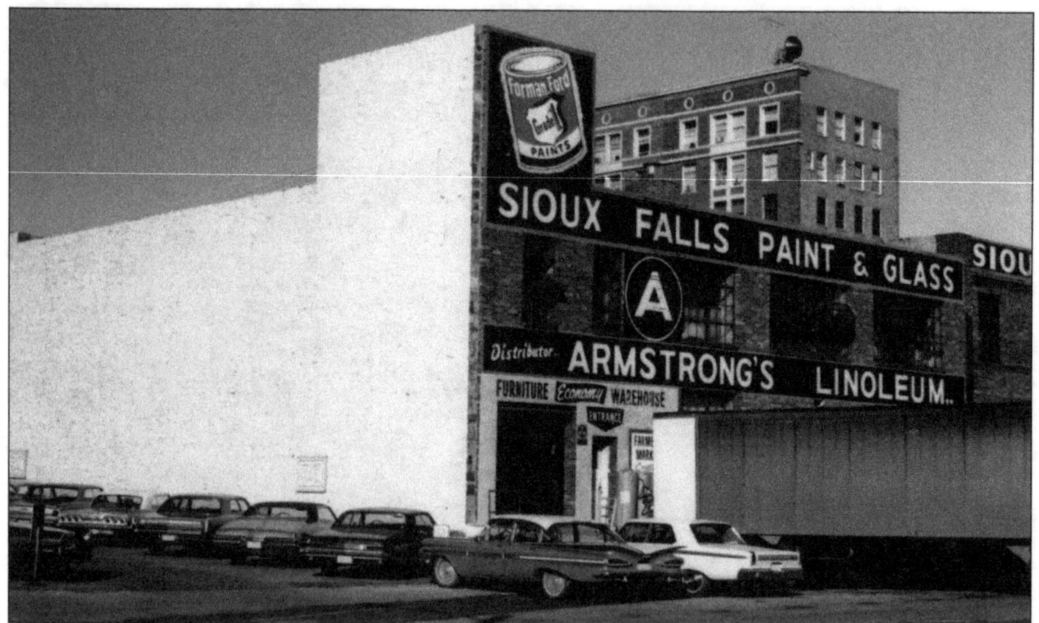

This is the Sioux Falls Paint and Glass Company building on the west side of First Avenue, between Ninth and Tenth Streets. This was one of the buildings torn down during the early 1970s that became a parking lot. There is a proposed mixed-use building plan to include office, retail, and residential spaces at this location. (Courtesy Siouxland Heritage Museums, Sioux Falls, SD.)

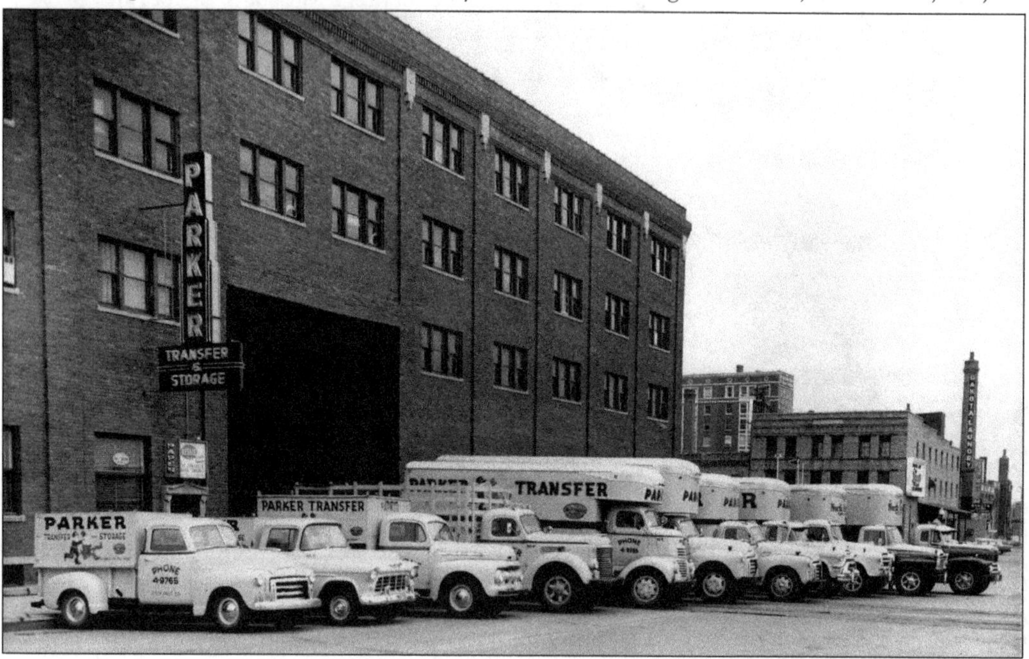

Pictured here is Parker Transfer and Storage on the west side of First Avenue between Tenth and Eleventh Streets. Note the large opening in the middle of the building. This is where the train would enter to be unloaded. The company used this location before moving to an industrial area. Parker Transfer and Storage has been moving Sioux Falls for 100 years. (Courtesy of Parker Transfer and Storage.)

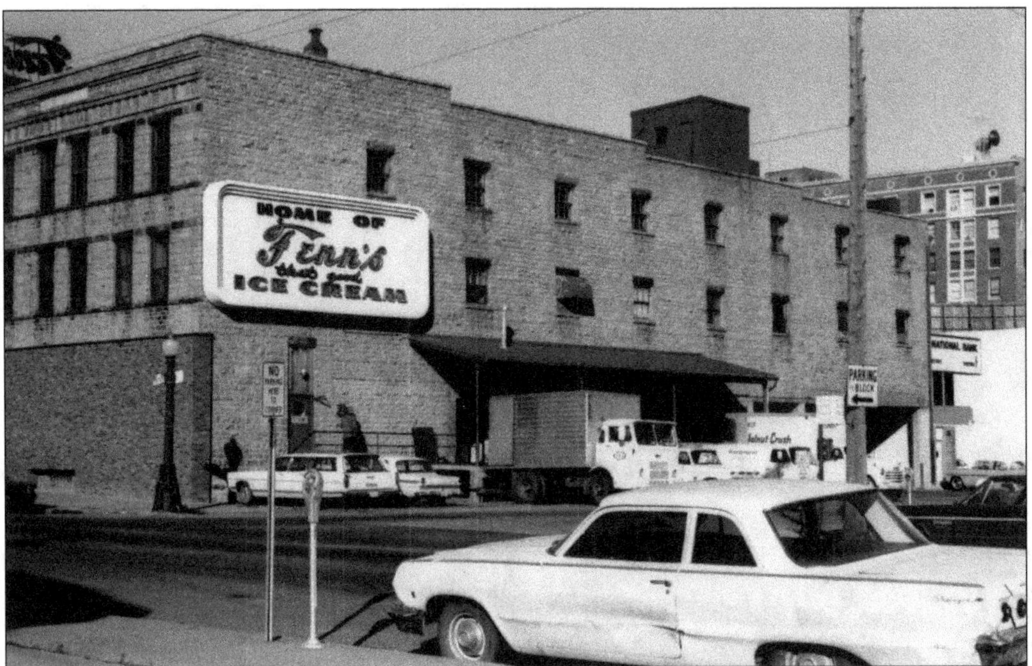

Fenn Bros. Ice Cream and Candy Co. was in business from 1898 to 1971. Their location was at the northwest corner of Tenth Street and First Avenue. Fenn Bros. invented the flavor of Butter Brickle ice cream. Their candy bars, including the famous Walnut Crush, were favorites as well. (Courtesy Siouxland Heritage Museums, Sioux Falls, SD.)

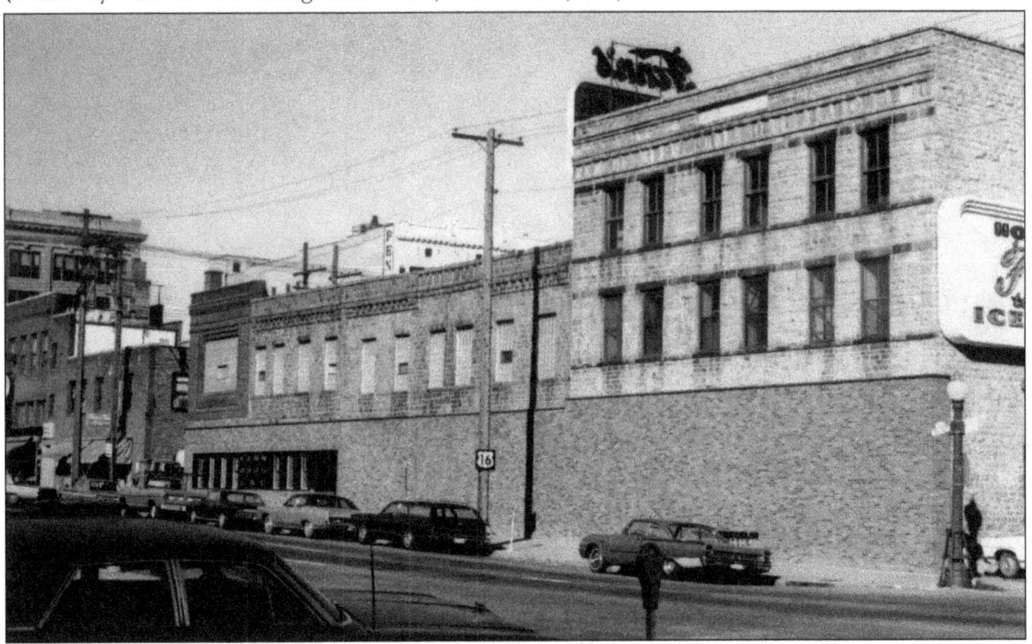

This view looking west on Tenth Street from First Avenue shows the south side of the Fenn Bros. Ice Cream and Candy Co. building. Note the Highway 16 sign. Highway 16 ran through downtown and was the main highway for travelers going from the Black Hills to Iowa or Minnesota. (Courtesy Siouxland Heritage Museums, Sioux Falls, SD.)

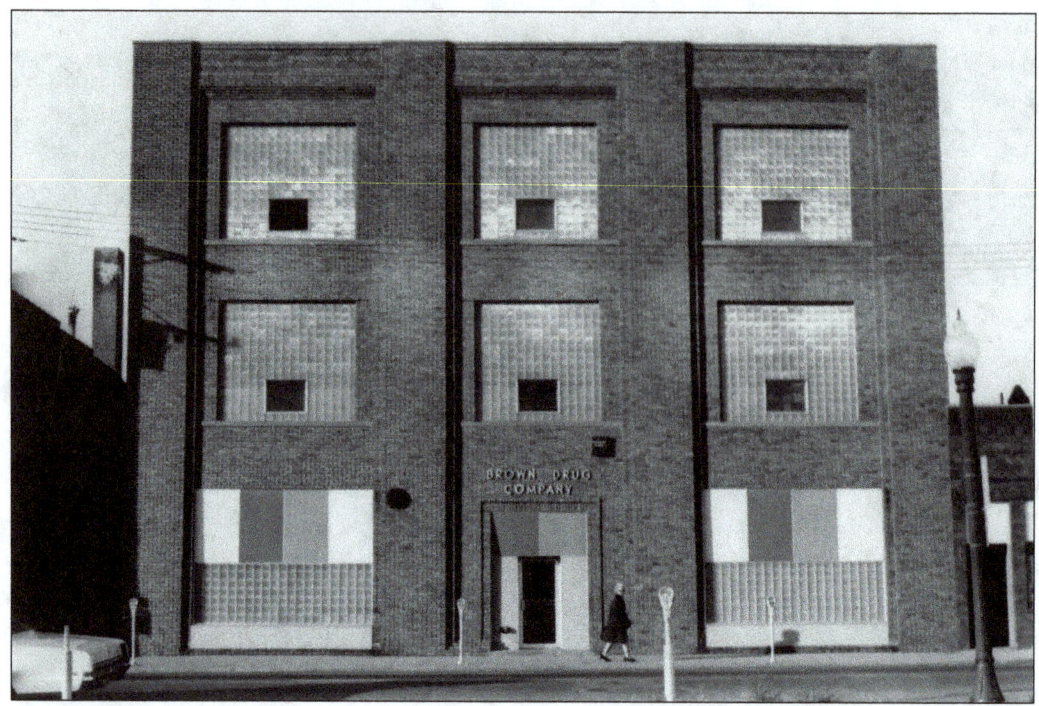

This is a rare picture of the Brown Drug Company at 212 East Tenth Street, on the north side of the street between First and Second Avenues. The drug company was organized in 1901 by Dr. R.F. Brown and was in business for nearly 100 years. (Courtesy Siouxland Heritage Museums, Sioux Falls, SD.)

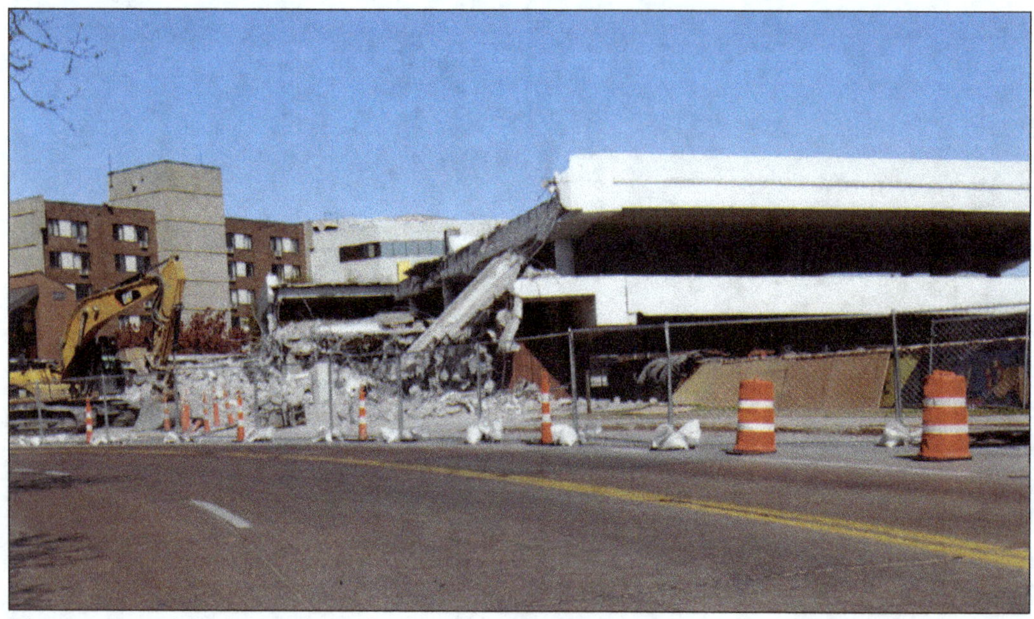

This is a view of the downtown parking ramp as it was being demolished. The River Ramp Parking Structure was located at 120 East Ninth Street. Cars had parked above the Big Sioux River on the ramp from 1962 until 2012, when it was torn down due to deterioration. (Courtesy Siouxland Heritage Museums, Sioux Falls, SD.)

Sioux Valley Hospital (Sanford USD Medical Center) was built at this location in 1930. This picture shows the entrance on the east side of the original building, when Euclid Avenue ran next to the hospital. Today, the cars at left would be sitting in the main lobby of the hospital. (Courtesy Olin Odland.)

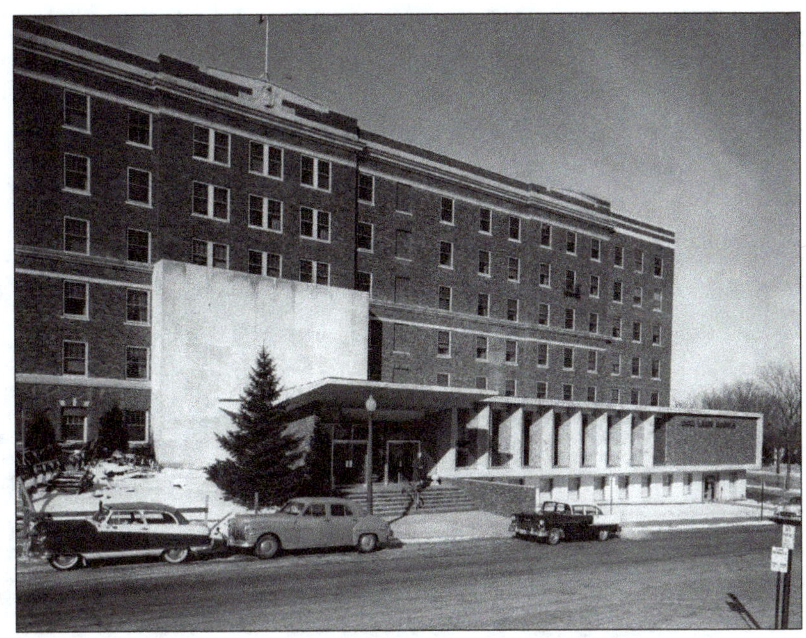

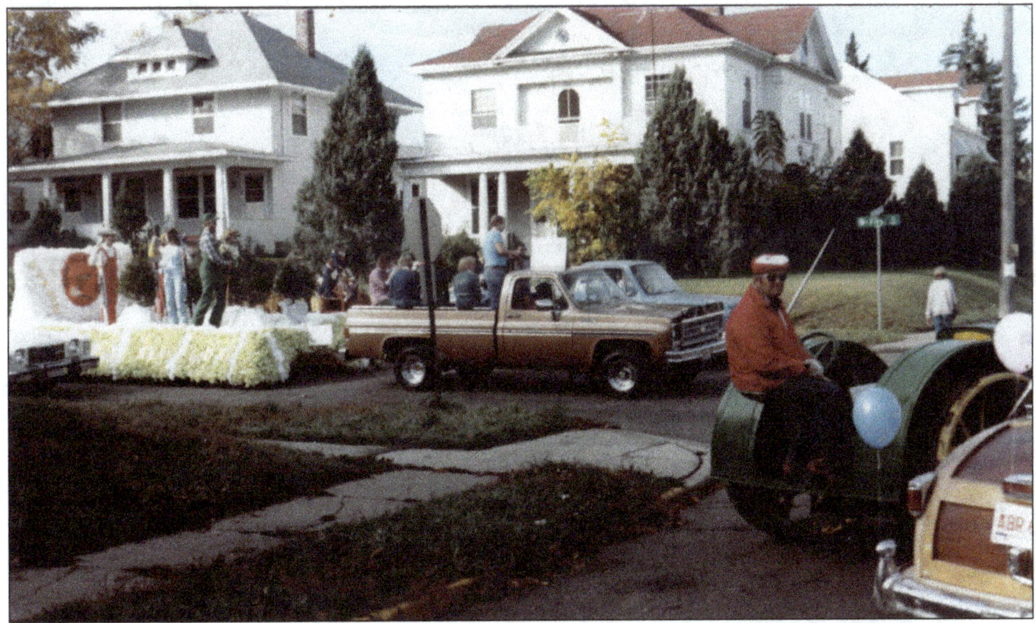

Parades have always brought many people downtown. Here, entertainers prepare for a parade at the corner of Fourteenth Street and First Avenue. Even more interesting is the apartment building hidden behind many trees. This building was constructed in 1896 on the southwest corner and was later used as Dunham Hospital from 1904 until 1912. Dr. Whitefield Otis Dunham had a general hospital with an operating room. (Courtesy Ed Limke.)

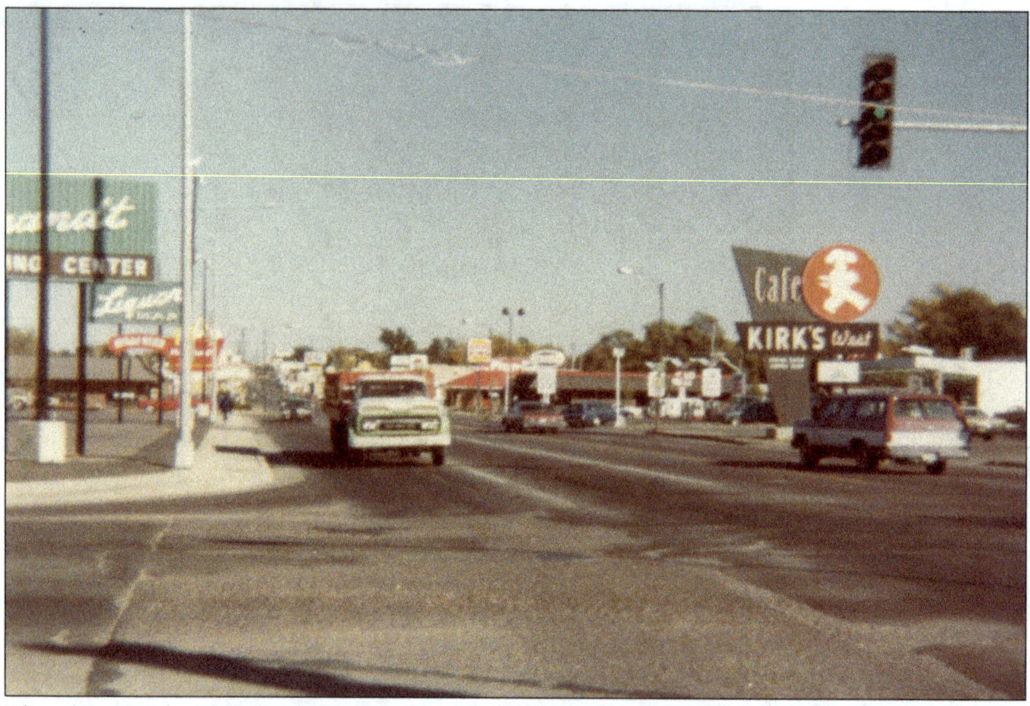

This photograph shows Twelfth Street looking east from Kiwanis Avenue. At right is Kirks Drive-Inn, which stood on this corner from 1955 to 1989. At left is the Brandt Shopping Center, which was once a Sunshine grocery store. Ace Hardware is located there today. (Courtesy Siouxland Heritage Museums, Sioux Falls, SD.)

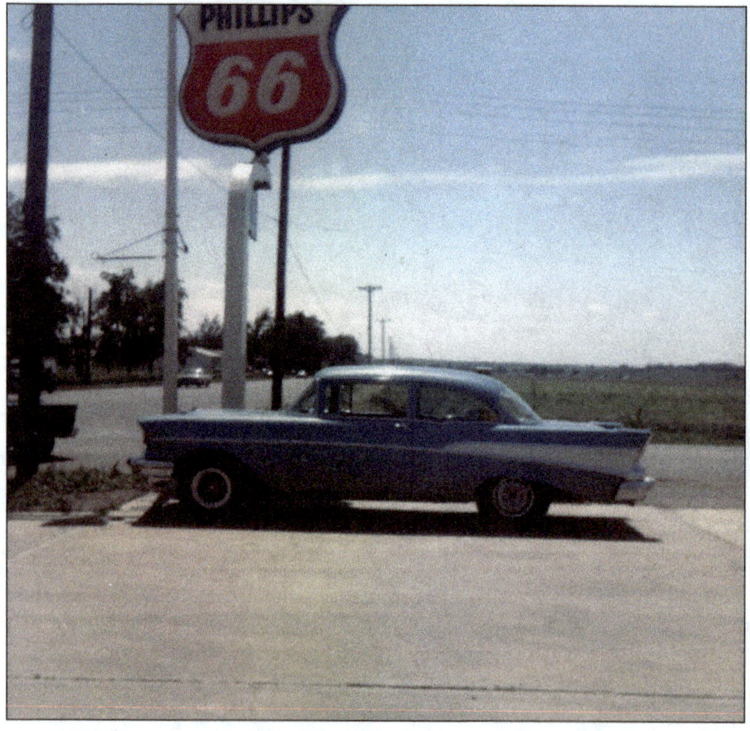

This view is looking south on Western Avenue from Forty-First Street in 1967. Today, this is one of the busiest intersections in the city. The grass area is where Graham Tire stands now, next to Western Mall. (Courtesy Tom Olsen.)

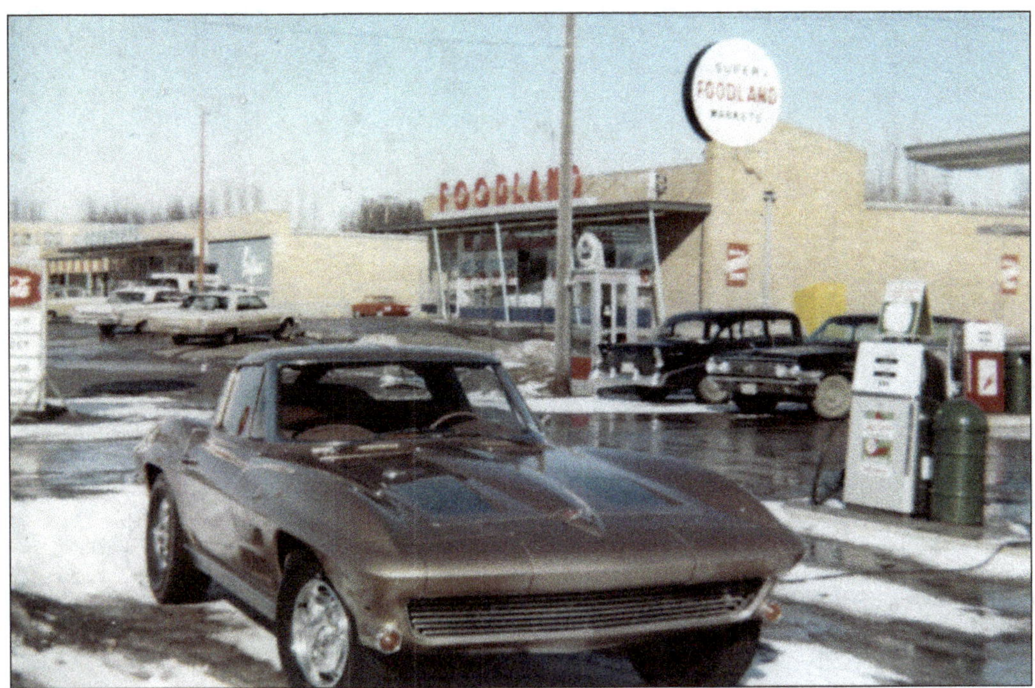

This view is looking northeast at the intersection of Western Avenue and Twenty-Sixth Street. Grill 26 restaurant is in the former Foodland Super Market building. At left is Parkridge Mall. (Courtesy Tom Olsen.)

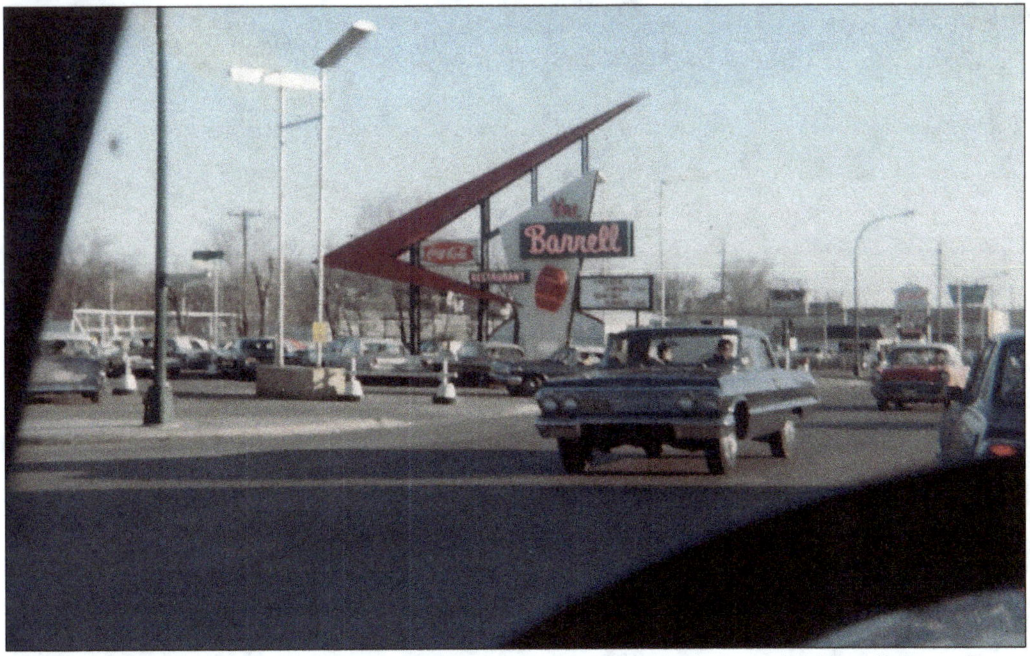

Locals have always loved to cruise. Tom Olsen is driving north past the Barrell Drive-In on Thirty-First Street and Minnesota Avenue. Note that the Avera Living Well building has not yet been constructed south of the Barrell Drive-In on the northeast corner of Thirty-Third Street and Minnesota Avenue. (Courtesy Tom Olsen.)

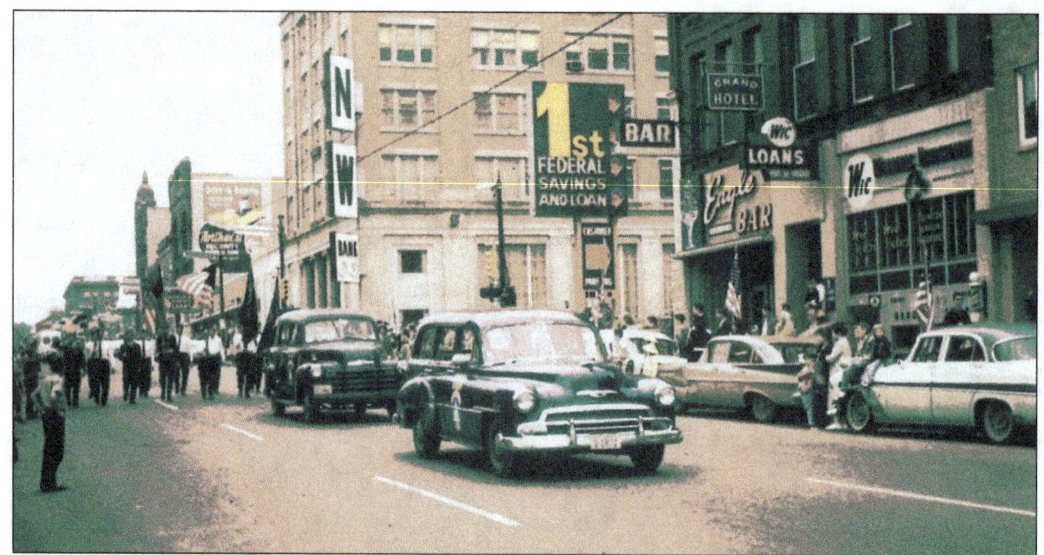

This picture was taken during a parade in the early 1960s from the north side of Ninth Street. From left to right are Washington High School; Union Trust Bank (with the dome), built in 1888 and razed in 1965; the Odd Fellows Hall; and Security Bank. The brown building on the right was the Metropolitan Block, constructed in 1886 and razed in 1965. (Courtesy Tom Olsen.)

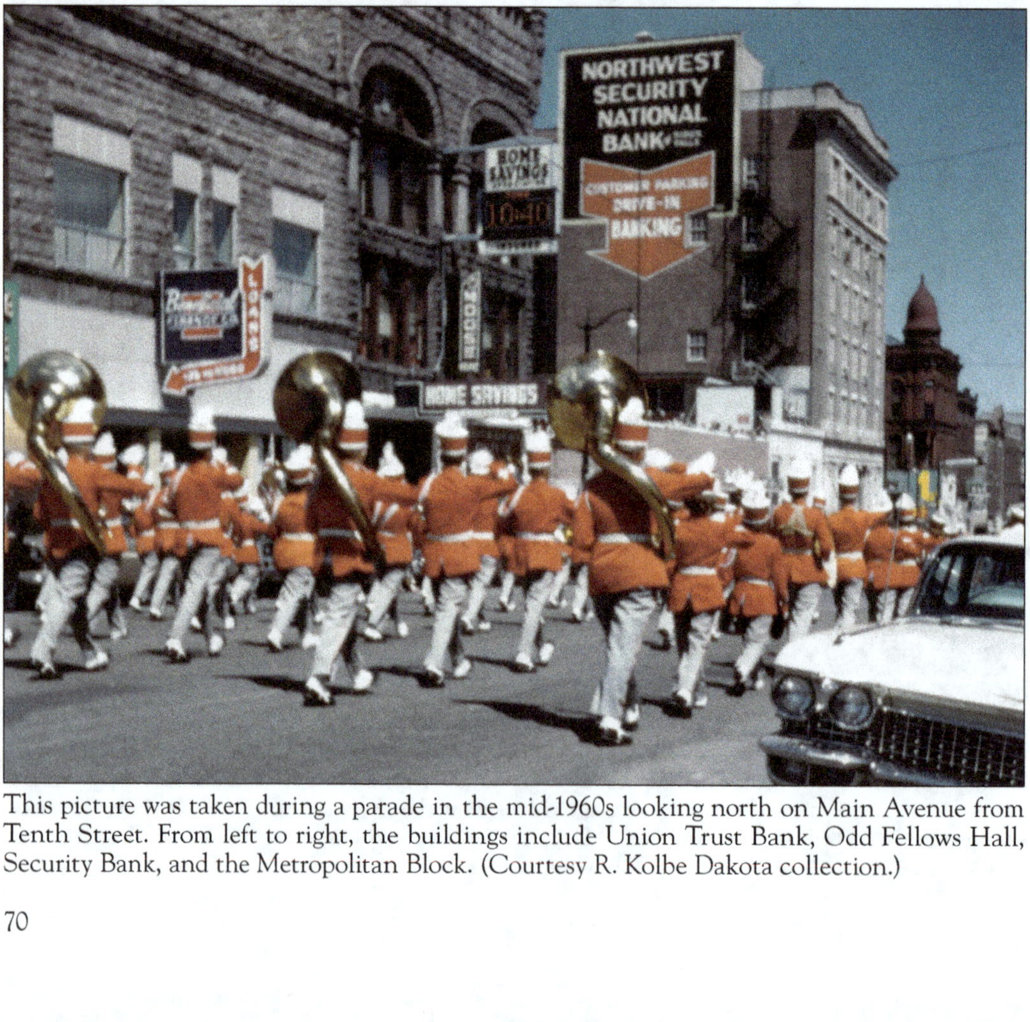

This picture was taken during a parade in the mid-1960s looking north on Main Avenue from Tenth Street. From left to right, the buildings include Union Trust Bank, Odd Fellows Hall, Security Bank, and the Metropolitan Block. (Courtesy R. Kolbe Dakota collection.)

Four

Landmarks of Sioux Falls

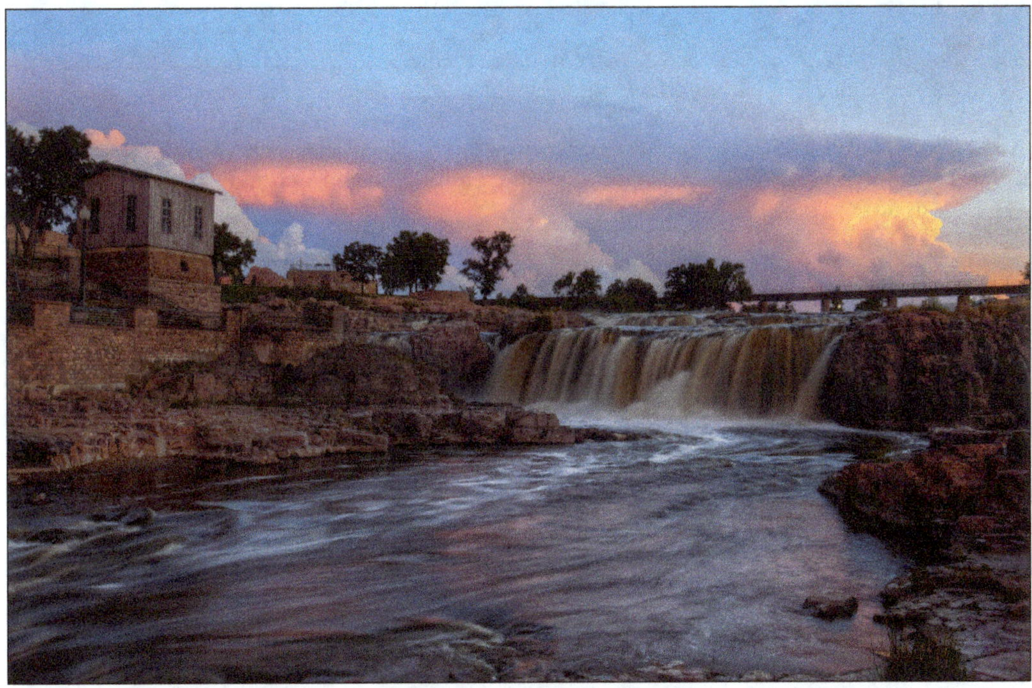

Is it any wonder why people have been drawn to the Falls of the Big Sioux River? This breathtaking picture was taken by local photographer Christian Begeman. It is amazing how much water has glided over the quartzite bedrock over the years, but this continues to be one of the most beautiful areas in the city. Were it not for the Falls, it is possible early pioneers may have traveled by and kept searching for a spot for their new village. If the stones could talk, they could tell many stories of the people who have stopped to enjoy the beauty and power of the Falls of the Big Sioux River. (Courtesy Christian Begeman.)

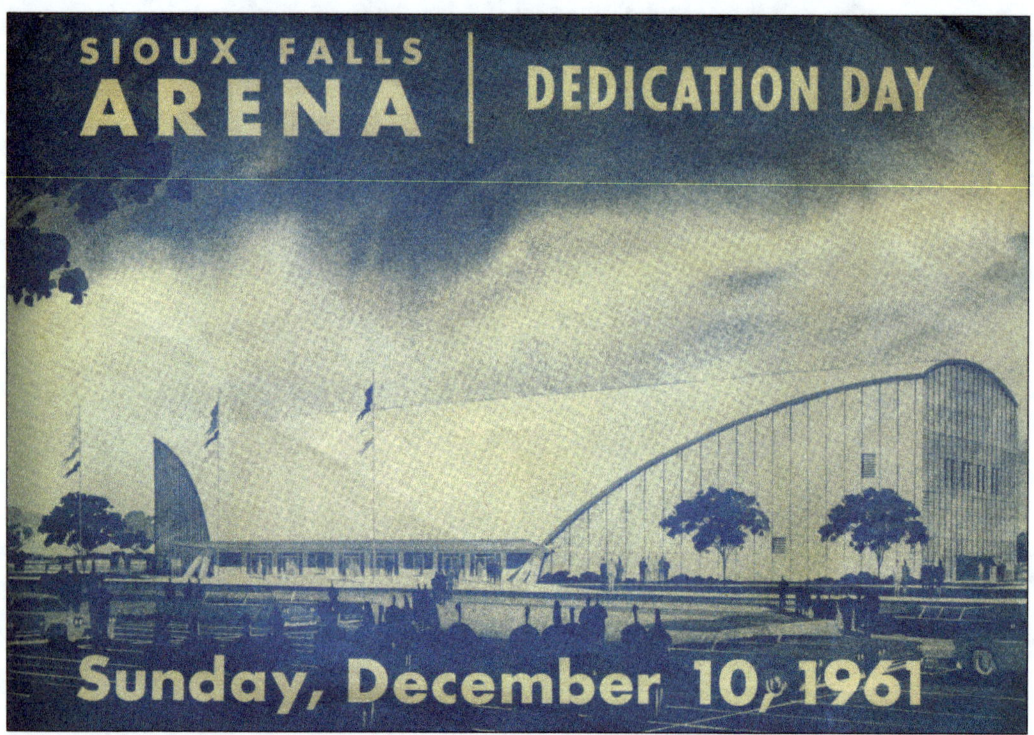

Thousands of Sioux Falls high school and college students have celebrated their graduation ceremonies at the Sioux Falls Arena. The Sioux Falls Arena has entertained millions of people with sporting events, musical performances, and other shows. No doubt some of the loudest screams at the arena were heard when Elvis performed on October 18, 1976, and June 22, 1977. Less than two months after Elvis left the building for the last time, he died of heart failure.

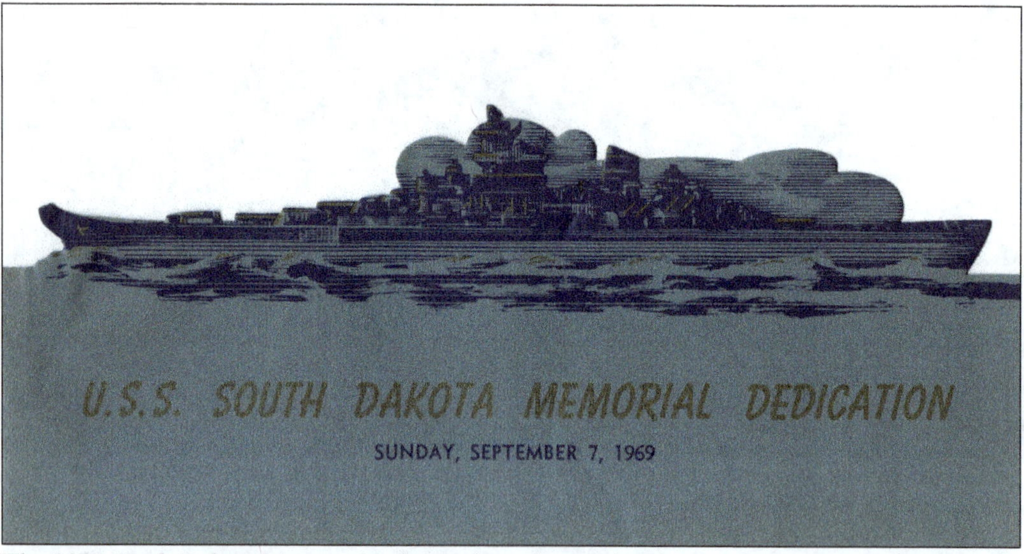

The USS *South Dakota* Memorial is located on the southwest corner of Kiwanis Avenue and Twelfth Street, north of the Great Plains Zoo. This memorial was dedicated on September 7, 1969. Battleship 57 (BB 57) was also known as USS *South Dakota*, *SoDak*, *Old Nameless*, and, most famous, *Battleship* X. This was one of the most highly decorated battleships of World War II.

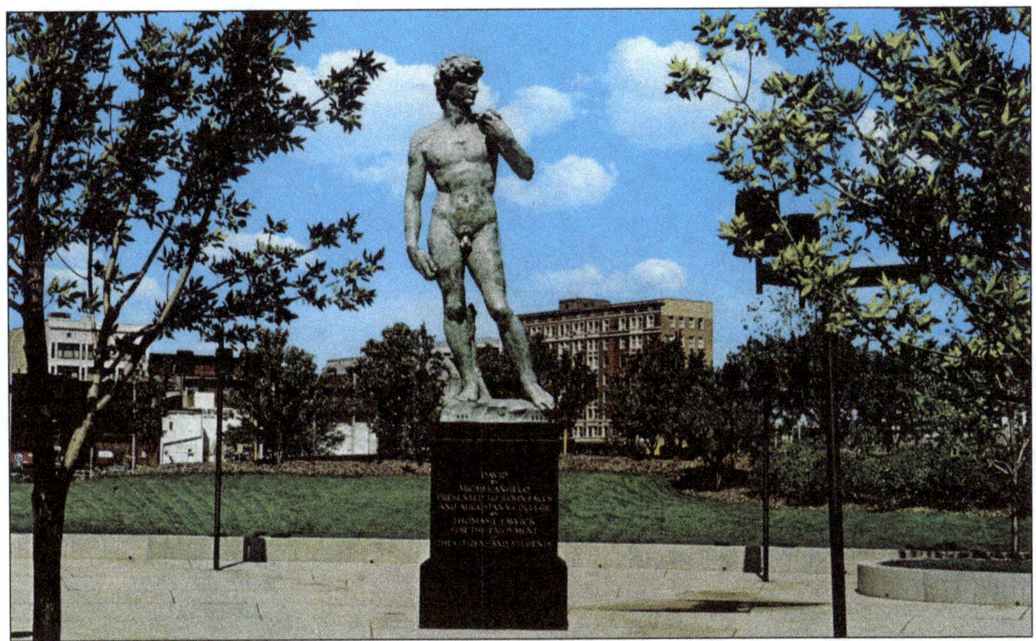

This sculpture represents David, from the Bible story of David and Goliath. Gifted by Thomas Fawick, a Sioux Falls native and inventor, the bronze statue had an estimated value of $350,000 when it was placed downtown in 1971. This was a controversial gift for the city, and to limit visibility, it originally faced southeast, away from traffic, and had trees planted around it with the goal to make it more modest. The above picture shows the original placement of David. In 1997, the sculpture was put in storage while the park was excavated and cleaned up due to contaminated soil. In October 2000, he returned to his former shadowland and was now placed facing north. The picture below shows David in his new location after the Fawick Park renovation.

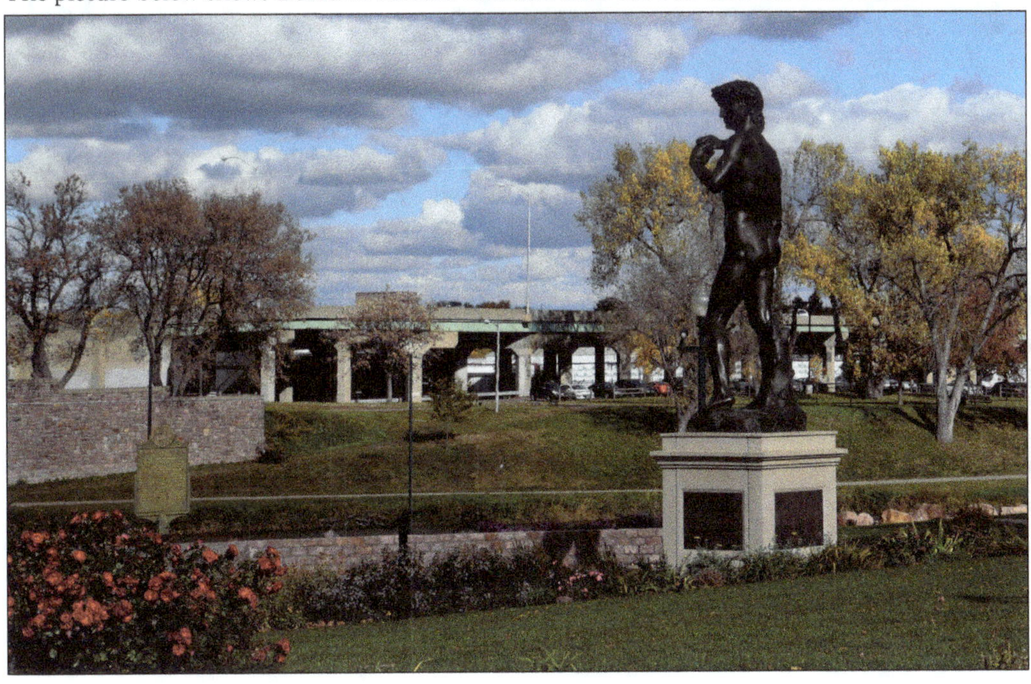

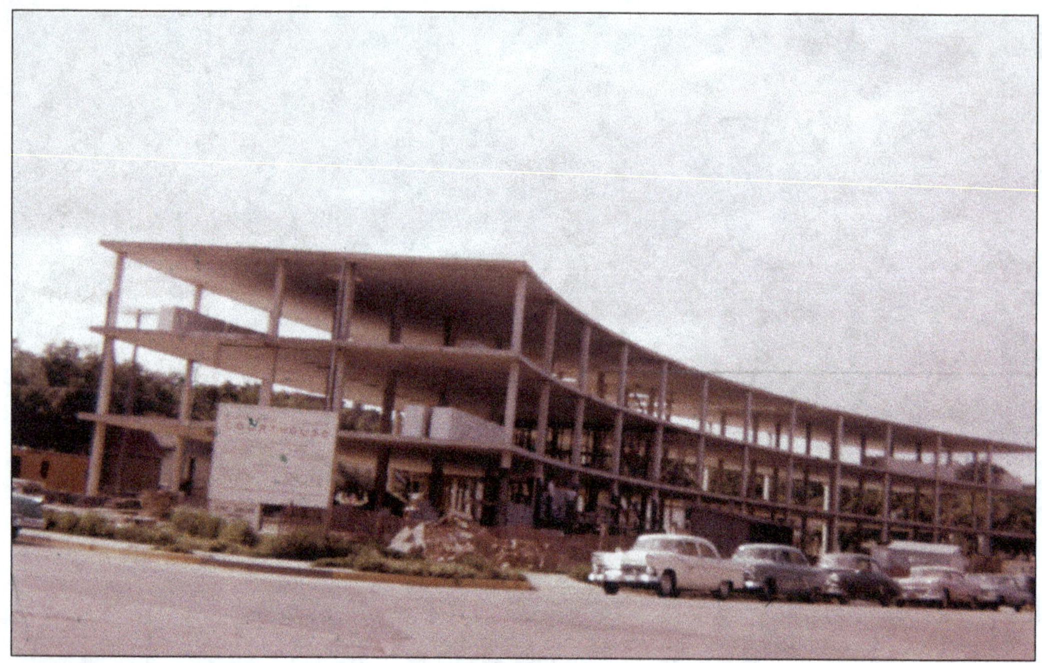

This picture shows the Minnehaha County Courthouse as it was being built to the west of the original courthouse. The unique contour of the front of the building gave a modern look to the structure, which was a contrast to the historical buildings in the neighborhood. This building was completed in 1962 and used until the next courthouse was constructed in 1996 to the north. (Courtesy Siouxland Heritage Museums, Sioux Falls, SD.)

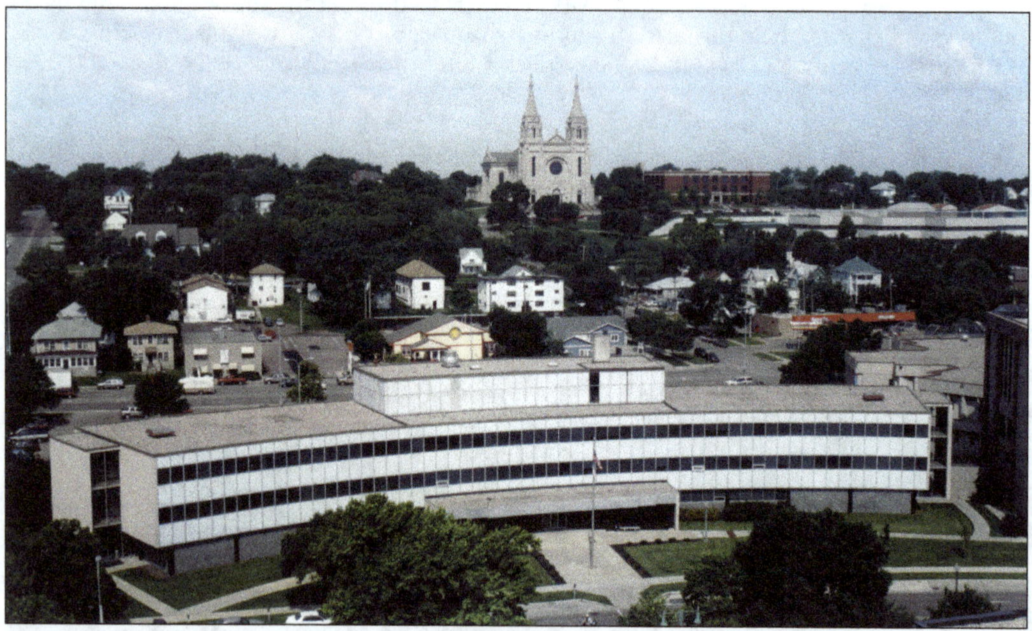

This picture was taken in 2003 from the bell tower of the Old Courthouse Museum. The view, looking west, shows the Minnehaha County Courthouse and the beautiful St. Joseph's Cathedral on the hill with St. Joseph Cathedral School to its right. Hawthorne Elementary School can be seen at center right. (Courtesy Tom Olsen.)

The Falls have always been an attraction for the local community. There was a certain period when they were not as attractive or as safe as today. This view taken in 1979 shows the Falls as they appeared for several years, overgrown with trees and brush and hiding the natural beauty of the area. Today, the Falls are beautiful year-round. (Courtesy Siouxland Heritage Museums, Sioux Falls, SD.)

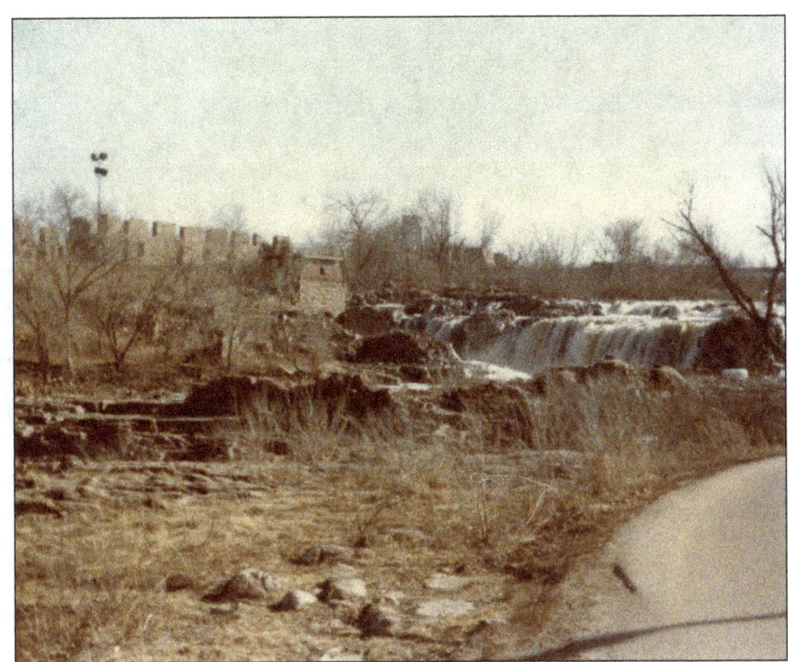

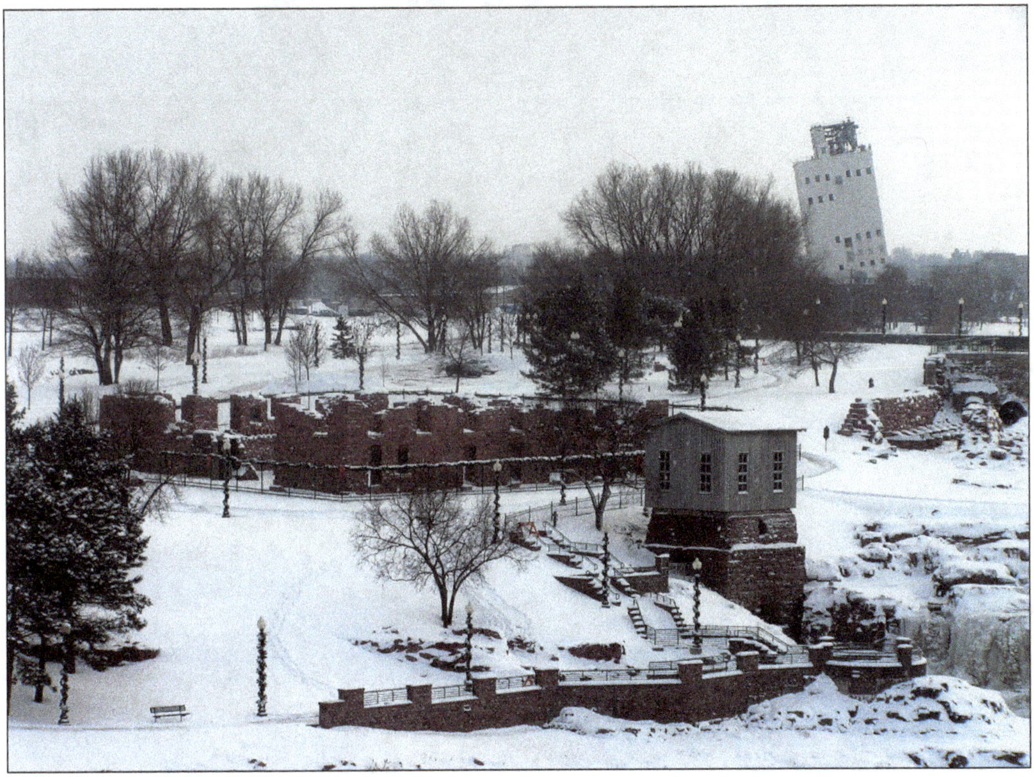

This winter view of the Falls shows a tilted Zip Feed Mill in the background. On December 3, 2005, efforts were made to implode the Zip Feed Mill. There was quite an explosion, but not enough to level the structure. The mill was built in 1957 and used as a grain elevator and feed mill. It was the tallest building in South Dakota at 202 feet tall.

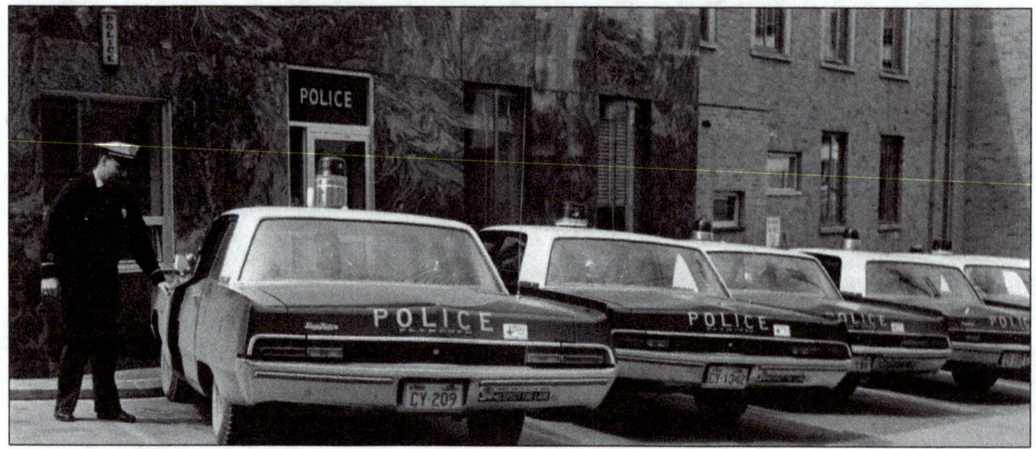

From 1936 to 1978, the Sioux Falls Police Department was in the basement of the city hall building on the northeast corner of Ninth Street and Dakota Avenue. This picture of the east side of the building was taken in the late 1960s. In 1978, the police department moved to its new location in the Public Safety Building at 500 North Minnesota Avenue, north of the Minnehaha County Courthouse. (Courtesy Tom Olsen.)

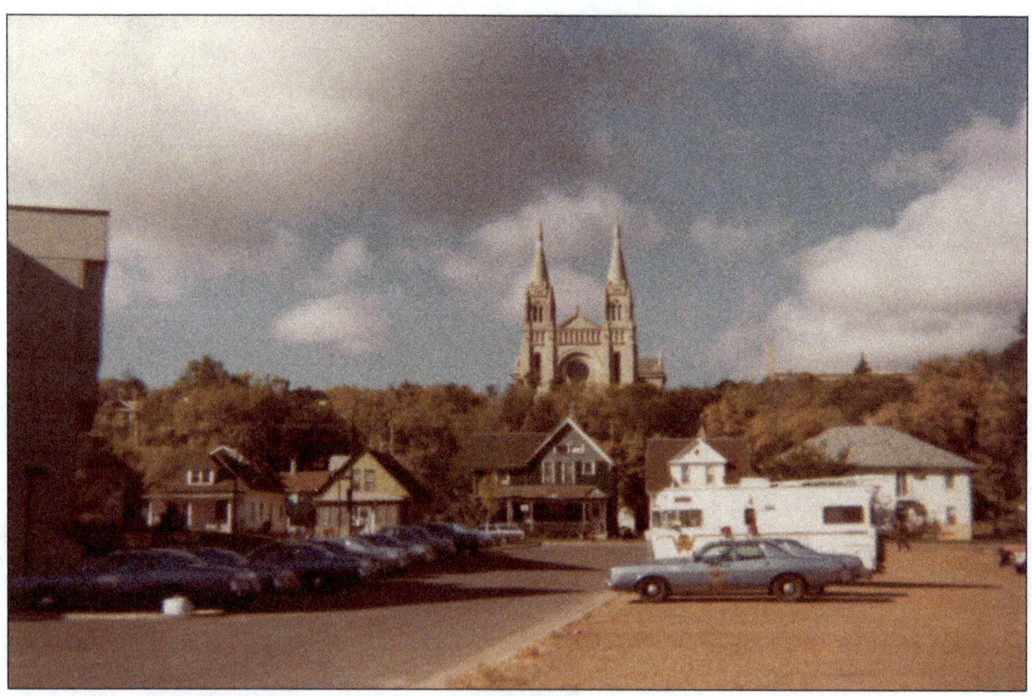

This view is looking west from Dakota Avenue, between Fourth and Fifth Streets. In the center background is St. Joseph's Cathedral, built in 1917. At left is the Public Safety Building, constructed in 1977. Note that the houses previously located on Minnesota Avenue have been torn down. (Courtesy Siouxland Heritage Museums, Sioux Falls, SD.)

Five

Aerial Views

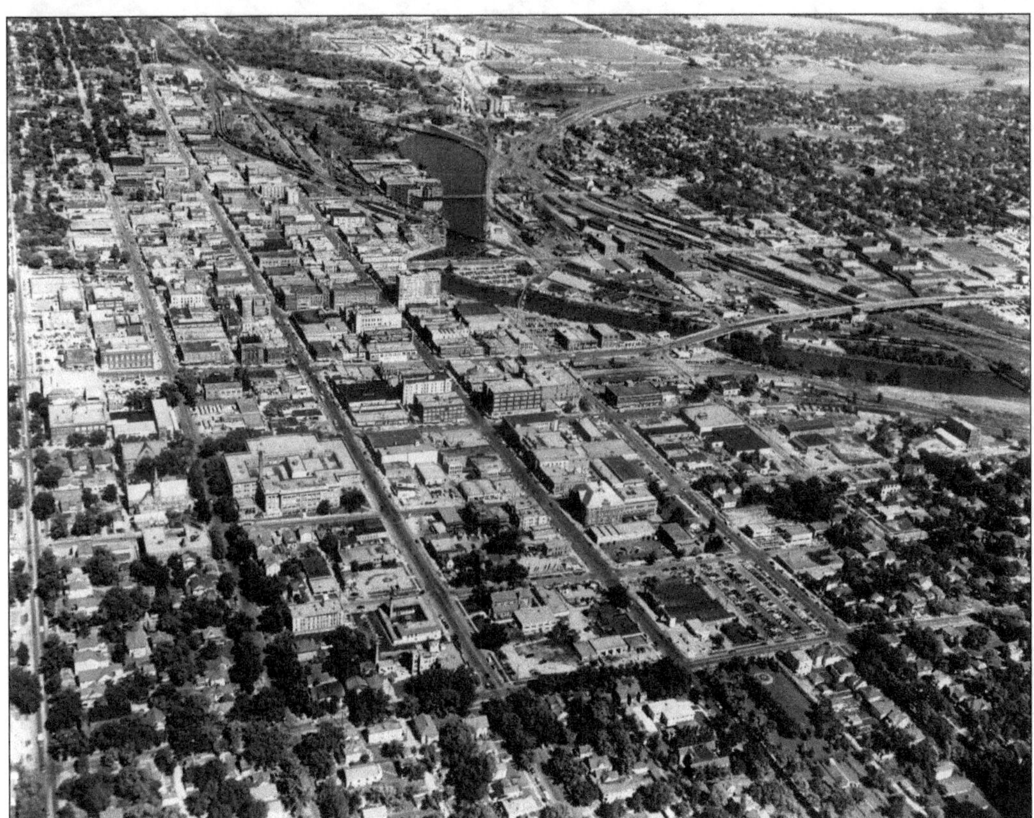

This is a very impressive view of the downtown area looking north in 1963. Beginning in 1973, urban renewal, a movement to replace the old buildings with modern structures or parking lots, began significantly changing the landscape of downtown. Most of the citizens are thankful for the buildings that were saved; however, many residents wished there could have been fewer demolished. (Courtesy William Pay.)

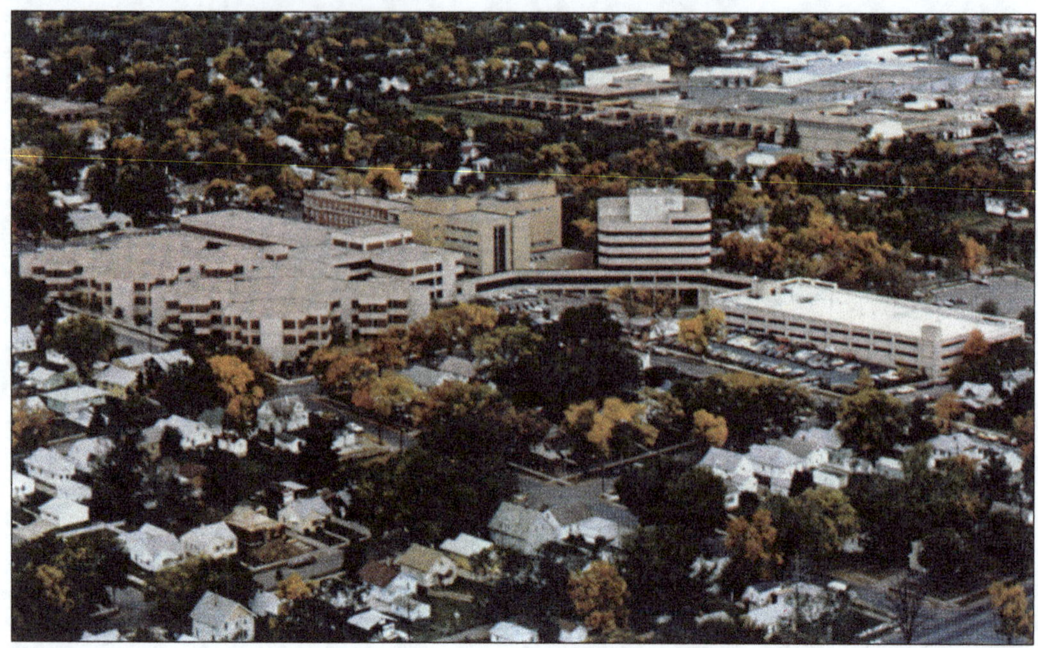

The above picture is an early aerial view of the McKennan Hospital campus, looking northwest. Since this picture was taken, many new structures have been built on the campus. The image below shows a more recent view of the Avera McKennan Hospital campus and how it has expanded. McKennan Hospital was built in 1911 and named after Helen G. McKennan, who left a large financial gift in her will for the hospital to be established. From the beginning, the Presentation Sisters of Aberdeen have operated the hospital. In 2000, the Presentation Sisters joined the Benedictine Sisters of Yankton to form Avera Health. Avera Health continues to grow and provide excellent medical care to the Sioux Falls community. (Below, courtesy Avera Health.)

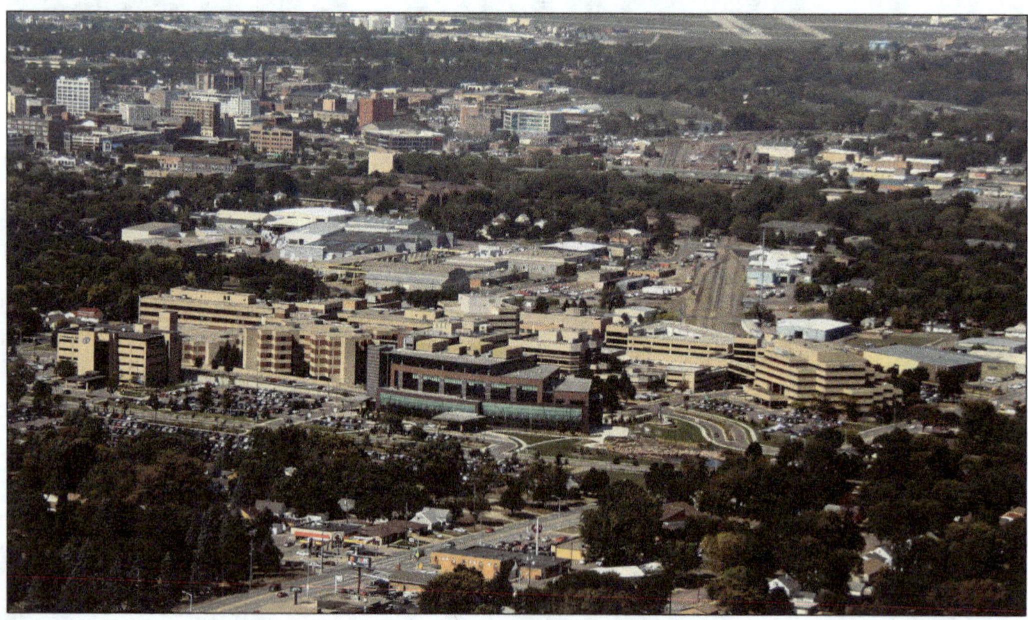

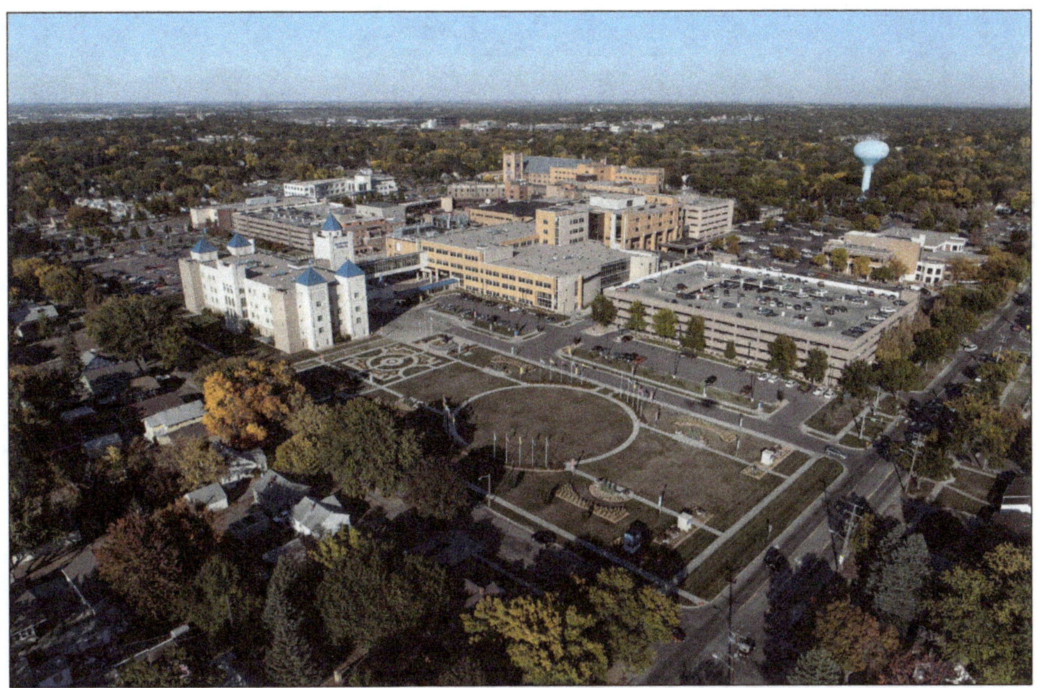

These are views showing the expansion from Sioux Valley Hospital to Sanford USD Medical Center. Over the last 10 years, Sanford Health has expanded to several locations throughout the community, region, and world. T. Denny Sanford has given close to $1 billion in financial gifts, which has fueled many new programs within the Sanford Health System. This expansion has provided many new jobs and improved the medical availability in Sioux Falls and in different areas of the world. Sioux Falls will be home to the Imagenetics program, which will mix genomics and primary care medicine to better predict and prevent disease. Below, at left, the construction of the Imagenetics building can be seen. (Both, courtesy Sanford Health.)

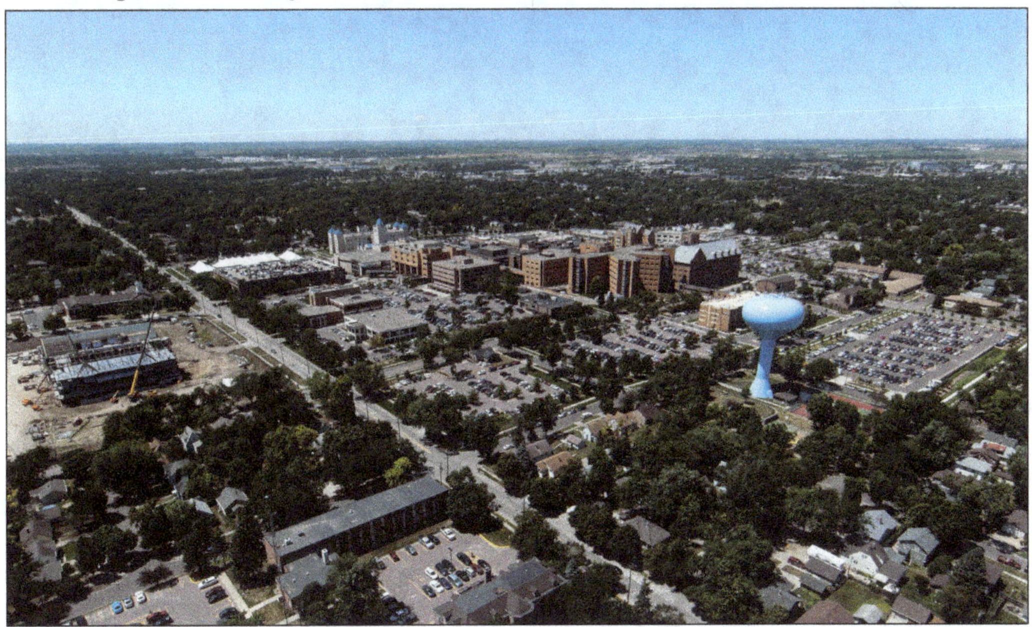

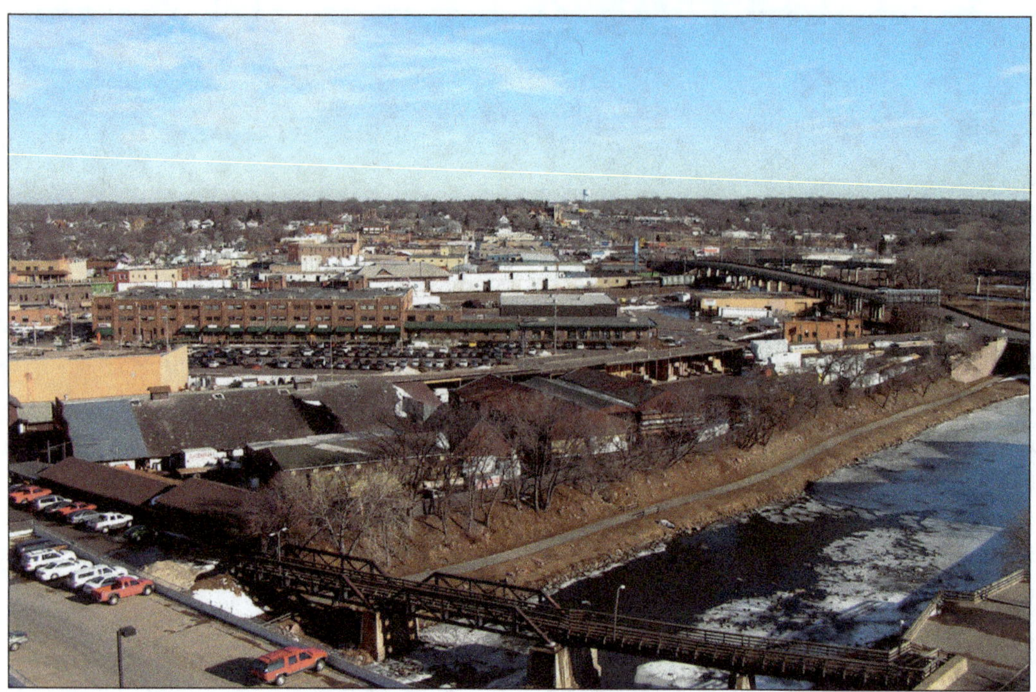

Both of these photographs were taken from the top of the bank building on the northeast corner of Ninth Street and Phillips Avenue. The above picture was taken in 2005, and the image below was taken in 2016. Two significant changes that took place during the 11 years between the pictures were the River Ramp parking structure being torn down and Schoeneman Bros. Lumber Company being razed and cleaned out to make room for the Hilton Garden Inn and the large office building at right. The lumberyard had been downtown for approximately 100 years.

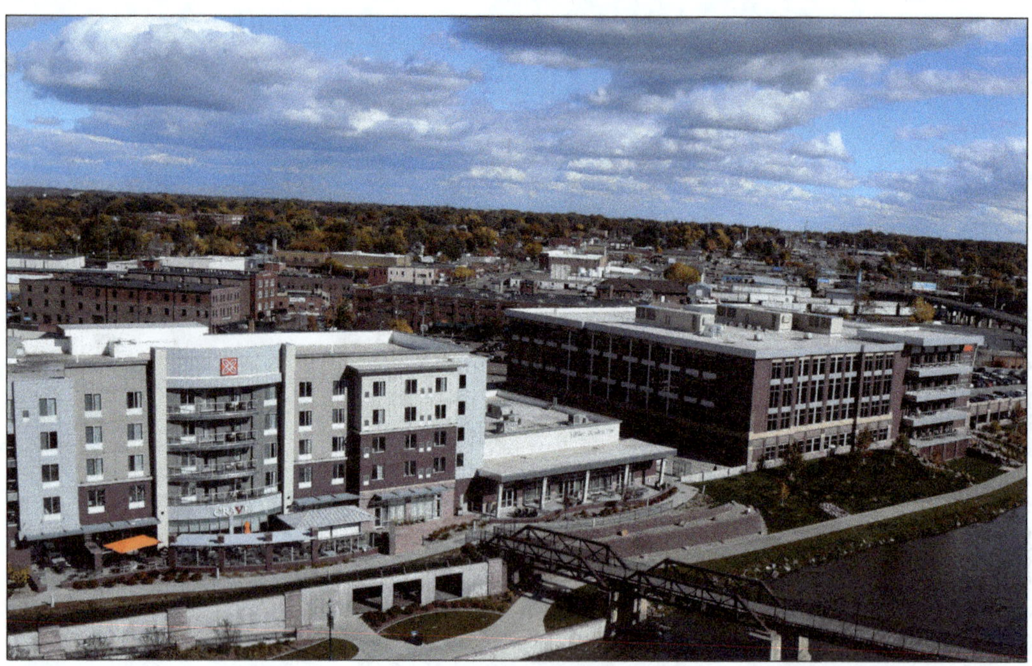

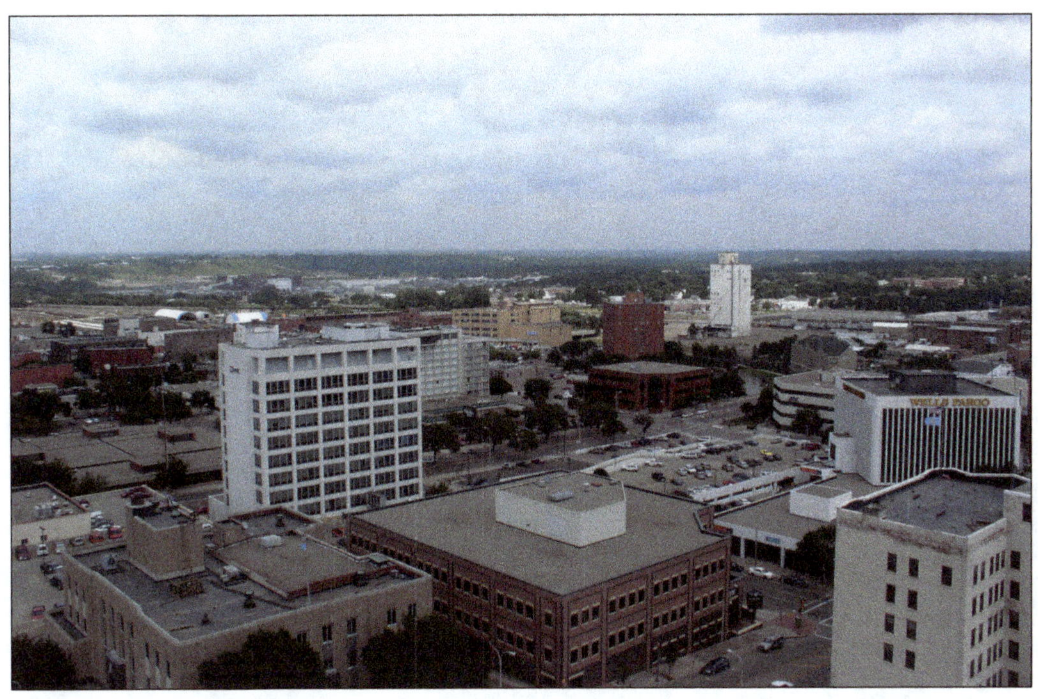

These two photographs were taken from the top of the Quest or Centurylink building on Tenth Street and Dakota Avenue. The above photograph was taken in 2005, and the image below was taken in 2016. Most of downtown looks similar. In the distance, the Zip Feed Mill was torn down and replaced with the beautiful Cherapa Place building. The view below shows some of the newer buildings at right.

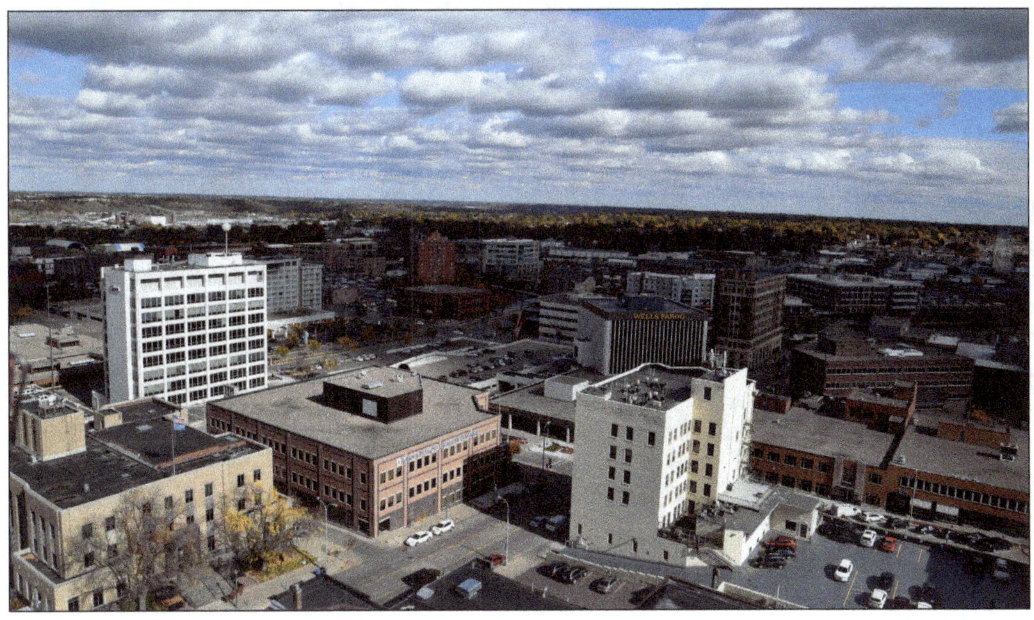

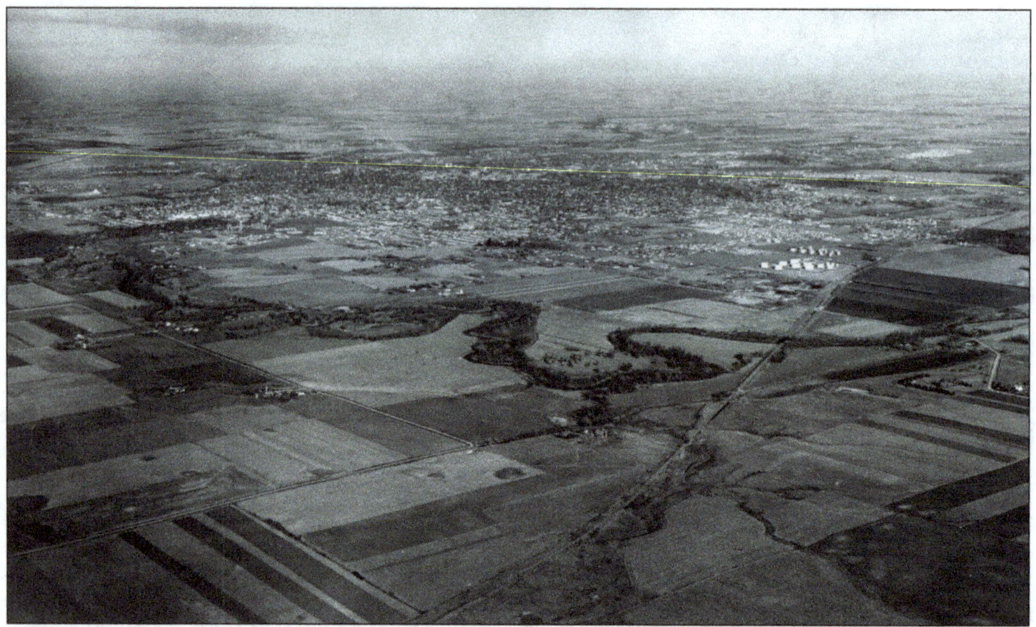

This picture was taken in 1954 looking northeast. The left center portion shows two roads that connect—this intersection is where Louise Avenue and Fifty-Seventh Street dead-end, before Fifty-Seventh Street extended across the city. Today, this is one of the busiest intersections of the city, and most of the open ground has been filled in with houses and businesses. (Courtesy William Pay.)

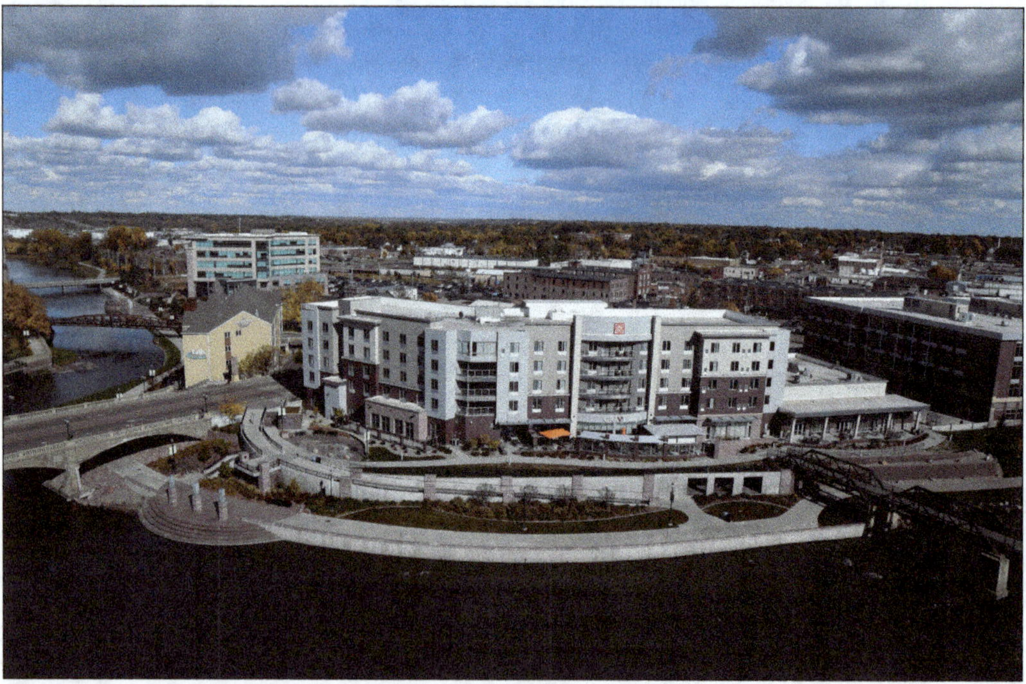

This area has been beautifully renovated in the last 10 years. The building at left, with the green windows, is Cherapa Place, which replaced the Zip Feed Mill. The building at center is the Hilton Garden Inn, which replaced the Schoeneman Bros. Lumber Company.

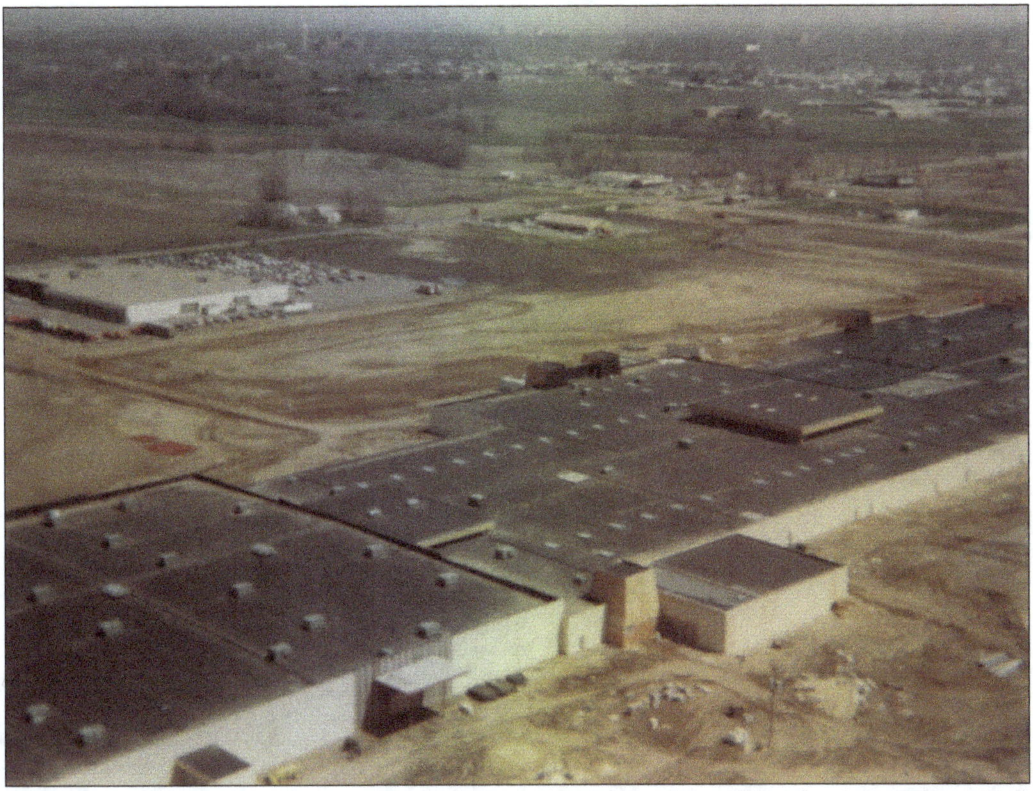

Taken from an airplane, this view is looking northeast from the south side of the Empire Mall as it was being built in 1975. The building at center left is the Ben-Hur Ford dealership, which had recently moved to this location from downtown. The small road in front of Ben-Hur Ford is Forty-First Street, which was a gravel road. (Courtesy Wally and Doris Johnson.)

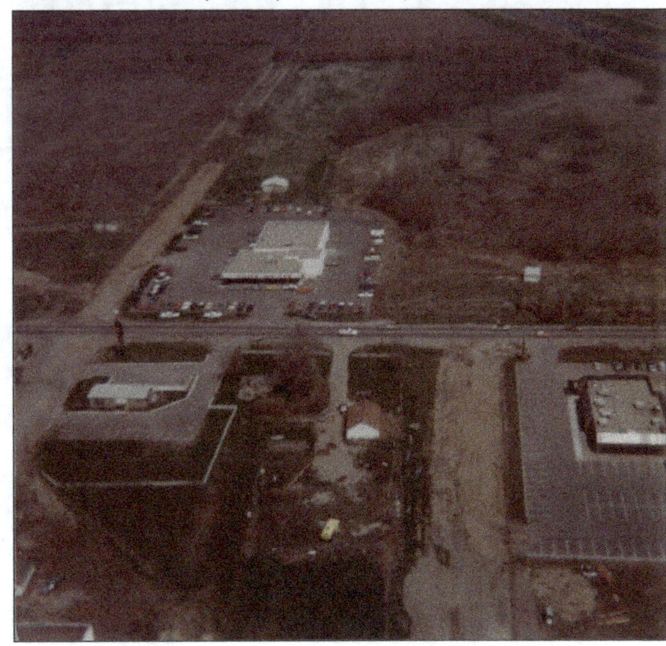

This view is looking north with Forty-First Street running horizontally through the picture. The gravel road at left is Louise Avenue, and the gravel road at right is Westport Avenue. At upper right is the river. The building at center is Tilton Motors, and the structure at right is the Billion Chrysler Plymouth Datsun dealership. (Courtesy Wally and Doris Johnson.)

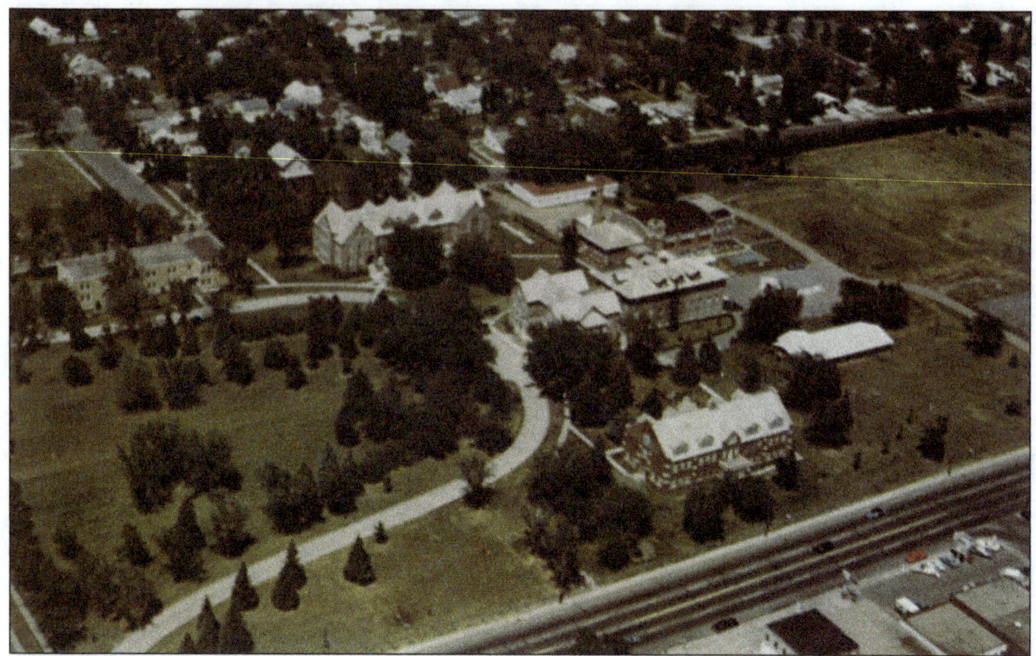

Education has been a priority for the South Dakota School for the Deaf since the school began in 1880. For over 120 years, the students stayed on campus for their education, with the highest enrollment at 135. Although there are no longer children living on campus or daily classes, the school is alive and well. In 2009, the school shifted to an all-outreach program and currently serves over 500 deaf and hard-of-hearing students in their home school districts across the state.

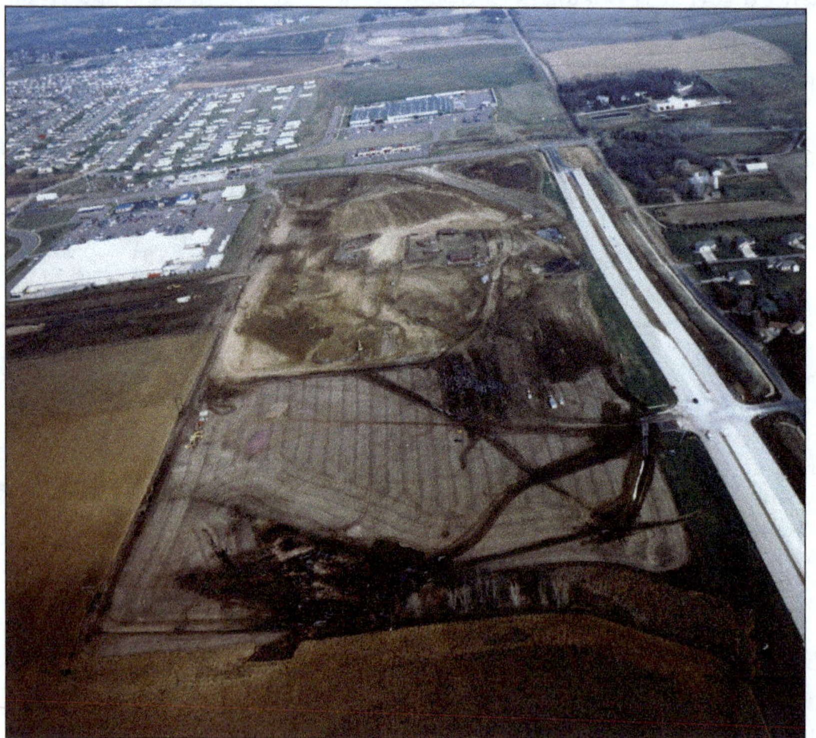

This aerial view of the Dawley Farm was taken in 2008 looking north. The white building at left is Walmart, and at upper center is Menards. The Century East Movie Theater was later built where the famous Powder House Blast occurred in 1936. At right is the new Veteran's Parkway, which replaced a stretch of Highway 11. (Courtesy William Pay.)

Six

Local Legends, Events, and More

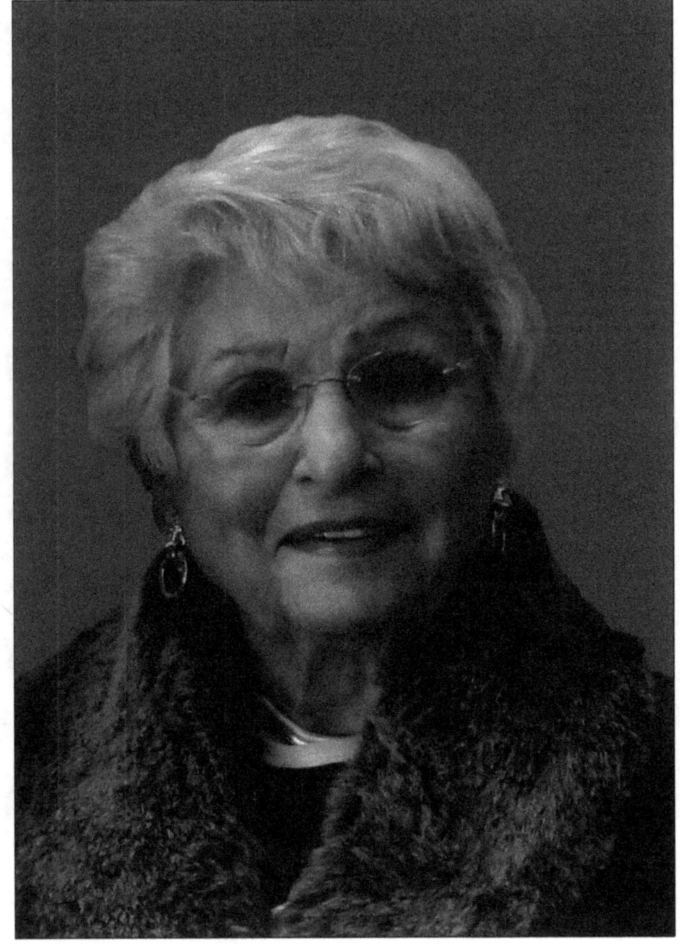

If there ever was a queen of Sioux Falls, it would be Sylvia Wolff Henkin. She has been a cheerleader for Sioux Falls for decades. Wolff was born and raised in Sheldon, Iowa. In 1940, she earned her private pilot's license and served in the Civil Air Patrol during World War II. She moved to Sioux Falls in 1944 when she married Sioux Falls radio and television pioneer Morton Henkin. The Henkins raised three children, Susan, Joseph, and Elizabeth. Sylvia started the Sioux Falls St. Patrick's Day Parade in 1979. In 1989 and 2013, she was honored as the grand marshal. She has been called the "First Lady of Sioux Falls" for what she has given back and how she has served the community for so many years. She has said she "hopes that friendly competition will reign in the future . . . and people will hold precious the culture of the community we have today." (Courtesy Susan Henkin McGowan.)

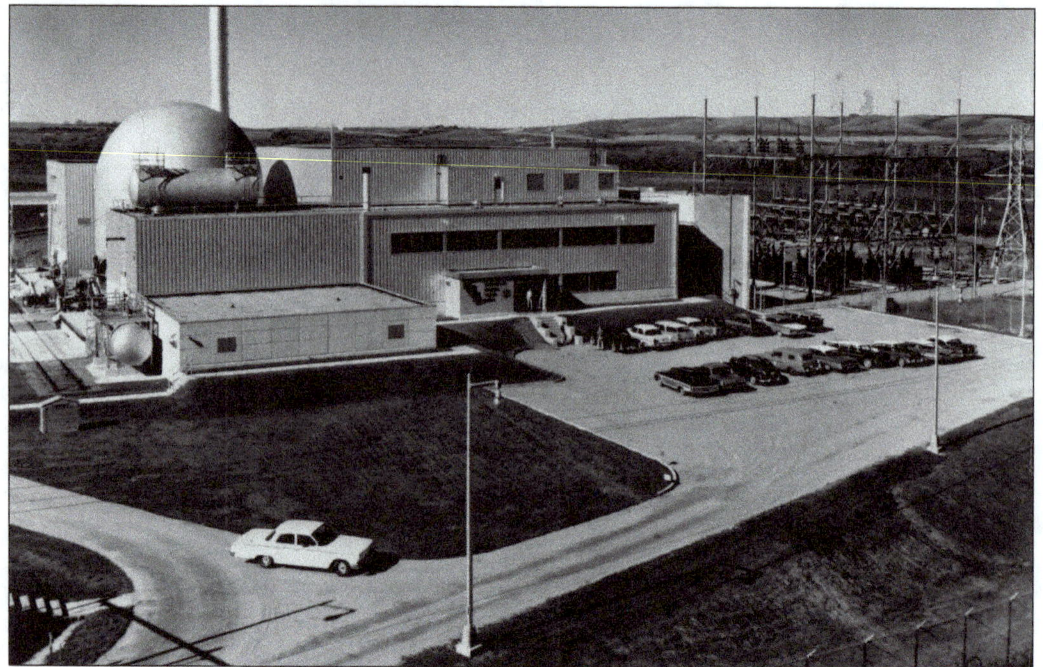

Pictured here is the Pathfinder Nuclear Generating Plant. This was the first of its kind in the world. It was built in 1962 but not licensed until 1964, and was completed in 1967. The goal was to use nuclear power to produce electricity. This was a time when alternative energy sources were being considered to replace coal and oil. In 1994, the Angus C. Anson Generating System (Xcel Energy) was built on the same site.

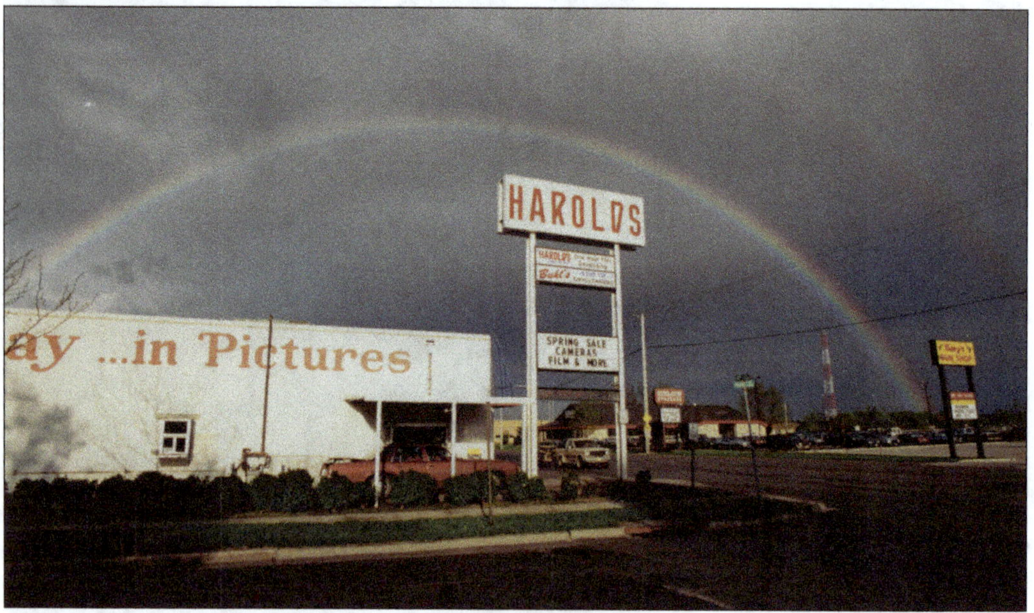

This beautiful picture of a double rainbow over the Harold's building at 912 West Forty-First Street was taken in the early 1990s. On the south side of the street were the Sirloin Stockade and later Coyote Canyon. The restaurant was torn down and today is the car lot of Graham Automotive. Gary's Gun Shop is at right. (Courtesy Harold's Photo.)

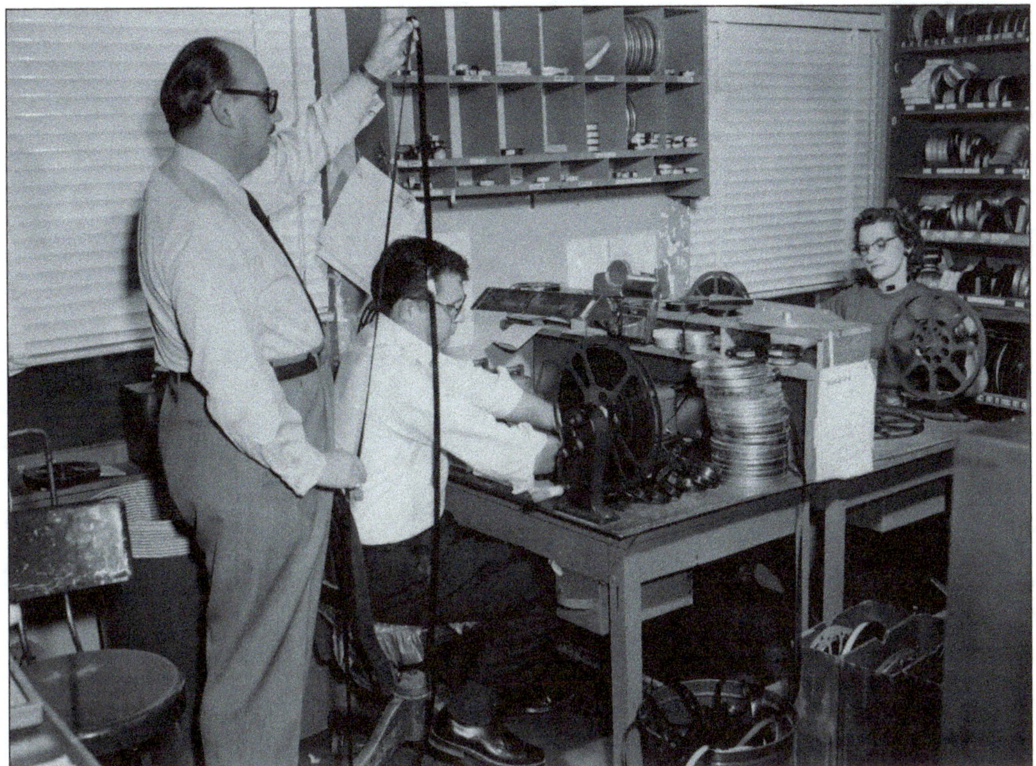

Joe Floyd is reviewing film for the television news. Daily, Floyd would review the film that was processed at Harold's Photography and would be played during the news. Floyd was a radio and television pioneer in South Dakota. He brought the first television station, KELO-TV, in Sioux Falls on air on May 19, 1953. (Courtesy Harold's Photo.)

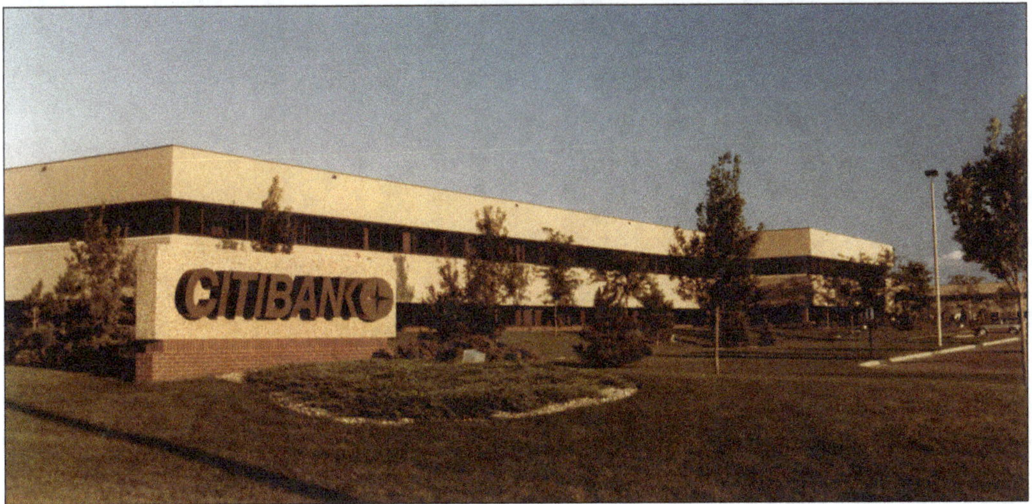

When Citibank came to Sioux Falls in 1981, it brought new opportunity for employment and a big boost in financial stability to the local economy. All three buildings were designed by Fritzel Kroeger, Griffin, and Berg and constructed by the Henry Carlson Company. Recent trends have shifted, and many employees now work from home, so only one of the three buildings is in use by Citibank. (Courtesy Olin Odland.)

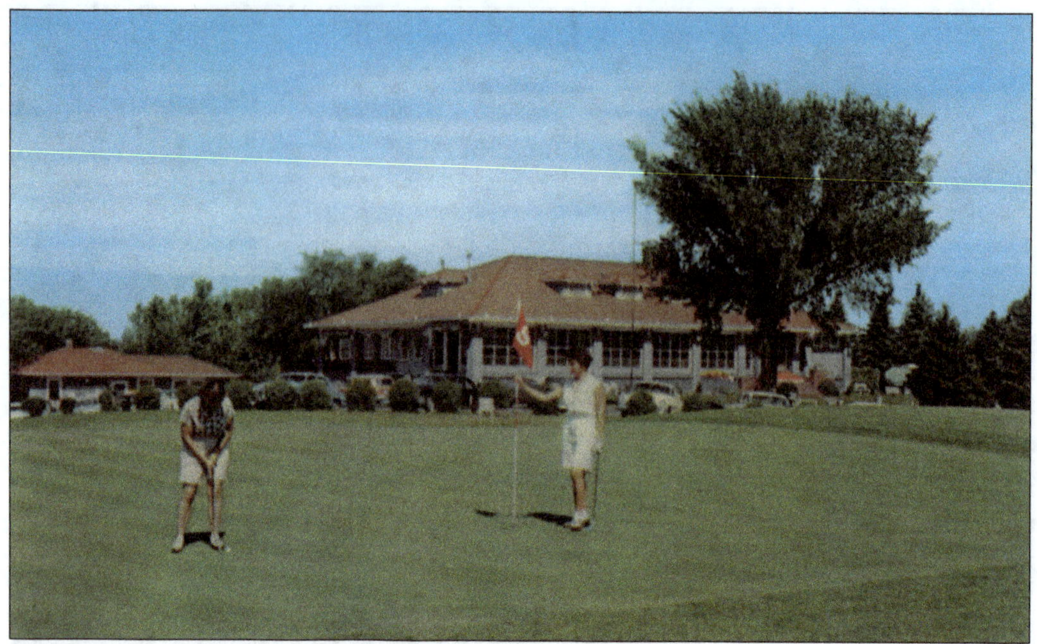

Golf has been a part of Sioux Falls history since 1905. Minnehaha Country Club was originally located near McKennan Park, between Twenty-First and Twenty-Sixth Streets, and Fourth and Seventh Avenues. In 1917, Minnehaha Country Club moved to its current location west of Kiwanis Avenue.

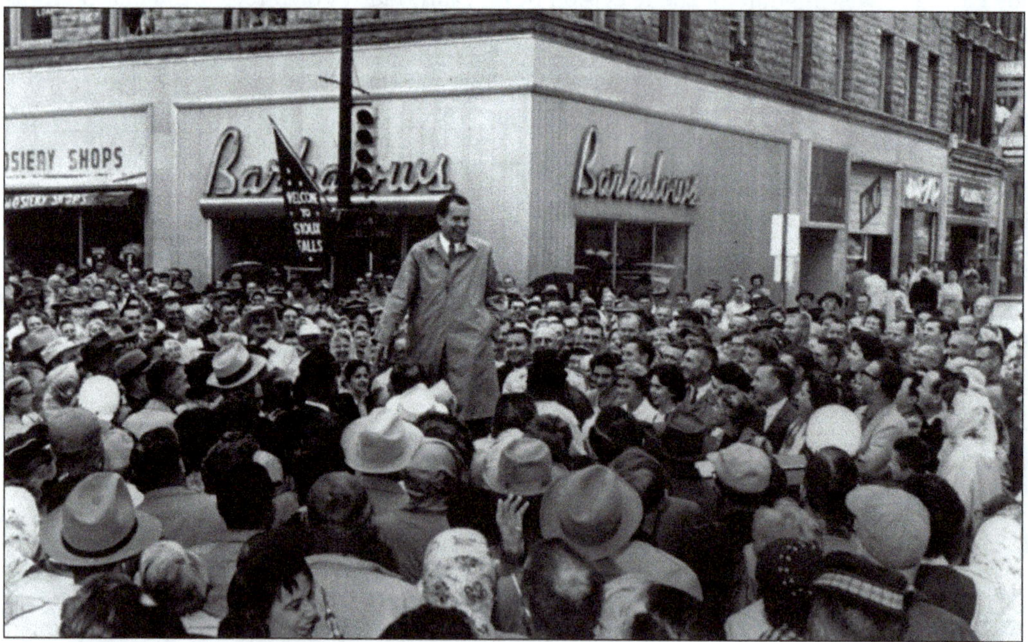

This picture was taken in 1960 and shows a crowd at the intersection of Phillips Avenue and Ninth Street looking west. They are welcoming presidential hopeful Richard Nixon. Two months later, John F. Kennedy would defeat Nixon. Nixon was later elected president and served from 1969 to 1974, when he resigned. As of 2017, he is the only US president to resign from office.

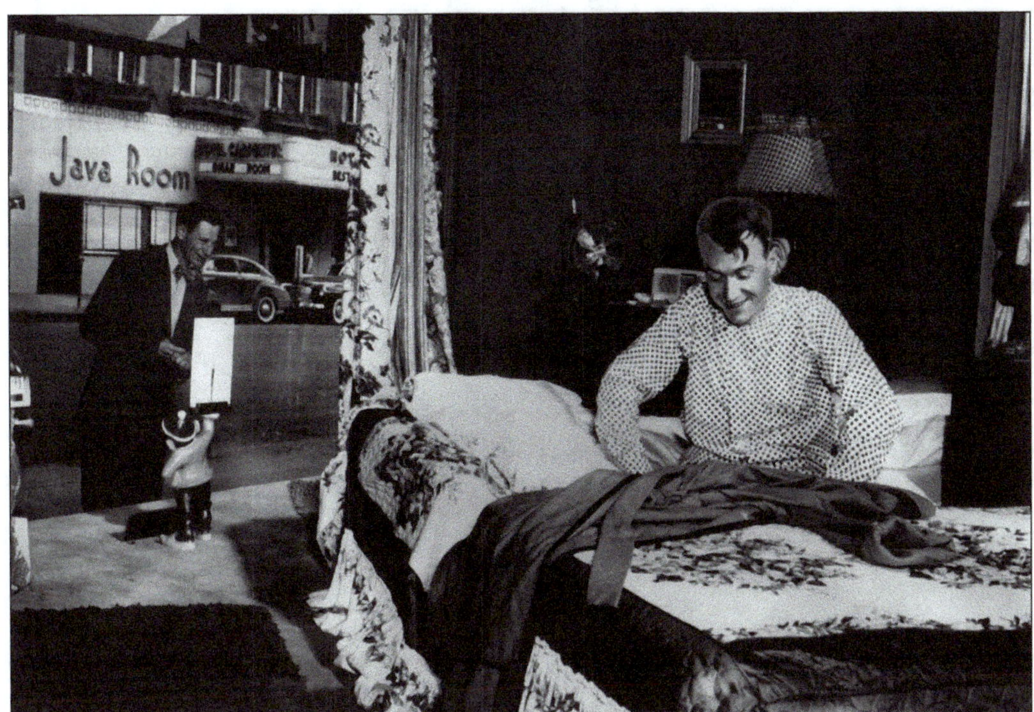

Wayne Pritchard is a Sioux Falls radio legend. In the radio business for approximately 40 years, he is best known for his morning talk show on KSOO radio. This picture shows Pritchard, age 29, after a night's sleep in the display window at the Shriver-Johnson Department Store. Pritchard was making a statement about the postwar housing shortage and lived in and broadcast his show from the store for about a week.

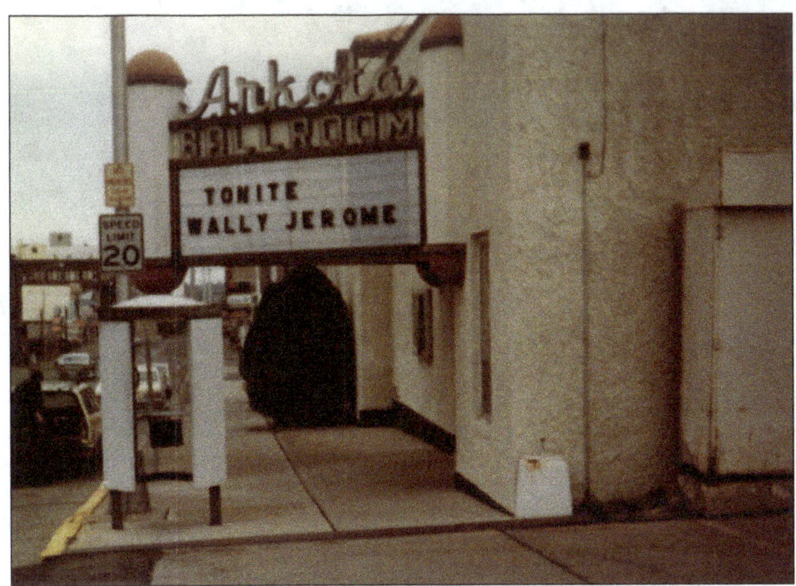

Wally Johnson, well known for being the owner of the Pizza Inn, is also a musician. He had a big band called the Wally Jerome Orchestra, which began in 1959. The band played around the region and was a regular at the Arkota Ballroom, now the Shrine Temple, on Phillips Avenue. (Courtesy Wally and Doris Johnson.)

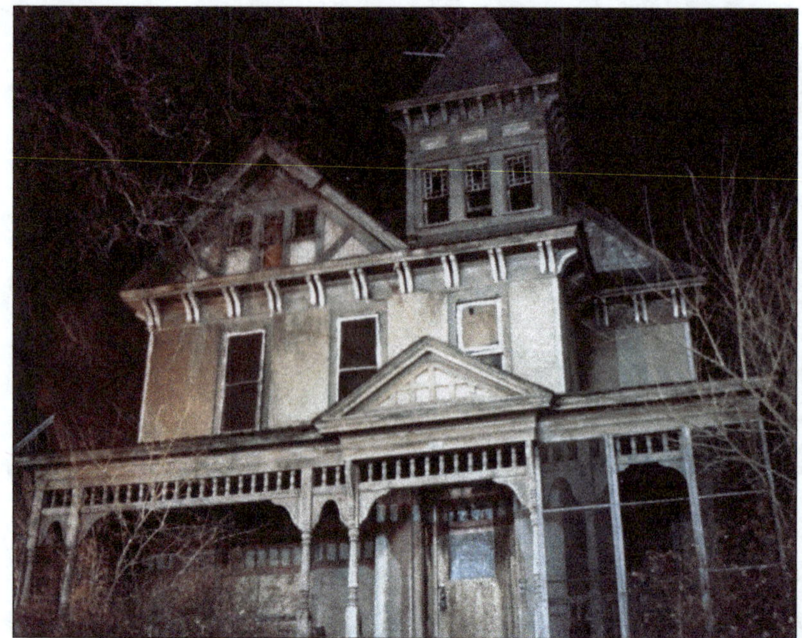

This picture shows the Abbot House, once located at 415 South Minnesota Avenue. Normally homes do not look this scary, but during the last years of this 100-year-old house, it was used as the Sioux Falls Jaycees Haunted House. Although the 1887 house is gone, the Jaycees continue the tradition of holding a haunted house fundraiser each year. (Courtesy Sioux Falls Jaycees.)

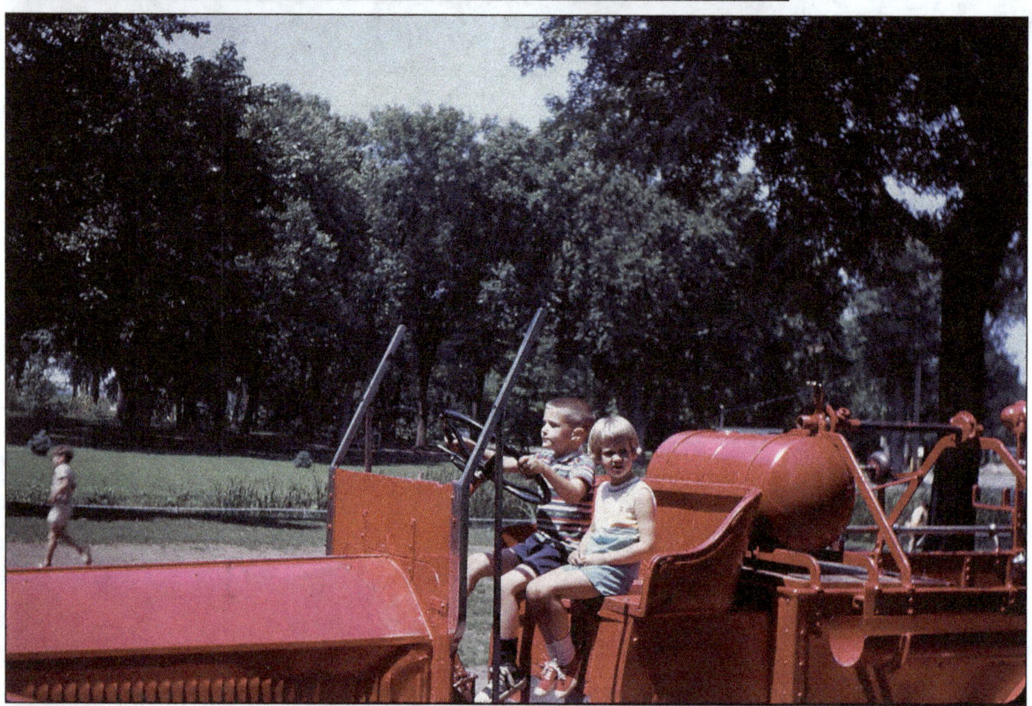

Many remember and others would be surprised to know that Sherman Park once had a playground named Dennis the Menace playground. Keeping the park consistent with the character of Dennis, the park was unique and had some unusual but awesome playground relics: an F-89 fighter jet from the South Dakota Air National Guard; a 1915 Seagrave fire truck, Sioux Falls's first fire truck; and a World War II tank. The park was established in 1959 and continued for many years until it was determined to be too dangerous. Today, the park is part of the African savannah at the Great Plains Zoo. (Courtesy Dean Musselman.)

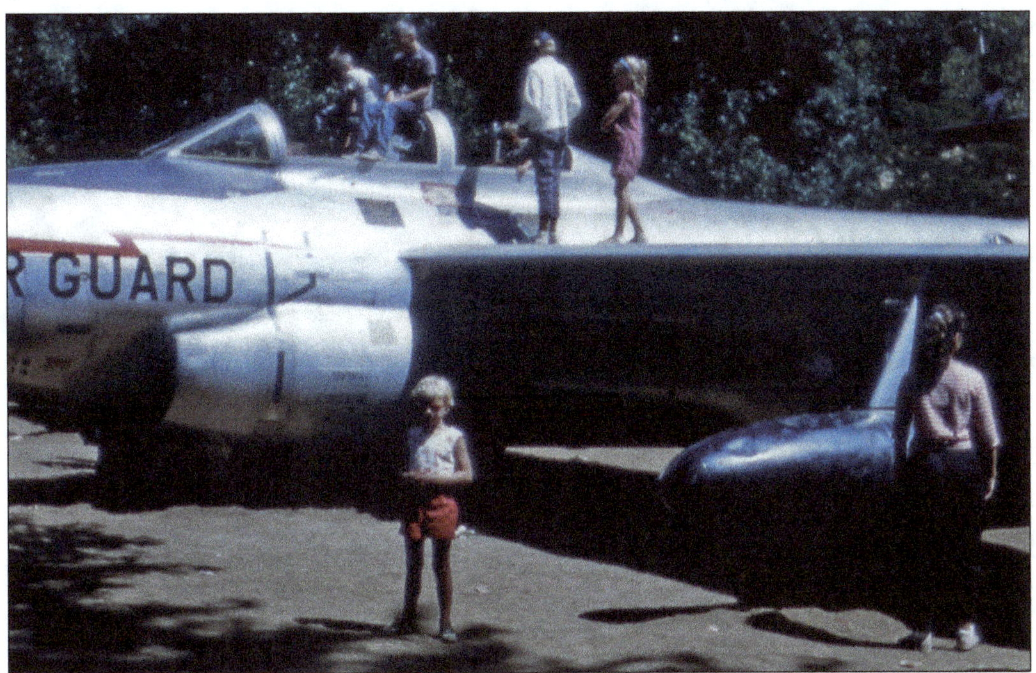

The airplane at Dennis the Menace playground has traveled many miles on South Dakota roads since its last flight in 1961. The F-89 retired from the South Dakota Air National Guard and was hauled to the Dennis the Menace playground at Sherman Park, where child pilots imagined great wartime flights until 1973, after which it was sold to Thomas Quigley. Quigley had the plane hauled to his land south of Newton Hills, where the plane was on display until September 23, 1998, when Verlyn Howe purchased it and transported it to his farm in Garretson, South Dakota. Howe once flew this same airplane. Today, the plane sits on Brian Howe's farm near Sherman, South Dakota; Brian is Verlyn's son. Both Sherman Park and Sherman, South Dakota, were named after E.A. Sherman, an early pioneer of Sioux Falls. (R. Kolbe Dakota collection.)

One of the coolest things a child in the 1960s and early 1970s had to play with was the World War II armored personnel carrier at the Dennis the Menace playground. A child could go into the tank feeling timid and scared but would crawl out feeling 10 feet tall and bulletproof. This tank was authentic and no doubt told children stories of its time fighting in World War II. (Courtesy Dean Musselman.)

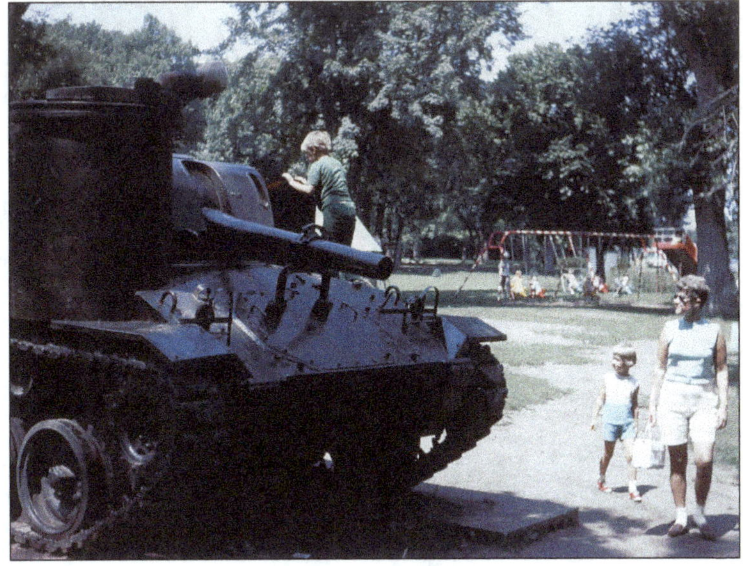

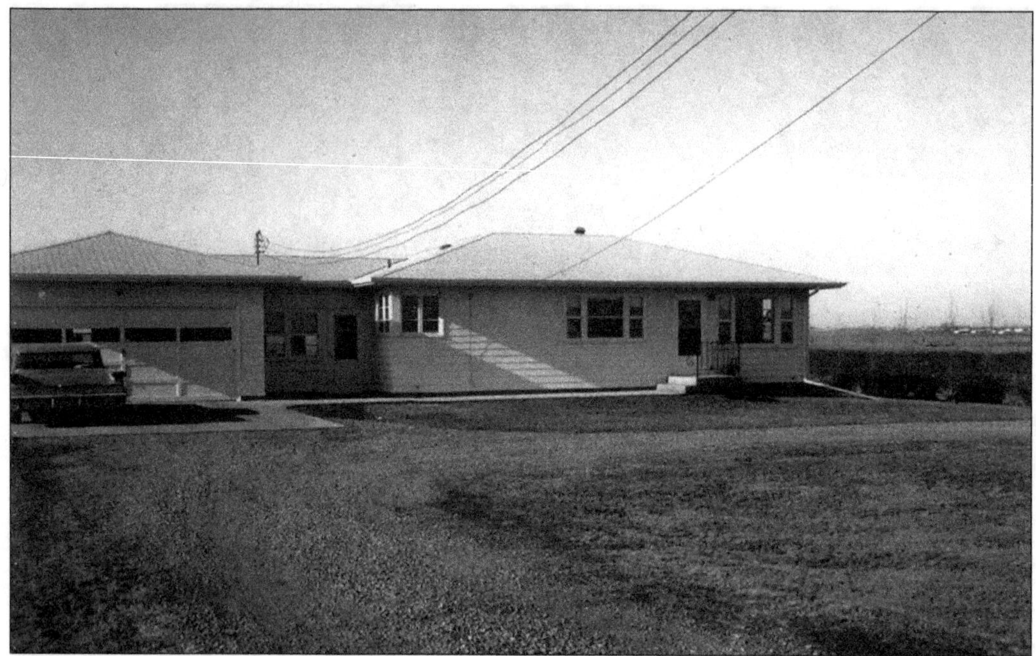

When this picture was taken, no one could have realized that this would become one of the busiest intersections in the state. When this house was built, it was practically in the country. A person standing in the same position looking west today would be facing the Spezia Restaurant on Louise Avenue and Fifty-Seventh Street. (Courtesy Marlo and Neva Opland family.)

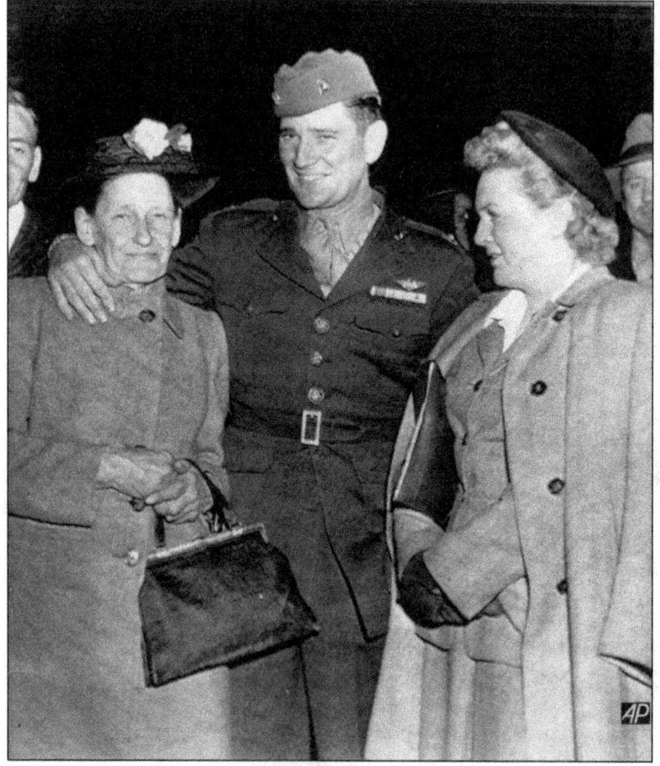

Capt. Joe Foss is pictured here with his mother, Mary, and wife, June. Foss was a national wartime hero as an ace fighter pilot. He helped to organize the South Dakota Air National Guard and was eventually promoted to brigadier general. Foss became a two-term South Dakota governor. He also was the first commissioner of the American Football League. (Courtesy Siouxland Heritage Museums, Sioux Falls, SD.)

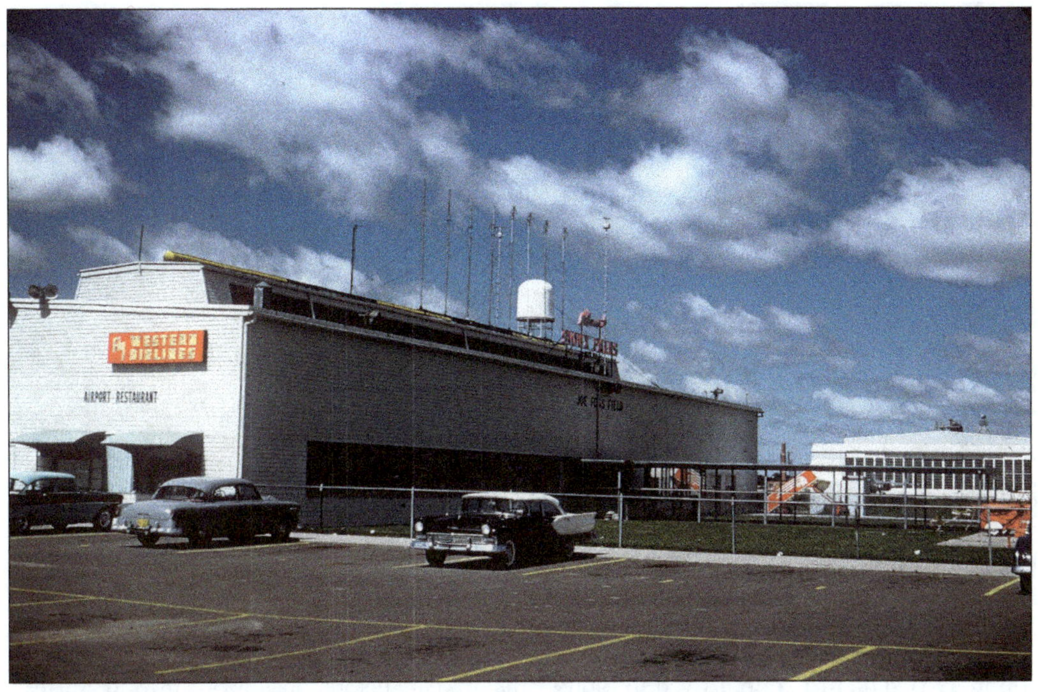

The Sioux Falls Airport opened on September 15, 1939. In 1955, the airport was renamed Joe Foss Field to honor the former South Dakota governor and World War II fighter pilot. Costello Terminal opened in 1970. Prior to 1939, the only airport in Sioux Falls was the Soo Skyway, which operated from 1929 to 1943 south of Forty-First Street, between Western and Kiwanis Avenues.

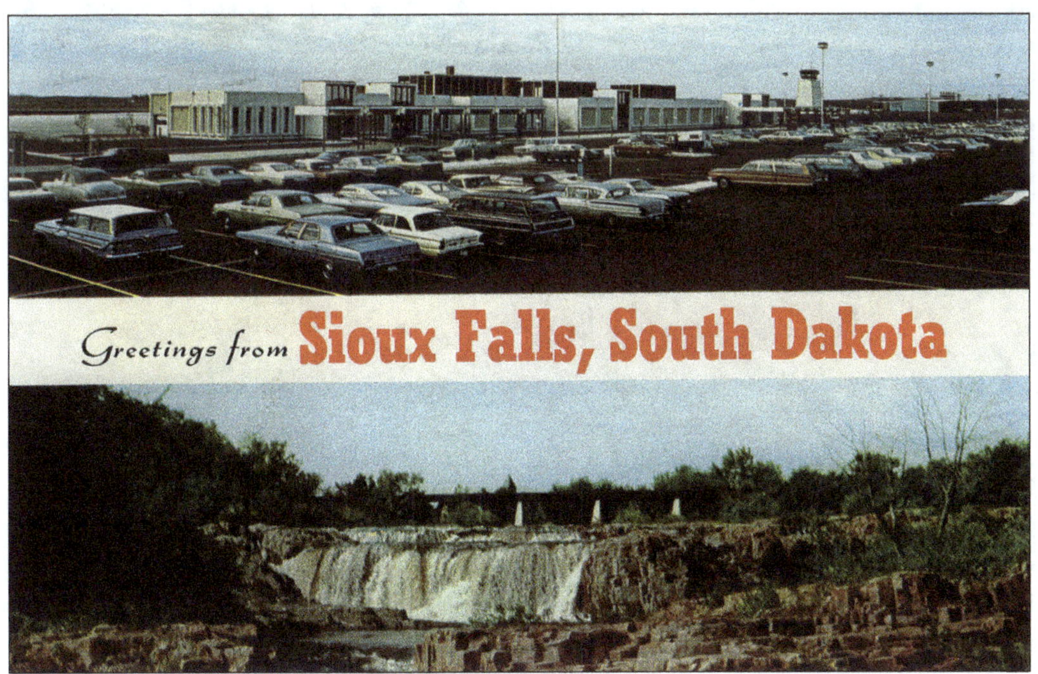

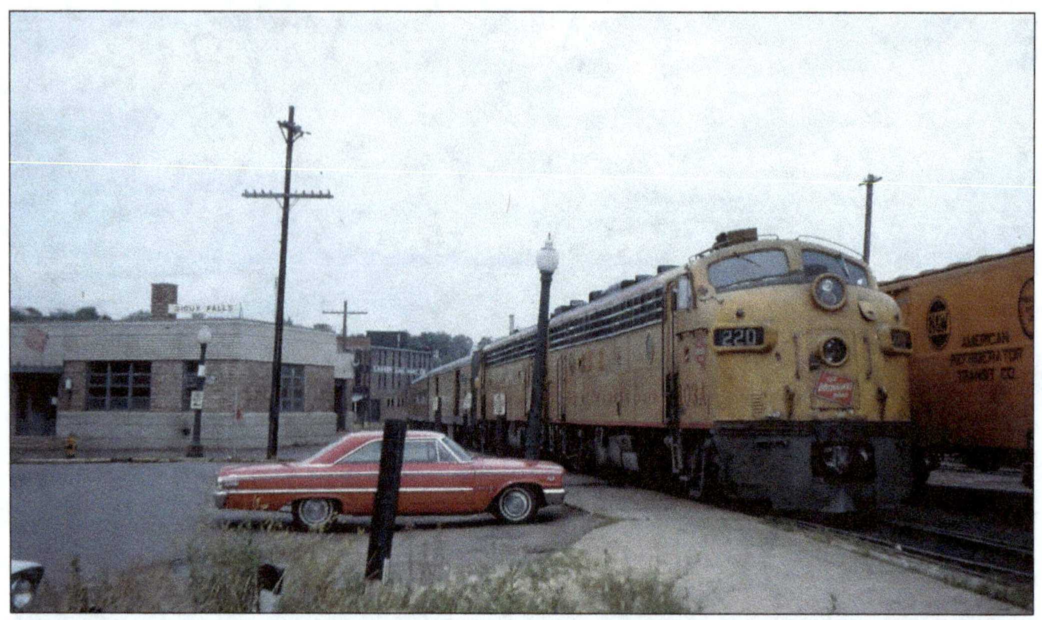

This photograph, taken in the summer of 1965, shows the Milwaukee Road's "Arrow" passenger train. This was the last train line to transport people to and from Sioux Falls and made its final trip in 1965. The first train arrived in Sioux Falls 87 years before, on July 30, 1878. (Courtesy Sean Cox.)

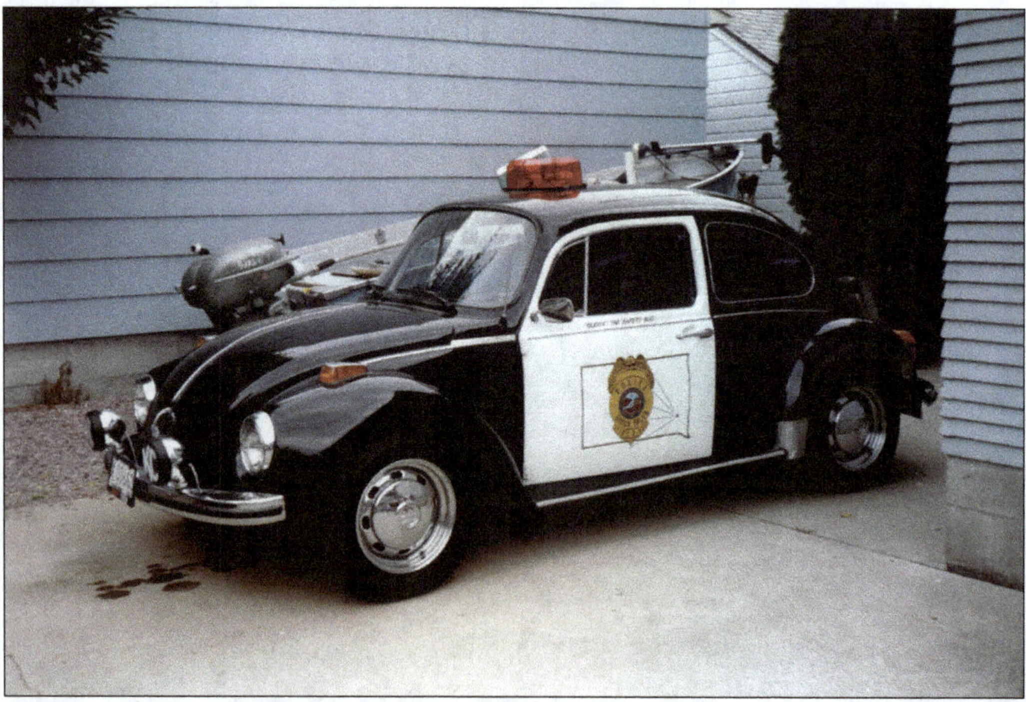

Buddy the Safety Bug hit the streets of Sioux Falls in 1991. The car and program were designed by now retired safety officer and former detective Bruce Millikan. Millikan's goal was for the car to be able to talk with children about pedestrian safety around cars. The 1973 car was later replaced by a 2000 version. (Courtesy Bruce Millikan.)

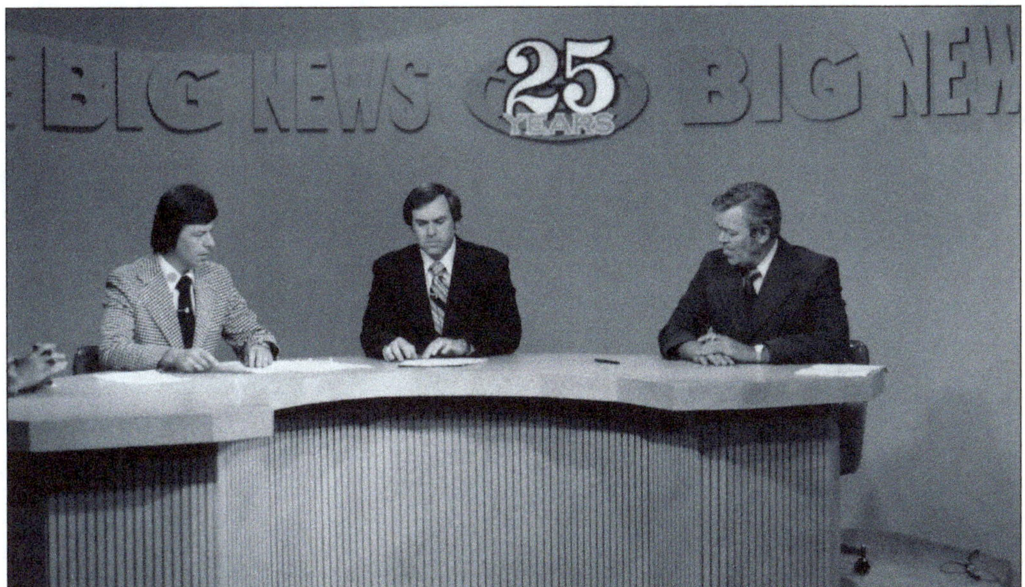

This is a great picture showing three KELO Television news legends. From left to right are Doug Lund, Steve Hemmingsen, and Dave Dedrick (without his Captain 11 uniform). This picture was taken in 1978, twenty-five years after the station signed on the air on May 19, 1953. (Courtesy Keloland Television.)

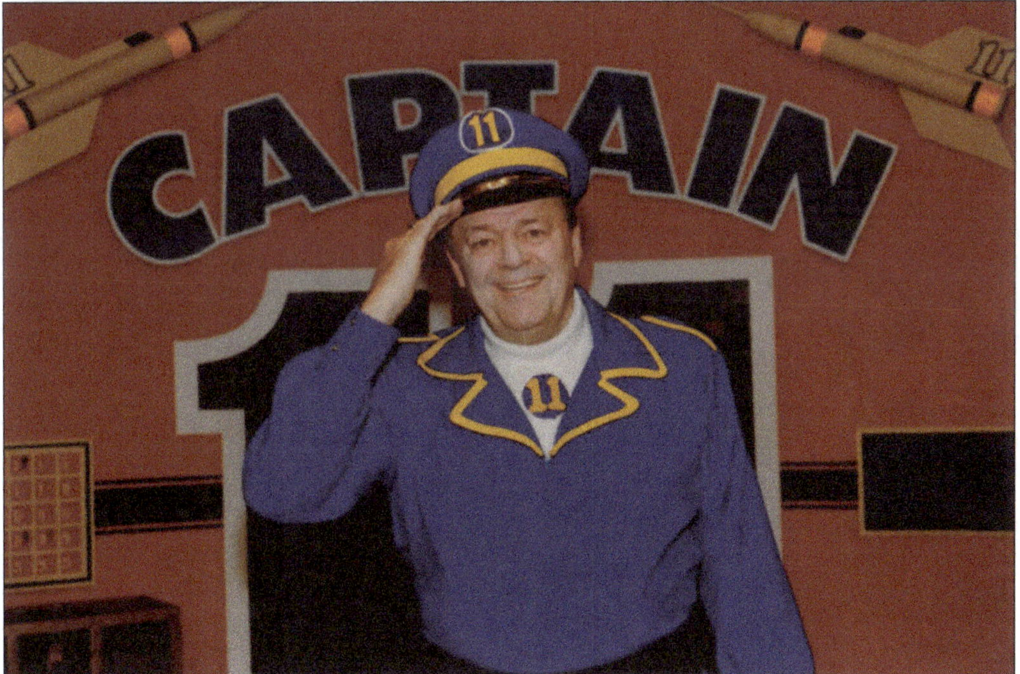

Dave Dedrick was the first voice heard when television began in South Dakota on May 19, 1953, as KELO Television took to the air. Two years later, he started the children's television show *Captain 11*. *Captain 11* ran from 1955 to 1996. He was the beloved hero to three generations of children. The set of *Captain 11* is on display at the State Historical Museum in Pierre, South Dakota. (Courtesy Keloland Television.)